Government and
the economy today

Politics today

Series editor: Bill Jones

Government and the economy today

Graham P. Thomas

Manchester University Press
Manchester and New York
Distributed exclusively in the USA and Canada by St. Martin's Press

Copyright © Graham P. Thomas 1992

Published by Manchester University Press
Oxford Road, Manchester M13 9PL, UK
and Room 400, 175 Fifth Avenue, New York, NY 10010, USA

Distributed exclusively in the USA and Canada
by St. Martin's Press, Inc., 175 Fifth Avenue, New York,
NY 10010, USA

British Library Cataloguing-in-Publication Data
A catalogue record for this book is available from the British Library

Library of Congress cataloging in publication data applied for

ISBN 0 7190 3074–9 *hardback*
0 7190 3075–7 *paperback*

Photoset in Linotron Ehrhardt
by Northern Phototypesetting Co. Ltd, Bolton.
Printed in Great Britain
by Biddles Ltd, Guildford and King's Lynn

Contents

List of figures and tables

Preface

As a teacher of Advanced Level Government and Politics I often complained of the lack of a textbook dealing with the role of government in the economy. Eventually my students got tired of my complaints and suggested I tried to fill the gap. Bill Jones was kind enough to encourage the enterprise, and this book is the result.

Clearly, no one studying politics, from GCSE upwards, can understand the subject without taking the economic dimension fully into account. This has been increasingly accepted by those responsible for preparing the various Advanced Level GCE syllabi, a number of which explicitly require a degree of economic understanding from both teachers and students. I hope that this book will aid both Advanced Level students and undergraduates to appreciate more fully the connections between the two areas of concern and that it will be of use to teachers of British politics, especially at Advanced Level.

The book is in four parts. Part One is an historical introduction to the growth of economic management by government. The Introduction examines the meaning of the twin concepts of politics and economics and argues that despite the changes in political fashion, all modern economies are 'mixed'. Chapter 1 outlines the changing attitudes to the role of the state, from *laissez-faire* to the modern mixed economy. Part Two examines the relationship between politics and economics since 1945. Chapter 2 considers whether there was a Keynesian revolution in economic management after the Second World War. Chapter 3 examines the decline in support for a managed economy in the 1970s. Chapter 4 looks at the record of the Conservative government from 1979 while Chapter 5 attempts to assess whether there was, as Mrs. Thatcher and her followers claimed, an 'economic miracle'. Part Three analyses the making of economic policy. Chapter 6 deals with the machinery of economic policy making. Chapter 7 traces the evolution of economic thinking in the Conservative Party since 1945, while that of the Labour and centre parties is examined in Chapter 8. Part Four considers the concept of corporatism. Chapter 9 looks at the role played by trade unions in British politics and Chapter 10 examines employers' organisations. A Conclusion considers various themes and hazards a guess at likely developments in the 1990s. Because various aspects of the relationship between government and the economy are examined from different perspectives, a certain amount of overlapping is unavoidable.

My debts are considerable. I am grateful to my students at Reading College of Technology, past and present, whose patience and fortitude has been endless (or perhaps they really *were* asleep). Particular thanks go to Bill Jones for his never-ending encouragement; I am honoured to contribute to the series which he edits with such distinction. I am grateful to Professor Michael Moran for his detailed and enlightening comments which have considerably improved what I have written. Richard Purslow of Manchester University Press has been the source of much help and support. Colin Kaplan generously gave the benefits of his editorial experience; he has improved the book out of all recognition and I am deeply grateful. However, I am responsible for any errors or inadequacies which remain. Above all, I wish to thank my wife and children for their loving kindness during the writing of this book.

Part One

Historical introduction

Introduction: Government and the economy

In 1969 Donald Winch wrote: 'there has been a remarkable sea-change in attitudes to the proper role of the state in economic life, not only in Britain but in most developed societies. The increase in the size of the government contribution to economic activity, and the widening in scope of its responsibilities, is one of the leading themes of twentieth century history. Broadly speaking, at the beginning of the century it was considered unnecessary, unwise and perhaps even impossible for governments to exercise detailed control over the direction of the economic machine. Now it is widely accepted that the economic performance of society, both in the large and in the small, is one of the primary responsibilities of the state.'[1] Despite the reaction against the role of the state in economic management since the mid-1970s, it is still a major task of government to ensure the economic prosperity of the country. Although one of the main themes of the New Right has been that politicians should desist from running the economy and leave it to 'market forces', political leaders are still held responsible for prosperity, economic growth, the level of unemployment and many other features of life which were once considered as largely outside the scope of government. This book aims to explore the interaction between the economic and political systems and to show that each depends on the other and that the connections between the two, despite changes in political fashions and rhetoric, have increased in numerous ways, especially over the last half century.

Being concerned with the interaction between politics and economics, we must begin with a definition of both terms.

The nature of politics

Neither politics nor economics can be defined precisely. Politics is a basic human activity, found not only at the national and international levels involving, for example, political parties and the nation-state; it is a fact of life at virtually every level of human existence. It is concerned, amongst many other things, with the use of power; fundamentally it involves disagreements between people and the settling of those disagreements. 'Politics is the study of conflicts of interests and values that affect all of society and of how they can be conciliated.'[2] Politics *is* because human beings differ, both as individuals and groups; they have differing aims, interests, ideals and characteristics. Throughout human history conflict has existed about the goals people seek and the methods they adopt to realise these goals. The essence of a political situation is conflict and the settlement of that conflict by methods ranging from discussion and compromise to the use of force.

The sources from which political conflict can spring are almost limitless. Differences in religious or moral attitudes, conflicting claims over territory and many others have provided the basis of political struggles of a range of intensity. Some differences have been seen as more important than others, and variations occur between the types of issue considered significant in different countries and in different periods. However, economic differences have been a perennial subject of dispute.

Economics

There is no one all-embracing definition of economics. It is concerned with the use made by human beings of those things which make life possible; because these things are not limitless, some kind of organisation is needed to ensure their availability. The recent emergence of the 'Green' issue has drawn attention to the danger in the unregulated exploitation of things previously regarded both as 'free' and 'limitless' such as the air we breathe and the water we drink, and their availability is rapidly becoming a major political, as well as economic, problem. Thus economics is concerned with how societies use scarce resources. Because of this scarcity conflicts arise over the distribution of economic resources; the economic system and the political system thus interact. Because resources are limited most communities are forced to make choices in what is to be produced, how that production is to be achieved and to whom these goods and services are distributed. The institutions of society which determine such matters are known collectively as the economic system, and there are various ways of classifying such systems, usually by reference to where decisions are made. In all but the most basic economy the government plays an important role.

The role of government in the economy

Throughout history, the part played by government in the economic system has been a major source of both political and economic controversy. At one extreme is the *command economy*, where the allocation of resources is determined primarily or almost exclusively by the state, as in the Communist countries of Eastern Europe before 1989; at the other is what has been described as a 'market' system. A *free-market* economy is one in which 'market forces' or the 'laws' of supply and demand determine who gets what and under what conditions. In this type of system (known as capitalism) the means of production are owned by private individuals intent on achieving profits and the allocation of resources is via the price system.

This gave rise to a school of both economic and political thought known as '*laissez-faire*' (leave alone), proponents of which believed that interference in the running of the economy by government was harmful except where it was necessary to ensure the efficient operation of the system. It was accepted that the state had a vital role in ensuring law and order, thus providing those social conditions of peaceful life without which any kind of economic transaction becomes virtually impossible, and a framework of contract and commercial law which is a necessary foundation of the market economy. In many respects, the maintenance of law and order is the most fundamental function performed by government in the economic sphere. *Laissez-faire* economists also accepted some additional roles for government, such as maintaining the value of money.

Apart from these basic provisions, the role of government was negative. Classical economists such as Adam Smith warned both on economic and political grounds of the danger of interference. 'The Statesman, who should attempt to direct private people in what manner they ought to employ their capitals, would not only load himself with a most unnecessary attention, but assume an authority which could safely be trusted not only to no single person, but to no council or senate whatever, and which would nowhere be so dangerous as in the hands of a man who had folly and presumption enough to fancy himself fit to exercise it.'[3]

The mixed economy

This book traces the growing political influence of those who argued that the state should have a minimal role in regulating economic activity. It will be suggested that even as the intellectual argument seemed won, government activity in the economic sphere grew rapidly because of the pressure of factors such as industrialisation and urbanisation, the expanding electorate and the influence of other philosophical outlooks. The role of the state in managing the economy grew throughout the twentieth century; the impact of the two world wars, the Great Depression of the inter-war years, the growing strength of socialism and of Labour parties, and the revolution in economic thought associated with John Maynard Keynes contributed to the emergence, in Britain and most other Western democracies, of what has been called the *mixed economy*. In this system both private and public enterprise have a role in economic activity and both market forces and the government determine the distribution of rewards. To a greater or lesser extent all contemporary economic systems are 'mixed', if only because of the great political significance attached to successful economic management. Despite the efforts of Mrs

Thatcher and her supporters to 'roll back the frontiers of the state', Britain remains very much a 'mixed economy', although the frontiers between the private and public sectors have changed.

In Britain the 'mixed economy' grew after the end of the Second World War, when market forces (on the whole) determined the level of prices and the supply of goods and services. Governments, however, increasingly intervened to achieve goals which they thought the market could not or could not do so fast enough to suit the economic and political priorities of the party in power. The market was thought to be deficient in two respects.

1. In the provision of what might be termed 'public goods'. These are goods and services the benefits of which apply to all members of society irrespective of the contribution made by individuals and of the use they make of the service. For example, there is general agreement that the provision of law and order and defence cannot be left to the market and that collective arrangements through the state are necessary. In the post-war period the range and variety of economic services provided by the state grew until Mrs Thatcher came to power in 1979; an example was the nationalisation of the basic utilities by the post-war Labour government.
2. It was thought that weaknesses in the capitalist market system involved a great deal of unfairness and inefficiency in both the provision of goods and services and their distribution. So governments intervened both in pursuit of a 'fairer' system of rewards, in which the wealth generated by the economic system would be used for the provision of 'public goods' and to ensure a more equitable distribution of resources, and of a more efficient economy.

In effect, the state has pursued goals which previous generations thought impossible or undesirable or both: such things as influencing the rates of inflation and unemployment, regional growth and even the well-being of the economy as a whole have become the proper and even essential concerns of governments. Governments have been brought into contact with an almost limitless range of interests in society and have had to exercise political skills in balancing the pressures exerted by groups as diverse as employers and unions, consumers and producers and so on. The growing complexity of the international economic system has meant that the health or otherwise of economies such as that of the USA has had a major impact on post-war economic and political developments in Britain, while the influence of international organisations such as the International Monetary Fund (IMF) and the World Bank has been pervasive. Governments have also been obliged to choose between a wide range of policy options and economic theories in implementing their aims and have been forced to balance both with what public opinion will accept. Thus political skills and economic judgements have become intertwined.

The post-war consensus

This mixed economy, based on a number of assumptions related to Keynesian economics and to a more general 'Butskellite' consensus dominated British politics for some thirty years. Occasional voices were raised in protest, but politicians who expressed concern at the growth of the state were whistling in the wind. The attempt by Edward Heath to challenge the consensus between 1970 and 1972 failed, and the 'U-turn' restored the status quo. But the shock to the Western economic system of the quadrupling of oil prices following the Yom Kippur War in 1973, which particularly affected Britain, led to a gradual loss of faith in the efficacy of economic management by government and to the rediscovery of classical economic theories. What are called 'New Right' economic and political values, of which the British variant is Thatcherism, dominated the 1980s in ways similar to the 'Butskellite' consensus of the earlier period. Clearly, however, the role of the state has not returned to that prevailing before the Second World War; the political pressures are too great. 'Whether a government decides to be "interventionist" or to allow market forces to operate, it cannot escape responsibility in the public eye for the economic consequences; in a mixed economy 'free-market forces' act only when a government creates the economic environment in which they can do so.'[4] Whatever the rhetoric, politicians still see their success largely in economic terms, even if the aims and methods have changed. 'Every British prime minister since the war has grasped with enthusiasm the opportunities for state involvement in the economy which Keynesian economics offered, not least Margaret Thatcher, who beneath an appearance of laissez-faire economics has placed herself more centrally within the mechanics of economic policy-making than any predecessor.'[5] The involvement of Mrs Thatcher and her Chancellors in the management of exchange and interest rates is an example of this continued preoccupation with economic management.

Much of the debate between politicians and economists of the various persuasions has been about performance; will things such as low inflation, economic growth and so on be better achieved by a free-market approach or by one in which there is intervention by the government? These questions can only to a limited extent be answered by economists; political priorities determine the context within which economic decisions are made (though economic constraints condition these choices). In turn, political pro-grammes are the result of a whole host of factors which make up social attitudes and beliefs, including moral and spiritual values. Mrs Thatcher's belief in 'Victorian values' of self-help and economic individualism seemed to her critics to exclude other values more related to community and the collective provision of services. Decisions about economic policy are largely related to the kind of society one wishes to live in. These fundamental questions and the kinds of dilemmas faced by public policy makers in dealing with the relationships between economic and political issues will be examined. This book is concerned with what has been called political economy, the interface between the economic and political aspects of public policy.

Notes

1   Donald Winch: *Economics and Policy: A Historical Study*, Hodder and Stoughton, 1969.

2   Bernard Crick and Tom Crick: *What is Politics?*, Edward Arnold, 1987, p.1. See also Bernard Crick: *In Defence of Politics*, Penguin, 1982, 2nd edn.

3   Quoted in Graham Bannock, R.E. Baxter and Evan Davis: *The*

Penguin Dictionary of Economics, Penguin, 1987, 4th edn, p.239.

4   Stephen Kirby: The Politics of the Mixed Economy, in Lynton Robins (ed.): *Politics and Policy-Making in Britain*, Longman, 1987, p.7.

5   Paul Mosley: Economic Policy, in Henry Drucker et al. (eds.): *Developments in British Politics 2*, Macmillan, 1988, rev. edn, p.176.

1

The growth of state intervention

This chapter examines the growth of government intervention in economic management. It considers the reaction against mercantilism, the development of *laissez-faire* ideas and the nineteenth century debate about the proper role of government. The challenge to orthodox economic thinking posed by J.M. Keynes is examined, and the chapter ends at 1945, when the climate of opinion about economic management by the state underwent a profound change.

The nature of the debate

Since the end of the Second World War, political debate in Britain has been dominated by the state of the economy. Both Labour and the Conservatives have largely based their respective appeals on trying to convince the voters that they have *the* answer to the problem of improving the material standards of living of the British people. The expectation has grown that the government will be responsible for the performance of the economy, and failure to meet this expectation has been punished by electoral unpopularity and defeat; this is the *major*, though not the *sole*, explanation for the various changes of government since 1945. The extent to which this affects politicians' attitudes can be seen in the speech made by Harold Wilson in March 1968. 'The standing of a government and its ability to hold the confidence of the electorate at a General Election depends on the success of its economic policy.'[1] This was a major aspect of the 'Butskellite' consensus of the 1950s and 1960s.

However, the belief in the capacity of governments to deliver economic prosperity was increasingly challenged during the 1970s, mainly from the Right, as economic crisis destroyed the earlier optimism. In the 1980s the Conservatives stressed the reduction of government involvement in economic management and emphasised the role of 'market forces' in achieving economic objectives.

The development of economic management

In various ways governments have always intervened in the economy hoping, for example, to increase national prosperity and therefore military and political power or to advance or safeguard the interests of particular groups in society.

1. The provision of a framework of law and the safeguarding of contracts has always been seen as one of the prime responsibilities of government.
2. Economic activity has always been regulated by government; the purpose and extent has changed over time, and today virtually every economic activity is affected, although since 1979 there have been attempts to reduce the range and extent of such regulations.
3. Governments have always provided services for the community; their nature has been the subject of political debate which has centred around whether they could be better provided by the market. The dividing line between the state and the market as the provider of services was one of the central arguments of the 1980s.
4. Governments have always had social objectives, the achievement of which has required some kind of economic intervention. The relief of poverty, the protection of the agricultural interest and so on, have caused government to intervene in the operation of the market. Taxation is not just an instrument for raising money to pay for the operation of government, it is also

a way in which the state can attempt to achieve its objectives. The progressive system of taxation is an attempt to reduce the inequalities produced by the market system. Governments have expressed through their interventions in the economy some idea of 'social justice'. This became more marked after 1945. The Labour Party emphasised an egalitarian view of society and the claims of the working class to a 'fairer' or more equal share of the national wealth. The Conservatives, while not denying the responsibility of the state to the poor, pointed to the importance of wealth-creation and stressed rewards for innovation and enterprise.

5. Governments have always had economic objectives, even though these may not have been explicit and were often expressed in non-economic terms. The pursuit of military and political power has been among the factors which have caused governments to encourage various forms of economic activity. Since 1945 this aspect of government responsibilities has grown and become more explicit. Governments have tries to stimulate economic growth, to deal with problems such as inflation and unemployment, the imblances between different regions of the country and so on.

However, the role of government as the manager of the economy with a range of explicit and purposive aims is something which has only developed since 1945. Before that, governments pursued the objectives listed above, but did not think of themselves as *managers* of the economy. This function of economic management is a relatively new one. Until the nineteenth century the role of government was very limited and largely concerned with protecting Britain from foreign invaders and maintaining law and order at home. Yet over the centuries the economic role of the state has grown.

Political economy

Political economy as a branch of knowledge can be traced back to the seventeenth century, when the development of trade and industry and the growth of European nation-states made it necessary to try to explain and predict the working of an increasingly important market economy. Profound social changes associated with the Reformation, the Scientific Revolution and the opening up of the New World led to the emergence of the merchant class and its alliance with ambitious monarchs. There was an increased recognition of the connection between national power and economic strength. The rulers of the emerging nation-states had to increase national wealth in order to maximise their own revenues so as to fulfil their expanding roles and deal with the discontent arising from the social changes associated with economic development.

Mercantilism

Mercantilism influenced policy makers in several European countries between the mid sixteenth and late seventeenth centuries. It concerned the relationship between a nation's wealth and its foreign trade, and favoured state intervention in order to maximise national wealth, which proponents identified with the possession of precious metal (gold and silver). The increasingly detailed control of economic affairs by governments led to growing resistance from those who wished to be as free as possible from all restraint, but mercantilism was important in helping to explain the forces behind economic activity. It stressed that the national economy would take an increasing share in international trade if the industrial, commercial and maritime branches were encouraged.

The emergence of England as an economic power

England was well placed, by a combination of circumstances, to take advantage of the opportunities for economic growth during the sixteenth and seventeenth centuries. The emergence of the merchant class and the increasing religious strife between the Stuart kings and Puritanism were factors in the Civil War and the Commonwealth which followed, although they were only part of a complex situation. Gradually a capitalist class developed whose individualism and sense of its economic and thus political importance made it increasingly resentful of the restrictions placed upon it by paternalistic, corrupt and inefficient governments. By the end of the seventeenth century the moral attitudes of capitalism – hard work, frugality, self-sufficiency and the pursuit of material wealth – were increasingly influential on public policy making.

In seventeenth century England, constitutional and political conflicts were the background to attempts to understand and explain the workings of the market economy. But only in the following century did writers began to describe an economic system separate from the political system. They began to argue in terms of impersonal forces stimulating economic development and spoke increasingly of the importance of self-interest in motivating individuals to act. At the same time, many were aware of the problem of reconciling this self-interest with some concept of the public interest. Increasingly, however, the role of government as an economic agent was questioned. 'The spirit of the age was set on course to embrace Adam Smith's view of the economy as a naturally harmonious, self-regulating system in which direct government intervention was more likely to reduce the national level of economic activity than to raise it.'[2]

The development of *laissez-faire*

By the mid-eighteenth century, an attitude amounting to *laissez-faire* dominated government thinking; individuals should be left to make economic decisions based on their own self-interest. At no time, however, before or after Adam Smith did the idea that the economy should be left to the profit motive ever totally dominate the minds of policy makers. The law of the market ruled unchallenged through nearly all sectors of the internal economy, even though there were many regulations on external trade. On the question of the need for state intervention to limit the free play of market forces, there was a pragmatic response in which, although there was a measure of social conscience, the main concern was for 'the interests of the moneyed classes who composed the political nation'.[3] Politicians and writers on the economy saw little need for government intervention; wealth was being accumulated as never before and where the market seemed deficient the state provided the necessary institutions, such as the control of the monetary system. From the mid eighteenth century the economy developed spontaneously in response to market forces. The state provided security at home and abroad within which those forces could flourish; it did not provide the momentum for economic change and social development. Regard for property rights was a cardinal feature of public policy, even though there was considerable acknowledgement that property had duties as well as rights.

It was against this background that Adam Smith (1723-90) wrote and taught. His most important and influential work was *An Inquiry into the Nature and Causes of the Wealth of Nations*, first published in 1776. It is generally agreed that this book was crucially important in the development of economic theory and in providing a theoretical justification for the limited role of government in economic management. Interpretations of Smith's work are part of the intellectual arguments which have resurfaced in the last decade as the tide turned against Keynesianism and as economic liberalism regained the adherence of policy makers in many Western countries.

His main idea was 'that all attempts to promote national economic progress by restricting the activities of individuals operating in fully competitive markets were destined to be self-defeating . . . the message was that there was an underlying order in the capitalist market economy which had a natural tendency to enrich the people. Governments concerned to promote national wealth should work within that order rather than against it, so allowing it to exert its full beneficial force.'[4] This theory greatly attracted the many producers and traders chafing under the restriction imposed by the mercantilist system, and it increasingly accorded with the new ideas of economic liberalism which were shaping political attitudes. Smith assumed that the prime objective motivating individuals was self-interest, the desire to maximise one's own gain from trade. He also believed that the pursuit of personal gain in a freely competitive market tends to maximise not just personal but also national wealth. Combined with a belief in a divine plan for society this provided a persuasive system of ideas in support of economic liberalism.

Smith believed that the entrepreneur was 'naturally' motivated to maximise his profits. In *The Wealth of Nations* he wrote 'Every individual is continually exerting himself to find out the most advantageous employment for whatever capital he can command. It is his own advantage indeed and not that of the society, which he has in view. But the study of his own advantage naturally, or rather necessarily leads him to prefer that employment which is most advantageous to society.'[5] Smith concluded with a passage which became one of the main foundations for economic liberalism; it is likely that Mrs Thatcher had this idea in mind when she referred to the primacy of 'market forces'. 'He generally, indeed, neither intends to promote the public interest nor knows how much he is promoting it ... he is in this, as in many other cases, led by an invisible hand to promote an end which was no part of his intention.'[6]

In the continuing debate over the role of the state in the running of the economy, Smith has been adopted by those who wish to minimise any 'interference' with market forces. Support for this extreme *laissez-faire* position can be found in *The Wealth of Nations*. However, Smith was concerned with a wider purpose than that of providing an ideological justification for greed. His main aim was to influence those responsible for public policy. In his view, the state had three functions.

1. To protect the society against invasion.
2. To protect, as far as possible, each individual from the injustice or oppression of every other member of it.
3. It had 'the duty of erecting and maintaining certain publick works and certain publick institutions, which it can never be for the interest of any individual, or small number of individuals, to erect and maintain; because the profit could never repay the expense to any individual or small number of individuals, though it may frequently do more than repay it to a great society.'[7]

Smith's work can be seen as encouraging governments to work with, rather than against, those things which promote economic growth, and not as a blanket attack on any kind of state action. The need to raise revenue for the purposes of protecting both the nation and the people within it implied intervention in the market place, while the third duty opened up a debate on the proper role of the state which is still of the utmost significance in contemporary political argument.

The state and the economy in the nineteenth century

The nineteenth century has been described as the '*age of laissez-faire*', while economics came to be dubbed the '*dismal science*'. These terms imply both that governments adopted a 'hands-off' approach to the economy, leaving society to the mercy of the ruthless greed and self-interest of the increasingly powerful entrepreneurs, and that their cruelty was sanctified by economists, both lay and professional, such as Malthus, Bentham and David Ricardo, whose attempts to divide the *is* from the *ought* left the poor defenceless. Ricardo in particular was the most articulate supporter of the ending of government controls over economic activity; he saw an inseparable connection between economic liberty and economic progress. In this, his opinion was even more fervently *laissez-faire* than that of Smith and reflected the attitudes of government, turning away from the mass of regulation over prices, wages and industrial practices.

However, rhetoric must be separated from reality. While the ruling tradition in economics held that government interference with the free market would be harmful, there were other pressures at work, particularly industrialisation and urbanisation. This was in the context of rapid population growth and, in the earlier part of the century, the fear of revolution. Governments were led to involve themselves in more and more aspects of life. This process was intensified later in the century by the emergence of a mass electorate as a result of successive Reform Acts. Different kinds of economic activity must be distinguished. To oversimplify somewhat, measures designed to give more protection and security to workers and to society at large through the provision of regulatory and welfare services were a feature of much state action throughout the nineteenth century, while policies aimed at affecting the overall performance of the economy developed in the twentieth century.

During the nineteenth century, government policy towards economic interests fell into two categories. Although free trade became increasingly dominant in the field of commercial policy, with a vigorous programme of tariff liberalisation the attitude to other economic questions was more pragmatic. *Laissez-faire* ideas influenced many of the reforms to the banking system; but there was considerable regulation of the railway system, while the government itself ran some industries and services such as dockyards, arsenals and, above all, the Post Office. There was also a very considerable programme of action undertaken by the newly established municipal corporations to improve the local environment and provide services such as gas, water and public transport. Later in the century, this came to be known as 'gas and water socialism'. These municipal reforms can be seen as both 'economic' and 'social'; they had both an economic rationale, for instance that clean water and healthier living conditions would make for a more efficient, productive workforce, and a social aspect, that there was a moral imperative to improve the conditions of life of the people.

Thus, as society grew more complex and social evils multiplied under the pressure of factories and towns, it became more difficult for governments to ignore their responsibilities. Intervention in the economy resulted from a shift in social values, of ideas of what it was proper for governments to do. It was increasingly felt that the poor and helpless should be protected from the worst consequences of economic change.

Another important influence was that of Utilitarianism, whose founder was the philosopher Jeremy Bentham. Benthamism aimed for 'the greatest happiness of the greatest number'; it urged either more or less state intervention, depending on the issue. Benthamites were concerned about the relief of poverty and were influential in the establishment of the Poor Law. Increasing destitution had led to various local initiatives to succour the poor.

Most economists, however, saw these well-meaning efforts as examples of the adverse effects of intervention. Foremost among these was the Rev. Thomas Malthus, who in his *Essay on the*

Principle of Population, published in 1798, said that human beings have a natural propensity to reproduce themselves faster than they can increase the basic means of subsistence: thus 'Population when unchecked increases in a geometric ratio. Subsistence increases only in an arithmetic ratio.' Nature rather than social injustice regulated population; poor relief of any kind only made things worse, since it encouraged those without work to have families and thus to increase the burden on the ratepayers and ultimately on natural resources. This theory justified opposition to government attempts to alleviate poverty; 'the objective laws' of political economy meant that, as the economic system was naturally self-regulating, man-made attempts to intervene in the distribution of rewards could only worsen the condition of the poor. Most nineteenth century economists accepted these harsh policy implications. 'The idea that the laws of political economy demanded punishment for poverty, rather than a more just redistribution of incomes from rich to poor, injected an ideological bias into economic debate, which could only be justified by detaching orthodox political economy from ethical considerations and which has never lost its power to persuade some policy-makers that governmental efforts to equalize incomes are inevitably counter-productive.'[8] This lesson in 'economic realism' was to be repeated endlessly by the Thatcher government during the 1980s.

Yet the actual Poor Law reform shows the difficulty of deciding which of the various philosophical approaches dominated policy making. The Poor Law Amendment Act of 1834 established local Boards of Guardians to build workhouses where they did not exist. All relief of poverty would be given in the workhouse, where conditions for the able-bodied would be made so unpleasant that they would be effectively deterred from applying and so forced to work. This was the 'less eligibility' principle, whereby the conditions of the able-bodied poor in the workhouse were to be harder and more unpleasant than those of even the poorest outside in order to deter people from seeking relief. Victorians commonly distinguished between the 'deserving' and the 'undeserving' poor, a distinction which some commentators claim re-emerged in the social policies of the 1980s. The attitude of the Commissioners typified the belief that politicians were an untrustworthy breed, who would spend public money in order to 'buy' votes. The Commissioners opposed national schemes of poor relief, preferring local 'unions' with elected Guardians supervising paid officials carrying out the policy of the Commission. A national system would mean that 'Vigilance and economy, unstimulated by any private interest . . . would be relaxed . . . candidates for political power would bid for popularity, by promising to be good to the poor.'[9] One of the main claims of monetarism was that it effectively prevented politicians 'bribing' the electorate with promises of increased welfare spending.

However, the practical effects of the Act were different from those intended. Outdoor relief continued, but the number of males receiving it fell, and to some extent the moral stigma involved in entering the workhouse meant that the Act was a 'success'. Yet the Act also stimulated even more state intervention, especially in the field of medical services. There was increasing legislation about working conditions, especially for women and children. In other aspects, the lack of national action was marked; for example where slum clearance occurred it was almost entirely due to local initiatives.

Thus although many Benthamites urged that the state must place as few restraints as possible on the freedom of the individual, the coincidence of interests was not absolute. The Benthamites were not totally opposed to state intervention, accepting that in certain circumstances the attainment of the greatest happiness of the greatest number might require more intervention not less. Gradually, the intellectual arguments were shifting in favour of greater state intervention.

The changing role of the state

Gradually and for a multitude of reasons not foreseen or desired by policy makers or economists the role of the state grew. With increasing foreign competition, Britain's economic predominance was threatened and many contemporary observers saw the last quarter of the nineteenth century as one of economic slump. 'This was the period when Britain's economic position in the world was being challenged by the growth of the German and American economies and when forebodings concerning Britain's economic decline were first raised.'[10] The effects on policy making were considerable, and the claims of classical economists such as Richardo to be able to predict the future were increasingly challenged. By the 1870s and 1880s orthodox economic doctrine had been overtaken by events. There were also vast changes in the social and political context of economic behaviour, such as the growing strength of the unions and the extension of the franchise. 'Though economic policy and attitudes towards it changed only gradually, it is possible to point to a number of events in the years around 1870, all significant in producing a change of attitude towards state intervention in the economy.'[11]

Thus by the 1880s, the setting for discussions about economic policy-making had changed drastically. Despite the influence on economists of the theory of evolution, where the 'survival of the fittest' seemed to justify *laissez-faire* policies, and despite the predominance in economic thinking of the strongly anti-socialist Alfred Marshall, pressure for greater state intervention grew. This was the period when collectivism became an important influence on public policy, challenging the individualistic orthodoxy of a minimal role for the state in the provision of services such as health and welfare. 'Collectivism' has several meanings but in late Victorian Britain it implied a change in the climate of ideas in which there was growing acceptance, firstly of the necessity of state intervention to rectify deficiencies in the market, and secondly that public provision of many things previously considered to be the province of the market was essential.

Despite the general agreement that large-scale economic intervention was undesirable, indeed disastrous, the area of acceptable state action had greatly increased. Education became a public responsibility, and there was a major change in attitude towards unemployment and poverty among the able-bodied. Their problems came increasingly to be related to faults in the organisation of society rectifiable by collective action rather than to individual moral defects.

These changes in the social and economic climate affected the political system. The 1906 Liberal government undertook a far-reaching programme of social reform which laid the basis for the 'Welfare State', turned into a comprehensive, 'cradle to grave' system by the Labour government after 1945.

The significance of these trends can be over-emphasised. Public expenditure had risen slowly during the nineteenth century, and as late as 1913 central government expenditure was only 7.5 per cent of gross domestic product.[12] Government spending had led to little redistribution of wealth. Yet the domination of *laissez-faire* in commercial policy, especially in external trade, coincided with greater interventionism in domestic affairs.

The state and the economy 1914–1945

In 1914 Britain still dominated the international economy. She was the largest trading nation, the City of London was the financial capital of the world, and Britain's vast earnings from overseas investments helped pay for the imports of food and raw materials needed to sustain the growing population. The Empire still seemed unshakable and a source of economic as well as political and military power. However, the impact of the 1914–18 war was so profound that Britain never again resumed that predominance despite the frantic efforts of policy makers in the inter – war years to return to what was described as 'normalcy'. The First World War fundamentally altered many established economic practices and patterns and challenged the beliefs of economists, politicians, and the public alike. Most of these changes were regarded as temporary, but it was impossible to return to the stability of the pre-war period. The attempt to put the clock back distracted attention from the new problems and led policy makers to suggest outdated policies.

The inter-war years were marked by heavy and persistent unemployment and by a prolonged slump in major sectors of British industry. The economist John Maynard Keynes challenged most of the accepted 'truths' of economics and suggested a fundamental change in the relationship between government and the economy. Yet several historians have pointed to a central paradox of the period: beside the evidence of unemployment, poverty, industrial decay (particularly marked in the staple industries such as coal, shipbuilding, and heavy engineering) and social distress, there was evidence of remarkable economic growth and increasing prosperity. It is against that background that the debate about the proper role for government in the management of the economy must be examined.

The First World War led to a marked increase in the scope and size of government, and a system of controls emerged to allow the mobilisation of the nation's economic strength. There was considerable direction of industry, restrictions on the raising of capital except for the war effort, controls on transport, rationing of foodstuffs and so on. The government tried to deal with the problem of inflation, largely by agreements with the trade unions to limit wage increases. There were promises of social reform once the war had been won: slogans such as 'Homes Fit for Heroes' were aimed at improving the morale both of workers on the home front and the armed forces. A Ministry of Reconstruction was established in 1917 to draw up programmes for post-war social and economic improvement.

Few of these promises were kept, and once peace returned most of the controls were abandoned. The cry was 'back to 1914'. Peden concluded that as far as economic policy was concerned 'most wartime measures were temporary . . . The greatest impact of war on economic policy was the indirect one of disruption of the pre-1914 international economy.'[13] Britain's export industries failed to recover, partly because of lack of investment and outdated methods, but also because of growing foreign competion and the imposition of tariffs (taxes on imported goods) by many countries in the inter-war period. Many markets were lost, thus weakening Britain's balance of payments, a problem intensified by the need to repay war debts, primarily to the USA. Britain was no longer an international creditor; the attempt to regain the pre-war position led to policy decisions such as the return to the Gold Standard which put further obstacles in the way of the competitiveness of British industry.

After the disruption caused by the war, orthodox opinion about the role of government in the economy quickly reasserted itself. Provided markets were allowed to work freely, the demand for goods would equal supply. As supply was fixed or could be increased only slowly, any attempt by government to influence the level of demand (in order, for example, to deal with unemployment) would be disastrous. Inflation would be the inevitable result of government borrowing to cover excess spending. The level of savings in the economy would also be reduced, and interest rates would have to be increased, discouraging investment in the private sector, which, according to orthodox theory, was the only real source of economic growth.

There was a chorus of criticism of government 'waste' and 'lavish' spending and demands that the burden of the National Debt be reduced. Thus there was very considerable pressure on governments to minimise their intervention in the economy, and the belief that public expenditure should be kept to a minimum was shared by politicians of all parties. These themes re-emerged to dominate economic debate in the 1970s and 1980s.

After a short post-war boom the economy went into sharp and sustained recession. Unemployment rose sharply, and the debate about dealing with the new phenomenon of mass, long-term unemployment was a dominant theme of the inter-war years. Unemployment above all gave the inter-war period the name the 'Slump' or the 'Depression', and for the unemployed or those who lived in fear of joining them, this was the central issue which dominated their lives. From 1921 to 1940 there were never less than one million people (one-tenth of the insured population) out of work. Following the Wall Street Crash of 1929, which led to economic and political crises in many countries, unemployment in Britain worsened, reaching almost 3 million (one-quarter of the insured workforce) in the winter of 1932–33. As the official statistics excluded a number of groups, it is likely that the real figure was higher.

The burden of unemployment was increased by the effects of the war and by the decline of the 'staple' industries, such as coal, heavy engineering, shipbuilding, etc. Thus unemployment was largely a regional problem, most serious in those areas dependent on these heavy industries. Debate among economists and politicians concentrated on how to revive these ailing industries and was part of the controversy over whether and how it was possible to return to 'normalcy', that is, to the pre-1914 situation.

Figure 1: Inter-war unemployment rates in the UK (percentages)

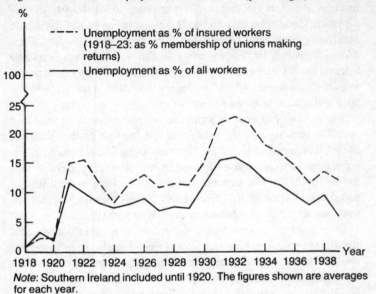

Note: Southern Ireland included until 1920. The figures shown are averages for each year.

Source: Charles More: *The Industrial Age*, Longman, 1989, p.239

Most politicians and economists blamed unemployment on what were seen as the high costs of British industry, which then found it hard to compete; the main cause of this was the 'excessive' level of wages, which must be reduced. During the 1920s employers attempted to cut wages, a policy executed with particular severity in the coal industry, and a major factor in the General Strike of 1926. But this was largely unsuccessful in dealing with the lack of competitiveness, mass unemployment and industrial stagnation. In the 1930s governments assisted industry to resist competition by a policy of rationalisation and amalgamation, which in practice meant closing uneconomic enterprises. The other alternative, that of tariffs to keep out foreign goods, was politically unpopular; the Labour Party was hostile, alleging that tariffs would raise the cost of living and thus harm the poor, while the Conservatives feared a repeat of the 1923 election, when they were defeated on a policy of tariff reform.

In fact, following the economic crisis of 1931, tariffs *were* widely introduced. This abandonment of free trade marked a dramatic break with classical economic theory. In the 1930s there was a growing realisation that unemployment was mainly a regional problem and governments tried to encourage people to leave the depressed areas. By the end of the 1930s rearmament began to make an impact, though as late as 1939 there were still over one and a half million out of work. Policy makers, believing mass unemployment to be unavoidable and insoluble, turned their attention increasingly to relieving its worst effects through the rather piecemeal extension of social security.

Another very important strand in the efforts to re-establish Britain's pre-war position was the decision in 1925 to return to the Gold Standard (at the pre-war parity of $4.86 to the pound) and fixed exchange rates between currencies. This was held to maintain confidence in the stability of the international trading system because it avoided the possibility of rapid and unforeseeable fluctuations in the values of the various currencies (arguments revived in the decision to join the Exchange Rate Mechanism in 1990). The constraints imposed by being on gold were supposed to prevent governments inflating the economy in pursuit of political popularity but at a cost of runaway inflation. The example of Weimar Germany, where the currency collapsed in the early 1920s, was used by supporters of a return to the Gold Standard. In general, it would reduce the ability of politicians to interfere with the 'natural' working of the economic system, something which was attractive to the Bank of England and other orthodox financial experts, and which enabled politicians to rationalise their own lack of action to deal with economic problems.

There seemed a number of good reasons for the policy. It would help to revive world trade, in itself good for Britain, restoring the primacy of the City of London and increasing British earnings from 'invisible' exports, such as insurance, shipping and so on. At a psychological level, 'there was a general assumption that the economic relationships and price levels ruling before the war were somehow real and absolute in a way that their post-war equivalents were not'.[14]

The decision, taken by the Chancellor, Winston Churchill,

under pressure from the City of London, the Bank of England and the Treasury, met with general approval. Even Keynes accepted it, though he criticised the return to the pre-war parity, correctly fearing that it would lead to over-priced British goods being even more uncompetitive. Most economic historians now see the return as a grave error. Its results included keeping interest rates high in order to persuade foreigners to hold sterling. This discouraged domestic investment, which worsened unemployment and delayed the structural changes needed to make British industries competitive. It distracted the attention of the policy makers from the deep-seated problems of an increasingly obsolescent economy and led to a concentration on wage-cutting as *the* way back to 'normalcy'.

London briefly regained its position as the centre of the world's money markets. But by tying the pound to a particular level against the dollar, Britain was becoming more and more dependent on the health of the American economy, and with the Wall Street Crash, which affected the whole international economic system, Britain went into a steep and calamitous decline. In 1931, following the formation of a 'national' government dedicated to saving sterling and remaining on the Gold Standard, the world economic crisis forced Britain to suspend payments in gold. Britain finally left the Gold Standard, though the pound remained closely linked to the dollar until currencies were 'floated' in the 1970s and their prices largely dictated by market forces.

Orthodoxy challenged: the impact of J.M. Keynes

Between the wars a school of thought developed which challenged orthodox economics and the prevailing view of the proper relationship between government and the economy. The growth of the economic role of the state had affected both economists and politicians, and despite the efforts to return to the pre-war situation, the climate of opinion was never the same. The main proponent of this new view was *John Maynard Keynes* who advocated more active government intervention in the economy. By the end of the 1920s he was demanding a policy of public works, such as road building, to reduce unemployment. His views helped to shape the Liberal Party's manifesto for the 1929 general election. 'Early in 1929 he translated the conclusions into popular terms with the ringing title, *We Can Conquer Unemployment* . . . This was a dramatic event: the moment when the new ideas towards which economists were fumbling first broke on to public consciousness. Here, implicity, was the end of Gladstonian finance and of the classical economics which followed in unbroken line from Adam Smith. Lloyd George's programme repudiated the system of *laissez-faire* and balanced budgets, under which Britain had once grown great and was now, it appeared, stagnating. Instead there were to be great public works – roads, houses, electricity, telephones, railways, paid for by a deliberate deficit. Idle capital and, more important, idle men would be set to work and would generate a prosperity which would ultimately absorb the expenditure involved.'[15]

These ideas were too new, appearing to most people to fly in the face of common sense. Though most economists were prepared to consider a public works programme, albeit as a temporary expedient, the Treasury view held sway. This was most clearly stated by Churchill in 1929: 'It is orthodox Treasury dogma, steadfastly held, that whatever might be the political or social advantages, very little additional employment can, in fact, and as a general rule, be created by State borrowing and expenditure.'[16] A later Chancellor, Neville Chamberlain, attacked public works programmes on the grounds of cost. 'He pointed out that it cost £250 a year to find work for one man and only £60 to keep him in idleness.'[17]

Keynes had not yet worked out his theory of the multiplier, that the money spent on public works programmes would then be spent by those receiving the wages; this expenditure on goods and services would in turn give employment to others. However, he argued that a programme of public works would not only generate some employment directly, but would also restore the confidence of the private sector and thus generate further employment. This was in contrast to the accepted view, which saw public expenditure as 'crowding out' investment in the private sector. This attack on the role of public expenditure in stimulating the economy was a feature of the monetarist theory which gained prominence in the 1970s and early 1980s.

Keynes gradually developed his theories, which culminated in the publication in 1936 of *The General Theory of Employment, Interest and Money*. He had become convinced that the dominant problem for Britain in a world depression was how to bring about a sustained economic recovery. He rejected the view of classical economic theory that recovery would eventually occur if governments allowed markets to work freely. As early as 1923 he had referred to 'the long run in which we are all dead'. Keynes believed an external stimulus was needed to raise economic activity to a level where mass unemployment would disappear. That stimulus was government expenditure, particularly on public works, to be financed if necessary by borrowing; the commitment to a balanced budget, far from being a sign of 'good housekeeping' was, in *the existing circumstances* a guarantee of continued depression. The multiplier was the mechanism for injecting this increased public expenditure into the economy. 'Keynes' originality was to suggest that the raised level of employment would generate extra savings which could be tapped to pay for the higher levels of government expenditure; consequently this would not eat into the savings available for private investment.'[18] However, if economic expansion fuelled inflation, counter-cyclical measures could be taken to reduce demand, including cutting planned expenditure, increasing taxes or adjusting interest rates.

Though state intervention in the economy grew in the 1930s, the most revolutionary aspect of Keynes' analysis lay in its advocacy of positive budgetary policy as a way of bringing the economy out of recession. Keynes was a Liberal in politics and believed in the free enterprise system as the most efficient way of delivering economic growth while at the same time maintaining individual liberty. But he believed that intervention was necessary to start the programme of economic recovery and to then ensure its momentum. 'Keynes' policy prescriptions, whether on domestic monetary policy, public works or the international monetary system, were all based on the same attitude towards the role of government in the economy.'[19] He criticised *laissez-faire* as a 'lethargic monster' and was equally critical of 'state socialism'. He set out his vision of the agenda which the government had a responsibility to undertake. 'The most important *Agenda* of the State relates not to those activities which private individuals are already fulfilling, but to those functions which fall outside the sphere of the individual, to those decisions which are made by *no one* if the State does not make them. The important thing for government is not to do things which individuals are doing already, and to do them a little better or a little worse; but to do those things which at present are not done at all.'[20]

The British economy recovered slowly and painfully during the latter part of the 1930s. The fall in prices of raw materials reduced the cost of living in industrialised nations, so that those in work prospered, while for the unemployed, life was a little less harsh. But despite the interest aroused among some politicians and commentators by Keynes' ideas, the government was still wedded to the ideas of good housekeeping and balanced budgets. Although some officials in the Treasury were becoming attracted to Keynesian ideas about economic policy, there were still fundamental differences of analysis. This was to alter under the pressures of another world war.

The state and the economy in the Second World War

The prospect of British defeat led to an almost complete national consensus on the need to utilise resources to the full and to allocate them as efficiently as possible. Britain's ability to win the war depended as much on her economic strength as on her military might. The government took powers to control almost every aspect of life. There was direction of labour and conscription, military and industrial, was extended to women. Non-essential industries were severely restricted and there was rationing of virtually every commodity. The health of the nation was improved, partly in order to maintain the ability of the civilian workforce to produce the goods and services needed to win the war. Half of the Gross National Product (GNP) was devoted to the military effort. This mobilisation of the nation brought the average citizen much more into contact with the state.

The economic dislocation caused by war was immense. To finance it, traditional economic policies were abandoned, especially the emphasis on a balanced budget and tight restraints on public expenditure. There was a marked change in employment policy. Britain still had around one million unemployed in April 1940, but the demands of the armed forces and the expansion of war work of all kinds led to a fall in unemployment and the recruitment of large numbers of new workers, such as women. By 1944 there were only about 50,000 registered unemployed, and increasingly employers were desperate for labour. The virtual disappearance of unemployment plus higher wages meant a rise in living standards for the bulk of the working class. With the increases in direct tax there was a slight change in the distribution of wealth towards the less well-off. There was an emphasis on paying for the war through taxation, rather than through borrowing as in the First World War, and there was a massive sale of foreign assets to pay for imports. Britain's financial resources were almost exhausted by 1941, though the full impact was masked by 'Lease-Lend' from the USA and by loans from members of the Empire such as Canada. Britain's debts in 1945 were £3,500 million, compared with only £496 million in 1939, while her foreign assets had almost disappeared. Only loans from the USA and Canada saved her from bankruptcy. The economy was distorted; the staple industries, such as shipbuilding, were propped up by the demands of war, and their adjustment to a peace-time economy was a long and often painful process.

There were radical and long-lasting changes to economic policy. The problems which faced the government were in many respects the opposite of those of the 1930s. It was feared that the virtually unlimited demands of the war, coupled with full employment, would produce rapid inflation, as in the First World War. For the first two years there was a lively debate among politicians and economists about both how to pay for the war and how to avoid dangers such as inflation. By the 1941 Budget, however, Keynesian ideas had become more accepted.

The 1941 Budget for the first time used a system of national income accounting designed to minimise inflationary pressures by relating government income and expenditure to the overall level of demand in the economy. This has been seen as the start of the Keynesian revolution in economic management. 'There, in the

1941 Budget proposals, lay the seeds of the British government's explicit commitment (in peace as in war) to a demand management stance, i.e. to manipulating its fiscal receipts and payments in such a way as to restrain demand when it was expected to be excessive and to stimulate it when it appeared deficient.'[21] However, the influence of Keynes at this period can be overstressed. Although he was given a room in the Treasury shortly after the outbreak of war he had no official position and much opinion in the Treasury and among academic economists remained unconvinced.[22] Official acceptance of Keynesian policies was piecemeal, related to specific problems. The first two years of the post-war Labour government were not marked by Keynesianism; it was the return of inflation and the balance of payments crisis of 1947 which led to the acceptance of macro-economic policies of demand management along lines suggested by Keynes.

It is a commonplace that one of the most significant legacies of the Second World War was the change in public expectations about the role of the state in relation to the social and economic well-being of the people. Although this change was partly a continuation of a trend present during the inter-war period, most commentators believe that the war itself was responsible for a major shift in public attitudes. Social factors such as the effects of conscription, the dislocations caused by the evacuation of people from the cities, the shared dangers of the bombing and the threat of invasion were said to have eroded (at least for a time) the barriers of class to produce a new social consciousness, an intense and genuine sense of national unity, a desire for 'fair shares' and a growth in collectivist attitudes and a widespread determination never to return to the 'bad old days' of mass unemployment, poverty and disease. Though both the extent of these feelings and their persistence after the war can be exaggerated, a major change in public attitudes clearly did occur and for a number of reasons the Labour Party was best placed both to reflect and to lead this mood. Labour ministers were largely in charge of the plans which were being made for post-war reconstruction, and the acceptance of Beveridge's plans for a comprehensive welfare state and the commitment in the 1944 White Paper on Employment Policy that 'This Government accepts as one of their primary aims and responsibilities the maintenance of a high and stable level of employment after the war' laid the basis for much of the Butskellite consensus which dominated British politics until the 1970s. A climate of opinion had emerged which accepted, indeed demanded, a peaceful revolution in the relations between state and society, one in which the economic role of government was to be of crucial significance.

Summary

This chapter has traced the evolving relationship between government and the economy. From a mercantilist system, involving detailed control of at least some aspects of economic life, through a largely hands-off approach, to the era of economic management associated with the ideas of Keynes, governments, whatever their philosophical attitudes, have been forced to take a view of how best the economy worked. Only with the election of the Labour Party in 1945 did governments accept explicit responsibility for the health of the economy as a whole. The next chapter will examine this new view of the responsibilities of the state.

Notes

1   Quoted in Rosalind Levacic: *Economic Policy-Making. Its Theory and Practice*, Wheatsheaf, 1987, p.11.

2   Phyllis Deane: *The State and the Economic System*, OUP, 1989, p.50.

3   Brian Murphy: *A History of the British Economy, 1740–1970*, Longman, 1978, 3rd imp., p.626.

4   Deane, *Economic System*, p.59.

5   Adam Smith: *The Wealth of Nations*, ed. R.H. Campbell and A.S. Skinner, Vol. i, p.454, quoted in Deane, *Economic System*, p.63.

6   Ibid., p.456, quoted in Deane, *Economic System*, p.63.

7   Ibid., Vol. ii, pp.687–8, quoted in Deane, *Economic System*, p.70.

8   Deane, *Economic System*, p.77.

9   Report of the Poor Law Commissioners, 1834, quoted in E.L. Woodward: *The Age of Reform 1815–1870*, OUP, 1954.

10   Roger Backhouse: *A History of Modern Economic Analysis*, Blackwell, 1985, p.241.

11   Ibid.

12 G.C. Peden: *British Economic and Social Policy. Lloyd George to Margaret Thatcher*, Philip Allan, 1985, p.40. GDP is a measure of the value of goods and services produced by an economy over a certain period of time. See G. Bannock et al.: *Dictionary of Economics*, Penguin, 1987, 4th edn.

13 Peden, *Economic and Social Policy*, p.57.

14 Charles More: *The Industrial Age. Economy and Society in Britain 1750–1985*, Longman, 1989, p.243.

15 A.J.P. Taylor: *English History, 1914–45*, OUP, 1965, pp.267–8.

16 Quoted in Backhouse, *Economic Analysis, p.253.*

17 Taylor, *English History*, p.268.

18 More, *Industrial Age*, p.245.

19 Backhouse, *Economic Analysis*, p.257.

20 J.M. Keynes: *The End of 'Laissez-Faire'*, 1926. Quoted in Backhouse, *Economic Analysis*, pp.257–8.

21 Deane, *Economic System*, p.170.

22 See Alan Booth: The 'Keynesian Revolution' in Economic Policy-making, *Economic History Review*, 2nd Series, Vol. XXXVI, February 1983, pp.103–23.

Part Two

Keynesianism and after: British politics and economic policy 1945–1990

2

The heyday of Keynesianism 1945–1964

For much of the time during which Keynesian theory (or versions of it) dominated British economic management, government policy was generally successful in maintaining rising living standards, a fairly comprehensive welfare state and full employment, while keeping inflation under reasonable control. However, this policy package (known as Butskellism) came under strain in the 1960s as evidence accumulated of economic weakness.

Labour in power

Although the Conservatives were expected to win the 1945 election, the result was a sensation. Labour formed its first majority government with an overall lead of 146. The swing, compared to the 1935 election, was 12 per cent, and Labour took seats from the Tories in every part of the country.

Broadly speaking, two factors caused this massive victory.

1. The public reaction against the past:
   a. people feared a repetition of the failed promises of the Lloyd George coalition at the end of the First World War;
   b. the Tories, who had dominated politics in the inter-war years, were blamed for the mass unemployment and poverty of the Depression and for the policy of Appeasement. Despite his popularity as a war leader Churchill was a prisoner of his party's record.

2. The positive image presented by the Labour Party, with its manifesto calling for:
   a. a programme of modernisation of homes, factories, schools and social services;
   b. 'Jobs For All' by using national resources to the full in order to avoid unemployment; there was a reference to the need to maintain high and constant purchasing power;
   c. the need to control rents and the prices of necessities to avoid inflation;
   d. planned investment, with a National Investment Board to 'determine social priorities and promote better timing in private investment';
   e. the Bank of England to be brought into public ownership and the other banks harmonised with industrial needs;
   f. an industrial system which could compete with the 'economic giants' by mobilising the knowledge and skill of the British people;
   g. the nationalisation of the coal, gas and electricity industries, inland transport (rail, road and canal) and the iron and steel industries (described as basic industries, 'ripe and over-ripe for public ownership and management in the direct service of the nation'), all on the basis of fair compensation;
   h. health services available to all, regardless of ability to pay, provided by the National Health Service (NHS) coupled with a system of social security for all, later to be dubbed 'cradle to grave' security.

Economic and social progress depended on the hard work and sacrifice of the British people. International co-operation was needed to ensure a recovery of the world economy and to avoid future warfare. Regulation would not be imposed for its own sake but as a safeguard 'against the chaos which would follow the end of all public controls'.[1]

This caught the mood of the time in a way that its Tory counterpart did not. Although Labour's policies established a *consensus* about the proper role of the state in the management of the economy and the provision of social welfare which lasted for almost thirty years, this did not mean that Labour embraced

Keynesian theories about demand management. 'The progress of Keynesian ideas slowed down with the advent of the Labour government in 1945, for although the Labour Party was committed to planning the whole economy, the planning they advocated was very different from that envisaged by Keynes.'[2] Hugh Dalton, Chancellor from 1945 to 1947, adopted a micro-economic strategy, concentrating on individual sectors of the economy, though this changed in 1947 under the strain of inflation and a serious balance of payments crisis.

Labour and the economy 1945–1951

The new government was faced with the dreadful economic consequences of the war.

1. Britain had lost about one-quarter of her national wealth, with much of her export trade lost to competitors, most notably the USA. Her whole economic system had been distorted by the overriding necessities of war.
2. Despite the war-time policy of 'fair shares for all' the standard of living of the British people was depressed; almost everything was rationed and the position worsened with peace. The *National Debt* (total government borrowing) had tripled. Massive efforts and huge sacrifices were required before her international position could be restored and industry returned to normal production.
3. A major problem was Britain's dependence on American aid. Much of the US government was hostile to what was seen as the 'dangers' of Socialism in Britain. American politicians wished to maximise the economic and trading advantages won from the war and saw Britain, despite her weakened state, as a serious rival. Policies to aid Britain were resisted; Lease-lend, under which the USA made loans to Europe during the war, was abruptly cancelled. In August 1945 Keynes was sent to America to negotiate a new agreement which would give Britain a breathing space to achieve economic recovery. Despite Britain's plight and Keynes' negotiating skill the loan was too small and was granted on terms that put Britain at a

disadvantage with America, the new economic giant. Sterling
was to be fully convertible into gold and dollars by July 1947,
i.e. holders of sterling could demand gold or dollars in
exchange. With convertibility there was an immediate and
massive run on the pound, and after five weeks it was sus-
pended and not fully restored until 1958.

This episode illustrates the extent to which the Second World
War had weakened Britain; this weakness placed major limits on
successive governments of both parties throughout the post-war
period.

Labour's aims

The government's programme of post-war reconstruction aimed
to implement Labour's socialist commitment to a fairer, more
socially just society while dealing with the economic consequences of the war.

Labour was above all dedicated to the notion of planning, as
opposed to what was seen as the chaos of private enterprise.
Instead of leaving the economy (and hence the well-being of
working people) to the vagaries of the market, Labour would plan
its development. This, it was hoped, would be more efficient and
would ensure that the benefits of economic growth would be
spread more fairly than in a purely market economy.

A number of basic industries were taken into public ownership.
Nationalised industries, it was believed, would recover more
quickly than under private ownership and thus make an essential
contribution to Britain's recovery. The government would be able
to pursue a policy of planning within a mixed economy.
Nationalisation did not aim to introduce a socialist society.
'Workers' control' of industry was never the aim. Labour intended
greater efficiency rather than a socialist transformation of the
relations between capital and labour. By the end of 1949 all of the
industries and services mentioned in the 1945 manifesto had been
nationalised although the House of Lords delayed the transfer of
the iron and steel industry until February 1951.

Later, there was much disappointment with the results of

nationalisation. The previous owners had been over-generously compensated, leaving the newly nationalised industries to struggle with a burden of debt. They were not integrated with each other or with the more general operation of the economy. The 20 per cent of the economy taken into public ownership was mainly the unprofitable part; the profitable part was left, largely unregulated, in the hands of private enterprise.

What Harold Wilson later called 'the commanding heights' of the economy failed to allow Labour to pursue successfully its aim of planning for an economic transformation in the lives of ordinary people.

Much the same could be said for other aspects of planning. Many of the war-time controls remained to ensure that production was directed to the needs of post-war recovery and especially to exports to enable Britain to earn the desperately needed dollars with which to buy food and raw materials. There was no mechanism for co-ordinating these controls and for integrating national planning. In particular, control over the movement of capital was weak; there was a considerable flow of capital abroad, much of it illegal.

In many respects, post-war recovery was marked; exports grew and industrial production rose impressively. War-time controls were retained and industry was directed to the former depressed areas. Dalton kept interest rates very low, to encourage industrial expansion and investment and thus to avoid the deflation and consequent high unemployment after 1918. Despite a sharp rise at the time of the 1947 fuel crisis, unemployment was not a problem in this period.

However, post-war reconstruction plus the cost of the social welfare programme proved too great a strain on the fragile economy. By July 1947 the American loan was almost spent and the convertibility crisis left Britain almost bankrupt. The government's economic policies appeared to have failed. In retrospect, the panic about convertibility was clearly a symptom of a much more deep-seated economic weakness accentuated by the war-time loss of export markets. The suspension and then abandonment of convertibility removed the immediate cause of the problems, but the basic weakness remained, compounded now by

Figure 2: Unemployment 1945-51

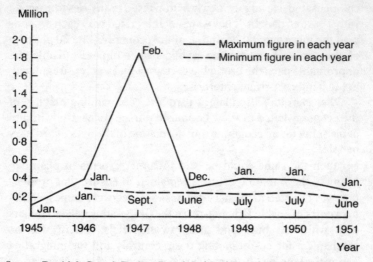

Source: David & Gareth Butler: *British Political Facts 1900–1985*, Macmillan, 1986, 6th. ed., p.372

a loss of confidence in Dalton's abilities. His resignation following a trivial Budget leak signalled the end of Labour's first, confident phase of economic management.

Cripps as Chancellor

In this period the government took explicit responsibility for avoiding unemployment but without risking inflation; these two policy objectives dominated the thinking of British governments at least up to 1976.

The appointment of Sir Stafford Cripps as Chancellor in October 1947 meant that Keynesian techniques were more fully accepted. Cripps began to cut government expenditure and impose *austerity*. The economic crisis produced virtually a seige economy, in many respects more severe than during the war. From the autumn of 1947 Labour began to lose the initiative, and Britain was increasingly affected by world economic events and more and more tied to the USA.

There were marked changes in the handling of the economy. Cripps aimed to control public expenditure tightly, relating it to the available resources, and to make Britain independent of American loans. The emphasis on exports increased as a way of ensuring national self-sufficiency. 'The broad intellectual pre-suppositions were Keynesian, with a reliance on budgetary policy and demand management that anticipates the 'Butskellism' of the fifties. Cripps, not Gaitskell or Butler, began the long reign of the Keynesians at 10 Downing Street down to 1979.'[3]

The emphasis on exports soon began to succeed. From the autumn of 1947 resources and manpower were diverted to the export trade in an effort to deal with the balance of payments deficit and to earn vital dollars. The benefits were rapid and spectacular. The economy boomed in 1948 in a way unknown since before the First World War; industry was regenerated, unemployment virtually disappeared, exports grew rapidly, the balance of payments deficit disappeared and a surplus was forecast for the second half of 1948.

Britain was again paying her way, with only the continued dollar imbalance as a major cause of concern. Britain was a major beneficiary of Marshall Aid, by which America assisted European recovery. Although it was enormously important, its impact should not be over-emphasised. The British economy was growing increasingly buoyant; Marshall Aid made a significant contribution to that process, it did not cause it.

Austerity

The emphasis on exports reduced even further the supplies of goods and services for the home market. This was the period of 'austerity'. Virtually every commodity, including bread, was rationed. It was a miserable time for most people and contributed greatly to the loss of support for Labour, mainly among middle class voters. Although rationing was gradually eased in the last two years of that Parliament, it was still a major feature of people's lives at the time of the next election. Working class people grumbled but accepted rationing as a system of 'fair shares'. Social reforms such as school meals and better medical services improved standards of health; poverty declined and full employment and a low rate of inflation helped those on low incomes. During the whole of this Parliament Labour did not lose a single by-election.

Political pressures led to less detailed, micro-economic planning. The emphasis during 1948 and 1949 was on loosening the war-time restraints on private business which it was hoped would be popular with electors – especially the middle class – at the next election. Harold Wilson's 'bonfire' of controls on Guy Fawkes Day 1948 was followed by a vigorous programme of scrapping restrictions on the manufacture of consumer goods.

Wage restraint

Working class support for the government was also seen in the policy of wage restraint; despite initial reservations, the Trades Union Congress (TUC), dominated by mainly Right-wing Labour loyalists, worked to ensure its success. Labour had agreed to the policy during the war, and the post-war shortage of goods and services made its continuance inevitable. Largely because of full employment and low inflation, the British people had money to spend but little to spend it on. Controls on incomes were thought necessary both as part of the fight against inflation and to ensure that goods were available for export. The government demanded that only exceptionally should wages, salaries or dividends be increased. A wage freeze became official TUC policy in March 1948 and held firm during 1949; 90 per cent of private firms also adopted a similar voluntary policy of dividend restraint. Although the TUC in September 1950 voted to end co-operation in the face of rising inflation brought about by the 1949 devaluation and the Korean War, the major unions were restrained in demands for wage increases until the fall of Labour in 1951.

Devaluation

By the spring of 1949 Cripps' policies seemed to be broadly successful. There had been a rapid rise in production and even more spectacularly of exports, and there were hopes that a balance of payments surplus would be achieved. But the outlook became very gloomy in the summer. A short-term recession in the USA weakened the trading position of the sterling area and world-wide speculation began against the pound. Pressure grew for devaluation. At first Cripps resisted, but following talks in Washington, in September the pound was devalued from $4.03 to $2.80. This was followed by deflation at home, involving heavy cuts in public expenditure, especially of capital investment. Reaction was generally favourable; the drain on the reserves was checked, exports were encouraged, especially to North America and the gold and dollar deficit shrank.

The 1950 general election

The government was confident that the economy was recovering. Inflation was under control, there was full employment and exports were rising. However, the election of February 1950 was a setback for Labour. Despite increasing its vote substantially, its share of the poll fell and its majority was reduced to 5, partly because of Britain's electoral system and partly because of a middle class revolt against austerity, controls and the general grimness of life under Labour. Nevertheless, Labour's working class support remained solid and Cripps' policies seemed to have been vindicated. His achievement was in holding the government together and in laying the basis for economic recovery. After the 1950 election Labour was physically and ideologically exhausted; consolidation rather than socialist reform was the agenda. Initially all went well. The Cabinet remained united and in good heart for some months, the post-devaluation boom showed every sign of continuing, and by the end of 1950 Hugh Gaitskell, Cripps' successor, announced that Britain would make no more calls on Marshall Aid.

The Labour Party was generally united, despite rumblings from the Left about the government's close ties with America, while the unions were still firmly in support of the cautious programme of consolidation, which stressed national unity and common sacrifice rather than an appeal to class solidarity and militancy.

The Korean War

The position was transformed by the invasion of South Korea by North Korea in June 1950. British forces were sent to Korea; expenditure on arms soared rapidly, gravely threatening economic strategy, social policy and the future of the Labour Party. The initial almost total unity about the need to respond to Communist aggression in Korea did not last long. Anxiety grew about the economy and particularly about the capacity of industry to respond to the scale of rearmament, especially as the government, under pressure from the USA, agreed a defence budget of £4700 million over the period 1951–4. Aneurin Bevan strongly criticised the decision as beyond the capacity of British industry. When Gaitskell decided to levy charges on prescriptions, dentures and optical services, Bevan resigned, to be followed by the President of the Board of Trade, Harold Wilson, and a junior minister, John Freeman.

Though the resignations led to divisions in the party, on the main issue Bevan and Wilson were right, and Gaitskell was wrong. The 1951 Budget was a political and economic disaster for Labour. 'The relative lack of growth in the British economy, compared with such nations as France, Germany or Japan, and its declining share of world trade in the fifties, had many sources, some of distant historical origin. But they can be traced, at least in part, to Gaitskell's one and only budget.'[4] In the end, the defence programme had to be scaled down by the incoming Conservatives. By the summer of 1951 the balance of payments position was deteriorating badly, more austerity was imposed, and there was a run on the gold and dollar reserves.

In the midst of this crisis Parliament was dissolved; Attlee's miscalculation has never been fully explained. The economy was in disarray, Britain was involved in serious political difficulties in the Middle and Far East, and the Bevanite rebellion was very much in the minds of the public. Despite polling its highest vote ever, increasing its share of the poll and actually gaining more

votes than the Conservatives, Labour had a net loss of 20 seats and
Churchill formed a Government with a majority of 17.

Labour in power: an assessment

Labour's first period of majority government had not brought
about the revolution some had eagerly awaited and others had
feared, but it was one of the most important administrations of the
twentieth century. Much of its legacy defies attempts by the New
Right to dismantle it. 'Labour had not engineered a social
tranformation or a significant transfer of wealth. It had sustained
capitalism, not destroyed it. But it had created a caring society, it
had transferred control of some industries to the state, and it had
broken with the divisive class politics of the inter-war period.
Perhaps, therefore, the message of the electorate in 1951 was that
it approved of all this, and that a future Conservative government
would need to move carefully if it chose to tamper with the
post-war consensus.'[5]

The period of consensus

By 1952, in spite of the strains imposed by the Korean War, a
sustained economic advance was under way. Investment grew and
private living standards began a steady improvement, from which
the Conservatives reaped a rich electoral harvest. With the fall of
Labour a consensus developed over the management of the
economy; there was a commitment to a mixed economy and the
use of Keynesian techniques of demand management. From the
outbreak of the Second World War to the early 1970s the British
economy was characterised by a high growth rate and by the
economic role of the state.

After the war the economy entered the longest period of sustained economic growth since the 1870s. Unemployment was
consistently below 2.5 per cent and for much of the time below 2
per cent. Industrial production rose by about 2.5. per cent a year
between 1939 and 1970, compared with 1.5 per cent between
1919 and 1939. From 1950 to 1969 it rose at around 3 per cent per
annum. Governments accepted overall responsibility for pro-

moting economic growth by applying Keynesian techniques, which the public, quickly getting used to rising living standards, saw little reason to question. However, the economy was increasingly affected by international political and economic developments. In particular the American economy played a major role in British economic fortunes just as the growing political and military power of America eclipsed that of Britain.

In 1942 Britain and America tried to establish an international economic order which would avoid a post-war depression. Keynes played a major role in designing what it was hoped would be a new system, comparable with but more stable than the pre-1914 Gold Standard. 'The basic assumption was that nations seeking to get on the path of steady economic growth could achieve their aims only within the context of an external monetary environment that was generally perceived to be both expansive and stable.'[6] The Bretton Woods Agreement established two new international organisations which have played a major role in post-war reconstruction.

1. The IMF was designed to maintain stability in the foreign exchanges by enabling participating countries to ride out short-term balance of payments problems. The IMF later played a crucial role as the weakness of the British economy became more apparent.
2. The International Bank for Reconstruction and Development, later known as the World Bank, aimed to provide investment funds to developing countries.

There were other initiatives aimed at increased international co-operation.

1. There were attempts to reduce protectionism and a beggar-my-neighbour attitude to international trade with the establishment of the General Agreement on Tariffs and Trade in 1947.
2. In the same year the USA launched the Marshall Plan, named after the American Secretary of State, which was a vast aid programme designed to supply the countries of Western Europe with scarce agricultural and manufactured goods.

3. In the 1950s a number of regional trade groupings, such as the EEC, were launched with benefits of various kinds, mainly for the developed nations.

This international co-operation mirrored the efforts of national governments to stimulate and direct economic recovery and expansion and contrasted with the situation following the First World War. From the start of the Marshall Plan in 1947 the world economy recovered rapidly and rates of growth in many countries reached historically high levels. Most governments were committed to high levels of economic activity and faster growth and the new international order aided the process.

In the 30 years following 1945, a period dubbed the 'age of economic management', the consensus which developed between the two major British parties was based on four specific economic objectives.

1. Stable prices.
2. A satisfactory balance of payments.
3. Full employment.
4. A rate of economic growth that matched the contemporary performance of other advanced economies.

These aims were common to all advanced nations, but in Britain were part of a wider consensus which came to be known as '*Butskellism*'. This expression was coined by The Economist in February 1954, in an article pointing to the similar policies of the Chancellor, R.A. Butler and his Labour predecessor Hugh Gaitskell. Butskellism largely reflected the policy agenda of the post-war Labour government and its belief in collectivism and state action.

There were five main planks.

1. The mixed economy in which the public ownership of the basic utilities and an active role in the management of the economy allowed governments to pursue a number of social and economic objectives. This was largely accepted by governments until the late 1970s, although Heath briefly tried to reverse the tide.
2. The commitment to full employment which was announced in

the 1944 White Paper and which was to be achieved by demand management along Keynesian lines.
3. Conciliation of the trade unions which had both advantages and disadvantages for governments and eventually collapsed in the 'Winter of Discontent'.
4. The Welfare State, with its promise of 'cradle to grave' security.
5. The retreat from Empire, counterbalanced by Britain's role as a nuclear power and membership of the Atlantic Alliance.

It was 'something of a social democratic package. It was a middle way, neither free market capitalist (as in the United States) nor state socialist (as it was to emerge in Eastern Europe)'.[7] There was a major paradox: 'There is no gainsaying that the first thirty post-war years of consensus politics coincided with both a steady reduction in Britain's international standing and a relative economic decline. Equally, one has to acknowledge that in every post-war year until 1973 [except 1958] the economy grew: the period saw the most rapid rise in living standards and social welfare. In this sense, the consensus coincided with economic success, even though Britain's economic performance was failing to match that of most other western states.'[8]

The period from the fall of Labour in 1951 until the shock of the oil price rise in the mid-1970s may have been one of general agreement about the aims of economic policy (although with often bitter arguments about which party could best deliver the various 'goods'), but it was also one in which there was a growing realisation of national decline. Both these themes need fuller examination.

Politics and the economy 1951–1964

After the 1945 election defeat there was a thorough review of Conservative Party organisation and policy in which the driving force was R.A. Butler. He restated Conservative economic and social beliefs, which had to show 'that we had an alternative policy to socialism which was viable, efficient and humane, which could release and reward enterprise and initiative but without aban-

doning social justice or reverting to mass unemployment'.[9]
Another important figure was Harold Macmillan who had been a
leading critic of the pre-war leadership's failure to tackle unemployment and other social ills. His book *The Middle Way*, written in
the 1930s, presented the case for the 'one-nation' Toryism which
dominated party thinking for much of the post-war period.

In 1947 the 'Industrial Charter' was produced, broadly
accepting the Welfare State and a managed economy. Despite
some rumblings on the Right, it was enthusiastically received by
most of party opinion. It was seen as an necessary prelude to
electoral victory and was followed by other reports which promised improved social services as well as reduced taxation based
on encouraging private enterprise.

The Conservatives won the 1951 general election with the
slogan 'Set the people free.' Voters were assured that, while they
would not be deprived of the fruits of six years of self-denial under
Labour, 'bureaucratic and unnecessary' controls on individual
enterprise would be ended. A combination of rising living standards, low unemployment and the Welfare State kept the Tories
in power for thirteen years. 'These were to be the years of
deregistration, of the burning of ration books, of growing
affluence among the working class, of the spread of material
benefits among all classes in a way never seen before. The benefits
were not equally spread but on the other hand nearly everybody
was better off. For ten years and three successive electoral victories there was no serious challenge to Conservative domestic and
economic policies and the comment attributed (erroneously) to
Prime Minister Harold Macmillan that the people had 'never had
it so good' seemed entirely appropriate.'[10]

Butler as Chancellor

Butler inherited from Labour a balance of payments deficit largely
caused by the Korean War and a worsening of the terms of trade
(i.e. the relationship between the cost of imports and the cost of
exports). However, although some deflationary measures were
necessary, a rapid and marked improvement in the terms of trade
transformed the position. Falling food and raw material prices

meant that Britain could buy much more imports with her exports. By the end of the decade the benefit to Britain was some £1,000 million per annum. This was not realised at the time, and the credit was given to Butler, who used the Bank Rate and changes in taxation either to stimulate the economy, or to cut demand if there was a fear of inflation or if a balance of payments deficit appeared likely. During this period there was a boom in demand encouraged by reductions in interest rates and taxation, both on individuals and on companies. Labour shortages appeared and inflationary pressures built up. It was easy for the voters to accept that the boom conditions and the rising standards of living were due to 'Tory freedom' as opposed to 'socialist austerity'. The programme of de-control continued, and by 1954 food rationing had ended. Many other controls were also scrapped; wages rose as did production. The slight increase in inflation was containable.

By now Britain was in the 'stop–go' era in which electoral considerations shaped economic decision making.

Stop-go

The fundamental problem was the perceived need to defend the value of sterling which was complicated by recurrent balance of payments crises.

Expanding economy – increase in imports and widening balance of payments deficit – increasing worries of foreign holders of sterling – sale of sterling holdings – international currency speculation. Bank of England buys pounds, reducing its reserves of gold, dollars and other 'hard' currencies to maintain exchange rate at predetermined level. Reserves fall – deficit continues – government reduces economic activity by (for example) raising taxes and restricting credit to reduce demand and thus imports to 'solve' balance of payments crisis. Contraction of economy – fall in demand – increased unemployment – fall in output – recession. But as general election approaches government reflates the economy – demand increases – election won – but balance of payments difficulties reappear. Cycle repeated.

'Stop-go' tactics were common from 1953, and despite denials by ministers, reappeared in the 1980s.

The 1955 Budget was affected by the imminence of a general election. A 'go' phase ensued, materially affecting the outcome of the election, won by the Tories with an increased majority. The

Figure 3: Stop-go

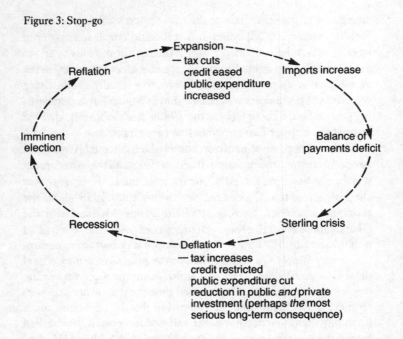

pressure on demand generated by this budget led to a 'stop' phase in the autumn. This inconsistent handling of the economy was later attacked as a significant cause of the British economy lagging behind its competitors. Although the Conservatives continued to heap praises on Butler for his handling of the economy, he was replaced by Macmillan who further tightened the screws.

Economic discontents during the short premiership of Anthony Eden were overtaken by the Suez catastrophe, which led to his resignation in January 1957 and replacement by Macmillan.

Macmillan's economic management

Suez did much damage to this country. Britain's international reputation was in tatters, the 'special relationship' with the USA was at a low ebb, opinion was divided at home and the economy had suffered great damage, both because of the costs involved and because adverse international reaction had led to pressure on sterling. The government's problems seemed so insurmountable that Macmillan himself believed that it could only last a matter of weeks. In fact, he remained Prime Minister for over six years, in 1959 leading his party to its third successive election victory in the midst of a sustained economic boom and rapidly rising living standards. This success was largely due to Macmillan's outstanding political gifts, though (as in the 1980s) the chronically divided state of the Labour Party provided an easy target.

At first things went badly on the economic front. Action was needed to restore the damage caused by Suez and the government was for the first time forced to borrow from the IMF. Growth was sluggish – less than 1 per cent per annum until 1958 – and the economy stagnated. During 1957 the Prime Minister and the Chancellor Peter Thorneycroft disagreed over the control of public expenditure. Thorneycroft believed it important to control the money supply – a view predating the *monetarist controversy* of the 1970s and 1980s. Feeling that the economy was overheating (growing too quickly) he introduced monetary measures such as an increase in Bank Rate, an indication that he preferred more unemployment to a decline in the value of the pound. Macmillan feared the electoral consequences of a rise in the jobless. He had differed with his party in the 1930s over unemployment, and refused to back Thorneycroft who, with his junior ministers, resigned. Macmillan shrugged off the loss of his entire Treasury team and quickly found replacements.

During 1958 the economy was stimulated and business confidence restored. The economic boom continued into 1959; taxes were cut and other 'sweeteners' were given to voters in anticipation of the 1959 election, which the Conservatives again won with an increased majority. Although this 'go' phase did not last long in the face of economic overheating, it enabled Macmillan to persuade the electorate that good times were here to stay. This was the 'SuperMac' phase of Macmillan's premiership.

The Labour Party seemed to face a bleak future. Conservative affluence, it seemed, had won over a significant section of the party's traditional working class voters. The 'embourgeoisement' theory stated that rising living standards had eroded the class solidarity of the workers who could no longer be relied on to vote

Labour, now the party of opposition, appealing to the shrinking number of the poor and generally disadvantaged. As in the 1980s, a long period of Tory rule was forecast by commentators.

The 'pay-pause'

The economic boom soon faded. The spending spree, much of it financed by hire purchase, led to fears about the balance of payments and inflation. A 'stop' phase began. Some economists argued that wages were rising too fast, leading to inflation which affected competitiveness. Rising incomes also led to excess home demand, which sucked in imports and diverted goods from exports. In July 1960 a nine month 'pay pause' for public sector workers was announced. This panic announcement aroused bitter anger among many groups of workers. Despite the growing feeling that unregulated collective wage bargaining needed to be reformed and that the trade union movement was a factor in Britain's increasing economic problems, the political insensitivity of the measure meant that this issue could not be dealt with by consultation and mutual understanding; instead, relations with the unions worsened. The introduction of other changes to economic management during the last months of Macmillan's premiership was made more difficult.

Growing interventionism

Government intervention increased. The National Economic Development Council (NEDC) was established in August 1961. It consisted of government, unions and employers and was intended to suggest ways of achieving more sustained and rapid economic growth. However, relations between the government and organised labour worsened. The National Incomes Commission, presented as an impartial pay review body, failed because the TUC refused to co-operate in further wage restraint, especially as other forms of income were largely exempt. There was a wave of strikes in the public sector, while in the private sector rises were considerably above government guidelines.

The 'dash for growth'

The appointment of Reginald Maudling as Chancellor to succeed
Lloyd following the 'Night of the Long Knives' (the episode
when Macmillan dismissed one-third of his Cabinet) at first
seemed to inaugurate a more positive era in economic management. He had had considerable experience in economic affairs
and was expected to turn the British economy round. Faced with
rising unemployment (which reached over 800,000 in February
1963, partly because of the harsh winter) and falling government
popularity, Maudling attempted to stimulate the economy out of
its depressed state, a tactic repeated by several subsequent Chancellors. The intention was to stimulate productivity and thus
exports, which would then end the balance of payments problem
without having to deflate the economy. The process would
become self-generating, because business confidence and
(especially) investment would not be adversely affected by 'stop–
go'. Economic growth could become sustained and continuous.

However, economists warned that a surge of imports, both of
raw materials and consumer goods would endanger the balance of
payments. The economy quickly went out of control and a huge
balance of payments deficit of around £800 million developed.

The choice of Sir Alec Douglas Home to succeed Macmillan in
October 1963 seemed to many voters to symbolise the decline of
the Tories into an irrelevant shambles. The Labour Party, united
now behind their new leader, Harold Wilson (Gaitskell having
died in January 1963), scented victory. Despite the recovery of the
Conservatives, aided by the short-term benefits of the 'dash for
growth', Labour won the narrowest of victories. The thirteen
years of Tory rule were over. Labour could inaugurate its 'brave
new world'.

1951–1964: Thirteen wasted years?

The Conservatives claimed that this was a time of rapid economic
growth brought about by wise and sensible economic management. But another view is that it was a period of lost opportunity,
in which the ground prepared by Labour was neglected by a

short-sighted and opportunistic administration, seeking immediate electoral advantages at the expense of the long-term prospects for economic growth. This is not simply an historical controversy; much the same debate is current about the economic
consequences of the Conservative domination of the 1980s.
Economic historians reflect the political controversy: 'paradoxically, while one widely expressed view of the 1950s and 1960s
sees them as years of steady growth made possible by wise
Keynesian policies of deficit financing, another sees inept
Keynesian counter-cyclical policies causing more problems than
they solved'.[11]

The years of Conservative rule from 1951 to 1964 saw the
appearance of the affluent, 'you've never had it so good' society.
Standards of living mostly increased, based on generally low inflation and the greater availability of consumer goods. Low (or vir-

Table 1   *UK comparative economic performance 1950–1973*

| | (i) Average % growth in GDP per annum | | | | |
	1950–55	*1955–60*	*1960–64*	*1964–69*	*1969–73*
UK	2.9	2.5	3.1	2.5	3.0
France	4.4	4.8	6.0	5.9	6.1
Germany	9.1	6.4	5.1	4.6	4.5
Italy	6.3	5.4	5.5	5.6	4.1
Japan	7.1	9.0	11.7	10.9	9.3[a]
USA	4.2	2.4	4.4	4.3	4.4

[a] GNP

| | (ii) National income per head 1960 and 1973 UK = 100 | | | | | |
	UK	*France*	*Germany*	*Italy*	*Japan*	*USA*
1960	100	92	91	51	34	206
1973	100	124	144	68	94	164

Source: B.W.E. Alford: *Economic Performance 1945–75*, Macmillan, 1988,
see pp.14–15 for full details of sources.

Table 2 *UK comparative trade performance 1945–1975*

(i) % shares of world exports of manufactures				
	1950	1960	1965	1970	1975
United Kingdom	25.5	16.5	13.9	10.8	9.3
France	9.9	9.6	8.8	8.7	10.2
Germany	7.3	19.3	19.1	19.8	20.3
Japan	3.4	6.9	9.4	11.7	13.6
USA	27.3	21.6	20.3	18.5	17.7

(ii) Volume of UK exports 1963 = 100			
1945	20	1965	108
1950	75	1970	140
1955	80	1975	182
1960	90		

Source: See Table 1.

tually non-existent) unemployment, coupled with the protections afforded by the Welfare State, relieved people from many of the anxieties which had been such a feature of pre-war Britain.

But how much of this prosperity did the Conservatives *create*? Instead of being responsible for a prosperous economy did the Tories limit and hamper growth?

The government was aided by a major shift in the terms of trade to the advantage of industrialised nations and by the enormous strength of the US economy. Although skilful short-term manipulation provided the Tories with three successive election victories, the signs of a relative decline in Britain's ability to compete in world markets were largely ignored until the early 1960s when the action which *was* taken was too little and too late. The struggle to maintain Britain's world role, the existence of an 'independent' nuclear deterrent, plus the enormous effort required to bolster sterling as a reserve currency, put a strain on the economy which led to massive overseas borrowing. Foreign realisation of the weak and exposed position of the British economy added to the loss of confidence. This seriously handicapped domestic economic management; the conditions attached to the IMF loan in 1976 demonstrated the increasing loss by Britain over its own economic destiny. Later economic decline may largely be blamed on these thirteen years of Conservative government whose complacency ensured that economic growth would be insufficient. 'Stop–go' policies undermined the confidence of industry to invest at home, while too much money went abroad. Defence expenditure, much of it wasted, was another drain on Britain's resources.

Summary

By the end of the Macmillan era the infirm foundations of affluence were increasingly realised. As the 1964 election approached Labour presented itself as the party of economic planning and industrial modernisation. Its slim victory can be seen more as a turning away from the past than as a positive indication of faith in this version of the consensus.

Notes

1   Quotations from *Let Us Face The Future*, The Labour Party, 1945.

2   Roger Backhouse: *A History of Modern Economic Analysis*, Blackwell, 1985, p.399.

3   Kenneth O. Morgan: *Labour in Power 1945–51*, OUP, 1984, p. 364.

4   Ibid., p.458.

5   Geoffrey Alderman: *Modern Britain 1700–1983*, Croom Helm, 1986, p.238.

6   Phyllis Deane: *The State and the Economic System*, OUP, 1989, p.173.

7   Dennis Kavanagh and Peter Morris: *Consensus Politics from Attlee to Thatcher*, Blackwell, 1989, p.6. See Chapter 1 in which they define consensus as 'a set of parameters which bounded the set of policy options regarded by senior politicians and civil servants as administratively practicable, economically affordable and politically acceptable'.

8   Dennis Kavanagh: *Thatcherism and British Politics, The End of Consensus?*, OUP, 1990, 2nd edn, pp.57–8.

9   Quoted in Stephen Ingle: *The British Party System*, Blackwell, 1989, 2nd edn, p.39.

10   Ibid., pp.39–40.
11   Charles More: *The Industrial Age, Economy and Society in Britain 1750–1985*, Longman, 1989, p.264.

3

The decline of Keynesianism
1964–1979

Although Labour from 1964–70 and the Tories under Heath after the 1972 'U-turn' followed generally Butskellite policies, Keynesian demand management fell apart when oil prices quadrupled following the 1973 Yom Kippur War. The economic shock and the accompanying political and social strains provided the opportunity for opponents of Keynes to apply *their* remedies to Britain's ills.

Labour in power 1964–1970

Labour inherited a serious sterling crisis which was the legacy of Reginald Maudling's ill-conceived policy. However, during the election campaign much had been made of the approaching crisis as a stick with which to beat the Tories and to some extent the run on the pound which followed Labour's victory was a self-fulfilling prophecy.

Wilson and his leading colleagues (who included James Callaghan as Chancellor of the Exchequer and George Brown, appointed to head the newly created Department of Economic Affairs, DEA) were immediately informed of the position of the pound. It was even worse than predicted. 'The likely balance of payments deficit was expected to be the largest since the war, the economy was overheated (with unemployment at just over 350,000) and the secret figures for the foreign exchange reserves showed that they were inadequate to defend sterling.'[1]

There were several policy options. One was to devalue the pound. This was rejected. The Treasury believed it would damage the standing of sterling and possibly the stability of the international financial system; it was expected to increase the price of imported goods (particularly food), which would reduce working class living standards. Wilson thought that devaluation would be a disaster; Labour must convince the electorate and international opinion that it could take 'responsible' economic decisions.

As with many decisions about the economy taken by post-war governments, there was a purely political dimension. 'With a majority of five the government had to plan on another election within a year or so and it was therefore in no position to sustain the difficulties associated with devaluation. Even though it would have been possible to blame the Conservatives, Wilson was convinced that devaluation itself – as well as the accompanying deflationary package that would be necessary – would be highly damaging to Labour's prospects.'[2] So it was decided not to devalue but to use other policies to generate the necessary economic growth to sustain Britain's international role and to increase domestic living standards.

Almost immediately the government had to appeal to foreign central banks to help contain a run on the pound caused by fears that Labour would put its social objectives above the need for economic restraint. The Governor of the Bank of England, Lord Cromer, put together a rescue package, in which support from the USA, fearing damage to the dollar if Britain devalued, was crucial. The immediate crisis was over, but the consequences were tremendous. 'The price of accepting this support gradually became apparent. It was not that strict terms were imposed but rather that the government recognised they would have to be "responsible" and not embark on programmes that alienated the international financial community.'[3] Increasingly British policy was constrained by international pressure: in particular, the US government closely monitored the efforts of Wilson and his colleagues.

The Department of Economic Affairs

The DEA under George Brown was intended to bring new vigour and adventurousness into economic management. The DEA was to be responsible for medium- and long-term planning while the Treasury retained short-term economic management. A highly ambitious National Plan was drawn up with the objective of securing a 25 per cent increase in real GDP between 1964 and 1970, 3.8 per cent per annum. In practice, the increase was only 14 per cent (2.2 per cent per annum). The Plan failed because of the over-optimistic targets set, the inadequate machinery for their implementation, and the friction between the DEA and the Treasury and their respective heads, Brown and Callaghan. Wilson's experiment in 'creative tension' failed.

Prices and incomes policy

Brown was responsible for a prices and incomes policy, another attempt to deal with Britain's floundering economy. A Declaration of Intent on Productivity, Prices and Incomes, issued by the government with the TUC and the main employers' organisations in November 1964, aimed to:

1. Relate wage increases to productivity.
2. Remove obstacles to efficiency.
3. Set up machinery to review both prices and incomes.

A National Board for Prices and Incomes was established, one of the many institutions (often short-lived) set up by Wilson. Initially it had no statutory powers and relied on voluntary co-operation, although later it became a statutory body to which the Secretary of State could refer wage and price proposals.

Cuts in public expenditure

Under increasing pressure, the government sought to cut public expenditure. Some of Labour's promises were abandoned or postponed and following a review of Britain's military capacity, cuts were announced which included the abandonment of plans to build aircraft for the RAF and the cancellation of the fifth Polaris nuclear submarine.

However, once the sterling crisis was over, the government appeared to be pursuing sensible policies. Callaghan was a cautious Chancellor and his Budgets managed to deliver some of Labour's promises to the less well-off while not frightening international financial opinion. A complicated international arrangement to support sterling was negotiated to counter speculation against the pound. Electoral opinion began to move in favour of Labour, who were helped by the inadequacy of the Tory opposition. By the autumn of 1965 most economic indicators seemed favourable, although this was deceptive. Both devaluation and severe deflation had been avoided. However, given the weakness of the economy, this was not a policy which could be sustained.

A worsening economy

Despite Labour's victory in the 1966 general election, the celebration did not last long. Despite the social achievements of the previous two years the economic problems had been postponed, not solved. Strikes damaged the economy. Foreign bankers felt that the unions had too much power over Labour and the pound came under pressure. By July there was a massive crisis of confidence among foreign sterling holders. There was renewed speculation about devaluation and the economy was deflated, including a legally binding freeze on wages and prices for six months, followed by a period of 'severe restraint'. Brown moved from the DEA to the Foreign Office. As Labour's hopes of economic expansion collapsed, the DEA was abolished in 1969.

Devaluation

The economic indicators worsened. The gold and dollar reserves fell, a balance of payments deficit appeared, and unemployment rose to 464,000 in July 1967, worrying for a party committed to full employment. Callaghan continued to argue publicly against devaluation, but pressure grew, especially because the government intended to seek entry to the EEC. Foreign speculators thought that entry would put a further strain on sterling. Despite Wilson's attempt to bolster confidence by an appearance of optimism, the situation worsened. Public confidence in the government declined, and by-elections and local elections went against Labour.

The crisis revived speculation about devaluation which Wilson and Callaghan had resisted. 'Wilson himself regarded the sanctity of sterling as so absolute that he allowed Cabinet to discuss the matter only once, on July 19th, 1966; and he refused to circulate the minutes of the meeting, even to the Cabinet ministers who attended it. Thereafter he vetoed all attempts to discuss the exchange rate in Cabinet, or even in any of the Cabinet committees on economic affairs ... Wilson continued to veto any formal discussion of the matter until the last minute, when he had already agreed with Callaghan that devaluation was inevitable.'[4]

In November the pound was devalued from $2.80 to $2.40. Central bankers agreed credits worth $3 billion, including $1.4 billion from the IMF, but on condition that deflationary measures were taken. To add to the government's woes, de Gaulle again vetoed Britain's application to join the Common Market. Opposition attacks on Callaghan's handling of the economy mounted and he changed places with Roy Jenkins, the Home Secretary. Labour slumped even further in the polls, there was growing discontent in the Parliamentary Labour Party (PLP) and in the Cabinet. Opposition to Wilson's leadership grew both inside and outside the party. However, he hung on, aided by the lack of agreement in the party about a likely successor and about the electoral consequences of a change of leader.

'In Place of Strife'

Britain's perilous balance of payments situation continued to dominate government thinking. Efforts to close the gap by increasing exports were hampered by lack of competitiveness and by strikes in reaction to the anti-inflationary incomes policy. The unions were thought to be too powerful and strikes, particularly unofficial ones, a prime cause of Britain's weak economic position. This led to the episode known as 'In Place of Strife' in which the government's relations with the union movement were strained. The humiliating climb-down of Wilson and Minister of Labour Barbara Castle contributed to Labour's defeat in the 1970 general election.

The 1970 general election

Though the economic situation remained gloomy throughout 1968, with further emergency measures in the autumn, by the beginning of 1969 it seemed that the worst was over. The financial markets began to stabilise and there were signs of a recovery of confidence in sterling. Public reaction to the 1969 Budget was favourable, largely because the increase in taxation was relatively small. The balance of payments situation began to improve and by September the deficit had been turned into a surplus. The changed situation was reflected in the polls, and the Conservative lead of more than 19 per cent in July fell to 12.5 per cent in September, and to 4 per cent in October. By-election results, though still poor, improved compared to those of previous two years. The pound strengthened and the Bank Rate, a crucial economic indicator, was reduced. Talk grew of an early general election.

The 1970 Budget found Jenkins walking a tightrope. Members of the Cabinet were pressing for a traditional, give-away Budget, 'doing a Maudling'. Jenkins resisted this, fearing it would not work in time and wishing to demonstrate prudence in this central area of policy. It was thus a neutral Budget, though much more optimistic in tone than its predecessors, and generally considered fair and realistic. Jenkins' reputation was enhanced, and Labour took the lead in the polls. After discussion in Cabinet Wilson opted for an early election rather than waiting for a further improvement in the economy. The date fixed was 18 June.

The Conservatives' policy review

The major policy review which culminated in a meeting at the Selsdon Park Hotel near Croydon (hence 'Selsdon man') marked a major shift to the Right and the first attempt to break the post-war, Butskellite consensus. The Shadow Cabinet formulated a five-point election strategy.

1. Stronger policies on law and order.
2. Free market economics ('rolling back the frontiers of the state').
3. The reduction of taxes.
4. The 'curbing' of the unions.
5. Tighter controls on immigration.

The Tories attacked Labour's record while promising a radical new departure in economic policy, and won a clear majority after a late swing in their favour. Several factors contributed to this unexpected result, but the publication a few days before the poll of adverse balance of payments figures for May (a freak and untypical statistic) probably revived concern about Labour's handling of the economy and allowed the Tories to exploit latent fears about their credibility. Healey sums up the election: 'there is no doubt that the 1970 general election was lost by the Government rather than won by the Opposition. The Wilson Government of 1966 to 1970 was not regarded as a success even by the Labour movement. It can now be seen as the turning point which started a long decline in the Labour Party's fortunes.'[5]

Labour's record considered

Despite some important social changes and attempts at institutional reform by the Labour Party, its handling of the economy has been much criticised. During the 1964 election campaign Labour had promised to modernise the British economy and to increase competitiveness and economic growth. However, in office, Labour's aims changed significantly, so that by 1970 it was able to claim that it had transformed a balance of payments deficit of some £700 million in 1964 into a surplus of the same amount. Yet this success was achieved at very substantial cost; unemployment and inflation had risen, and Britain's foreign debt had soared. The Wilson government had inherited a difficult economic situation but the major reason for its poor economic record lay in the handling of the devaluation issue. The main error was Wilson's determination to defend the pound, a measure of the government's conservatism. An early devaluation probably would have transformed the prospects for Labour.

The political effects of the policy errors were considerable.

1. The incoming Tory administration began an experiment in economic management which was intensified by the Thatcher government.
2. The concept of economic planning was delivered a major blow.
3. There were serious repercussions for the Labour Party and the wider labour movement. The failures led to a serious split in the party. The disillusion on the Left resurfaced during the next Labour administration and led to an assault on the consensus from the Left as well as the Right. This infighting contributed heavily to Labour's long exile from power.

In comparison with the other non-Conservative governments of this century (the Liberals from 1906 and Labour 1945–51) the 1964–70 Labour government was a failure. Its limited achievements could not match the scale of disappointment felt by many members and voters, and Labour's return to power four years later was more an accident of history than another step on the road to socialism.

The Heath government 1970–1974

During the election the Conservatives called for an end to the post-war consensus, blaming it for producing a stagnant economy, industrial indiscipline based on over-powerful trade unions and a lack of incentives for wealth-creating entrepreneurs.

After 1970, a new approach seemed to be on offer. The new economic policies 'encompassed trade union reform, reduction of state intervention in the economy, avoidance of a formal prices and incomes policy, cuts in public spending and direct taxes, and greater selectivity in welfare. These measures, it was claimed, would encourage enterprise and initiative; promote economic growth and reverse the country's relative economic decline. Entry into the EEC, combined with reforms of industrial relations and economic policies, would sharpen British industry to face new challenges and grasp new opportunities.'[6]

However, the 'quiet revolution' was of short duration. The 1972 'U-turn' reversed most of these policies. Though the reversal was partly the product of circumstances, the impression given by Heath in opposition had been misleading, though differing conclusions have been drawn about Heath's actions and motives. Some believe he was not a forerunner of Thatcherism; he 'was determined that his government would lead Britain into a new era of political honesty and economic prosperity. A true 'One Nation' Conservative, Heath wanted to make both the government and the economy work better to the advantage of the nation as a whole . . . his task was to reconcile and unite a class-based nation.'[7] Heath, a Tory in the Macmillan mode, was above all a moderniser and an expansionist, not someone who wished to bring about a return to an outmoded and irrelevant *laissez-faire*. If these interpretations are correct the 'U-turn' is easier to understand.

Supporters of Mrs Thatcher portray Heath as someone who accurately analysed what needed to be done in order to 'turn Britain around' and to begin the process of reverse the national decline. They see the 'U-turn' not as a principled decision but as a loss of nerve; Heath is accused of a lack of 'intestinal fortitude'. Martin Holmes bitterly attacked Heath's record: 'the Heath government was a disaster for the Conservative Party, and for the people of Britain, leaving only the lessons of failure'.[8]

These differing views are not solely of historical interest; they get to the heart of the gulf in the Conservative Party between those who advocate free-market solutions at virtually whatever cost in terms of social cohesion and those who argue for a more pragmatic and humane 'One Nation' approach.

Heath's new approach

John Campbell outlined four phases in Heath's premiership.[9]

Phase One

This period of 'quiet revolution' lasted through 1970 and 1971. The death of the Chancellor Iain Macleod shortly after the election was a major blow; his successor Anthony Barber lacked comparable stature. It is possible that some of the policy errors of the Heath government stemmed from this loss. The new government announced a series of radical measures.

1. Free collective bargaining was restored and the National Board for Prices and Incomes was abolished.
2. There was to be an end to state aid for ailing industries. According to John Davies, the Trade and Industry Secretary, 'lame ducks' would no longer be propped up and British industry would be 'leaner and fitter'.
3. The Industrial Reorganisation Corporation was abolished.
4. The 'lame ducks' policy would reduce the burden on public expenditure and also encourage employers to resist 'unrealistic' wage demands, unmatched by increases in productivity.
5. In the public sector the government would keep pay settlements as low as possible and public expenditure would be reduced.
6. Fighting inflation would be a major aim.
7. There would be tax cuts, especially aimed at the better off to encourage 'initiative', with cuts in social benefits (somewhat balanced by aid aimed at the poorest).

Almost immediately there was a departure from the 'hands-off' strategy towards industry; the giant Rolls-Royce company was on the verge of bankruptcy; it was given a loan of £42 million and in February 1971 was taken into public ownership. The strategic importance of the company for Britain's defence capability was the justification; however, it was a portent of things to come.

The most controversial piece of legislation was the Industrial Relations Act, which established the National Industrial Relations Court. The Act attempted to make bargains between employers and unions legally enforceable. It was an almost total failure. For various reasons, one of them the Act itself, industrial disputes increased during the Heath government. The miners' strike of 1973–74 contributed directly to its downfall. Heath's inability to 'tame' the unions was a theme taken up by Mrs Thatcher when she became leader and proved a potent weapon both against

Labour in the 1979 election campaign and against 'wet' critics within the Tory party.

The first phase soon ran into difficulties. Because of Barber's deflationary measures a recession quickly developed. Business confidence declined and investment fell. The slightly reflationary 1971 Budget failed to restore the situation and the economy slid further into recession. By January of 1972 the unemployment total approached one million. Most commentators concluded that the economic strategy was failing. At this point the government performed the 'U-turn' and the second stage began.

Phase Two

The 1972 Budget reversed the previous strategy; it was highly reflationary and aimed to produce growth of 5 per cent per annum. Taxes were cut by £1,380 million and a variety of welfare benefits increased. But the economy was dangerously out of control.

1. Inflation was rising sharply.
2. The balance of payments was in deficit and the pound was coming under pressure.
3. The 'lame ducks' policy led to many bankruptcies and to rapidly rising unemployment.
4. Despite the increasing number of jobless, wage costs were increasing much faster than productivity, and were passed on in the form of higher prices.
5. There was a deterioration in Britain's international position with exports increasing only a little while imports, especially of consumer goods, rose sharply.

A balance of payments surplus in 1971 became a deficit of almost £700 million in 1972. Sterling fell rapidly and Barber decided to allow the pound to 'float'; the Treasury ceased to fix the rate at which the pound traded on the foreign exchanges and its value was fixed by the supply and demand for sterling and other currencies. This major development in the international economic system was soon followed by most other nations, but brought little immediate benefit for Britain. The balance of payments remained in deficit, while the lower value of the pound added to domestic inflation. Unemployment became the major problem, topping one million (4.3 per cent) in January 1972; Heath was shouted down in the Commons.

Nothing so clearly distinguishes the change in the political climate in the 1980s as that no such clamour resulted from far higher rates of unemployment. It was on this issue that the 'U-turn' was most dramatic.

Starting with the rescue of Upper Clyde Shipbuilders, industrial policy was reversed. The Industry Act allowed the Secretary of State for Trade and Industry more extensive powers of industrial and regional subsidy than had been the position under Labour. The ending of the 'lame ducks' period is another stick used by Mrs Thatcher and her supporters to beat Heath.

A failed attempt to negotiate an agreement with the Confederation of British Industry (CBI) and the TUC to deal with inflation led to a prices and incomes policy, another humiliating reversal. In November came a statutory prices and incomes standstill, aiming to freeze most prices, rents, dividends, wages and salaries. This measure went through several stages of varying severity and involved the creation of a Price Commission and a Pay Board. The unions were bitterly opposed to the legislation, which they saw as limiting wages while doing little to deal with spiralling price rises; the climate of industrial relations worsened during 1973.

The main explanation for the 'U-turn' was Heath's acceptance of the consensus that unemployment was both an avoidable evil and a source of electoral disaster for the Tories. The conventional wisdom was that a government which allowed unemployment to reach over one million would be defeated. Though Heath defended his prices and incomes policy as necessary to deal with unemployment, economic policy was becoming increasingly inconsistent; each change of policy was making it more and more likely that the whole experiment would fail. 'The whole moral and political thrust of the Industrial Relations Act, that by encouraging a tougher, rational market system in industrial bargaining a more effficient and dynamic economy would emerge, was undermined by the Conservative economic policy after mid-1972. The Conservative government itself helped to kill its own baby.'[10] Despite all the work done in opposition, the Tories were unprepared to face the possibility that if the policies to control inflation failed, full employment might have to be abandoned. This dichotomy also confronted the Labour government of 1974–79.

Phase Three

During 1973 public expenditure was increased in a 'dash for growth' as part of 'the Barber boom'. By the end of the year unemployment had fallen to half a million. Stages Two and Three of the counter-inflation policy had some success. But the attempt to get a 5 per cent growth rate was frustrated by balance of payments problems and by May the government was obliged to cut public spending.

Phase Four

This final phase was marked by bitter confrontation with the National Union of Mineworkers (NUM) over pay. Stage Three of the counter-inflation policy came into effect as the Yom Kippur War in the Middle East cut oil imports. The fourfold increase in the price of crude oil not only reduced supplies, but also had a disastrous effect on the balance of payments. In November 1973 the NUM imposed an overtime ban in support of a pay claim in excess of Stage Three. The rapidly worsening situation led to a State of Emergency, a three-day week for factories and a number of other highly unpopular restrictions on the use of energy. An all-out strike began in the coal fields in February 1974. Pressure built up for an early election, although Heath initially resisted on the grounds that negotiations should be allowed to continue, while refusing to make an offer beyond Stage Three. When discussions ended Heath called an election for 28 February.

The government said it was a battle between a democratically elected government and an unelected body of union militants; the issue was 'who governs'. But a series of desperately worrying economic statistics undermined Conservative claims that the unions were to blame for the country's problems and their credibility was further eroded when a report from the Pay Board seemed to indicate that the miners had a good case for a pay rise. The election was a disaster for the Tories and their leader. The

Conservatives lost seats and votes and Labour emerged as the largest single party; Wilson formed a minority government, the first since 1929, and Heath had lost his gamble.

The Heath government: an assessment

Most historians have echoed the contemporary disillusion with Heath. 'Apart from membership of the EEC, the Heath government has probably left the fewest policy legacies of any post-war government, apart from the short-lived Home government of 1963–4.'[11]

Heath's failure to defeat the unions has attracted the greatest abuse, especially from those, such as the Thatcherites, who blame them for Britain's economic decline. Yet not all historians share this view and some contrast Heath's reluctance to use unemployment as a weapon against union power with Mrs Thatcher's less compassionate attitude. 'To his credit, he was not prepared to cow the unions by means of unemployment; instead he tried to buy their support for a form of social partnership now criticised as corporatist. But for the miners and the oil crisis, it might have worked. As it was, it ended in confrontation, blackouts and defeat. Yet it was a brave, honourable and high-minded attempt.'[12]

Labour in power 1974–1979

Wilson appointed Dennis Healey rather than Roy Jenkins as Chancellor. Although Jenkins had won much applause during his time at the Treasury, he was unpopular with the Left for his orthodox handling of the economy and for his enthusiasm for the EC. The government was a mixture of Right and Left. Jenkins became Home Secretary, with James Callaghan as Foreign Secretary while the Left was represented by Michael Foot at Employment, Tony Benn at Industry and Barbara Castle at Health and Social Security.

For the first two years the government sought to reverse economic decline by combining a number of strategies.

1. To deal with the balance of payments deficit it borrowed

heavily from abroad and encouraged exports, rather than adopt Treasury policy, namely that the economy should be deflated to reduce demand.

2. To ensure the growth of the world economy, a vital consideration for a country as dependent on exports as Britain, it tried to encourage other major nations, especially the USA and Japan, to adopt expansionary economic policies.

3. To deal with wage rises that outstripped production by an agreement with the unions.

4. To produce an 'irreversible shift in wealth and power' to working people by higher taxes on the rich to pay for increases in social spending.

The centrepiece of the strategy was the 'Social Contract.'

The 'Social Contract'

The economic scene was very bleak, with rising inflation and wages. Between March and October 1974, prices rose by 8 per cent and wages by 16 per cent, partly because of the miners' settlement. Following the oil price rise the world economic system was in disarray and inflation was worldwide. Labour and the unions while in opposition had accepted the need to deal with inflation. Both were also searching for a way to heal the wounds caused by 'In Place of Strife'. The 'Social Contract' was the result. Labour promised that, once in power, it would repeal the 1971 Industrial Relations Act and give the unions additional rights. The unions were to persuade their members to co-operate in voluntary wage restraint, thus avoiding a formal incomes policy which would put strains on the relationship. There should be a twelve month gap between wage claims, which would be related to price rises, while legislation would protect the economic and social position of the working class, such as improved social security benefits. In the event, the 'Social Contract' was a rather one-sided affair; Joel Barnett, who as Chief Secretary to the Treasury was involved in negotiations with the unions, said 'To my mind, the only give and take in the contract was that the Government gave and the unions took.'[13]

Healey as Chancellor

Healey's policy decisions had major consequences. His decision to reflate the economy, though soon reversed, while more powerful nations such as the USA and Japan deflated in an effort to deal with the consequences of the oil shock, was based on the hope that it would encourage working people to moderate their wage demands. Healey's task was made harder by errors in Treasury forecasting; in particular, the underestimate of the Public Sector Borrowing Requirement (PSBR) was to have serious repercussions.

The March to October Parliament was dominated by the imminence of another general election and by the serious state of the economy. The miners' strike was quickly settled, the three day week and state of emergency ended and the statutory incomes policy abolished. Other measures implemented manifesto commitments and the ground was prepared for an early election.

In October Labour won a slim majority of three which soon disappeared through by-election defeats and defections. The government struggled to deal with mounting economic and other problems with the party split on virtually every issue. However, by means of a variety of short-term deals and helped by a divided opposition, the minority Labour government managed to survive until it fell following the 'Winter of Discontent'.

Inflation, which dominated economic management, rose rapidly, partly because of increasing import prices (especially of oil) and because of rising wages. Britain's international competitiveness was threatened. Unemployment grew and the balance of payments deficit worsened. By early 1975 wages were rising by over 30 per cent and the 'Social Contract' was failing. Healey was forced into a deflationary Budget in 1975 and to impose large increases in direct and indirect taxation with major cuts in public expenditure. In July 1975 wage restraint was introduced. Increases were limited to £6 per week with no rise at all for those earning over £8,500. The reluctant consent of the TUC having been obtained, the policy was at first voluntary, although sanctions were imposed on firms to ensure that they could not increase prices to finance pay settlements.

Partly because of the exposed position of sterling during a time of world economic uncertainty but mainly because of fears that the government was unable to control public spending, sterling began to decline on the money markets, leading in 1976 to a major crisis.

The IMF loan

Attention shifted to the level of public expenditure and to the borrowing needed to sustain it, a concern orchestrated by the US Treasury, almost certainly with the connivance of some British Treasury officials, anxious for monetarist remedies to be applied. It contributed to a fall in the value of sterling which reached crisis proportions during the summer of 1976. By the autumn the position was so serious that the Chancellor obtained a loan amounting to $3,900 million from the IMF, granted on condition that measures be taken to get the economy back into balance. Taxes were to be increased and public expenditure cut; most significantly, the money supply was to be strictly controlled.

This marked the first major break in the post-war consensus and was a challenge to the predominance of Keynesian economics, more far-reaching than the unsuccessful and short-lived experiment by the Heath government from 1970–1972. The change in direction was set out in the speech that Callaghan, who had succeeded Wilson in March 1976, made to the Labour Party Conference in September, in which he formally buried Keynesian deficit financing. 'We used to think that you could spend your way out of a recession and increase employment by cutting taxes and boosting Government spending. I tell you in all candour that that option no longer exists, and that insofar as it ever did exist, it only worked on each occasion since the war by injecting a bigger dose of inflation into the economy, followed by a higher level of unemployment as the next step. Higher inflation followed by higher unemployment.'[14]

The IMF loan had been a panic measure by Labour. In retrospect the necessity for such an extreme course of action appears less clear. The Treasury had made some crucial errors. Officials had overestimated the PSBR deficit and had mismanaged what had been intended to be a controlled devaluation of the pound during the summer of 1976.

But it is clear that Keynesian policies of full employment were abandoned, to be replaced by the fight against inflation. This

opened up a wide gap within Labour and left an opening for the
Tories, who were increasingly taken over by free-market, monetarist theorists.

An improving economy

Following the IMF loan definite signs of improvement appeared.
The deflationary measures led to a fall in demand and a consequent rise in unemployment. However, North Sea oil began to
make a significant contribution to the balance of payments and by
the end of 1977 the deficit had been turned into a surplus. The
value of the pound rose and inflation fell.

The April 1978 Budget was somewhat reflationary. The
economy gradually recovered and living standards again began to
rise. Callaghan was expected to call an election in the hope of
securing a majority. Labour's position in the polls began to
improve and the party even managed to hold seats in by-elections.
In September, to general astonishment, he announced that there
would not be an autumn election. He believed that the government should continue until the economic improvements became
more apparent. Feeling that wage settlements were too high and
without consulting the TUC, Callaghan announced a 5 per cent
norm for the following year. The 1978 Labour Party Conference
rejected all pay restraint and in particular the 5 per cent limit, by 4
million votes to 1.9 million. From then on Labour's time in office
was limited.

The 'Winter of Discontent'

Support for Labour fell sharply. Living standards had been depressed
and pay differentials distorted by the successive phases of pay restraint.
Two prominent trade union supporters of the government, Jack Jones of
the Transport and General Workers Union and Hugh Scanlon of the
Engineering Union retired. Their successors were advocates of free
collective bargaining. Other new union leaders were more militant and
less able to control their increasingly restive members. In the winter of
1978–79 there was a rash of strikes. In January lorry drivers began a
national strike for a 25 per cent rise; this led to a mass of other claims,
mainly involving public sector workers.

In the 'Winter of Discontent' the government had other problems.

Pressure for devolution led to referenda in Scotland and Wales. When these failed to produce the results the nationalists desired, on 28 March 1979 the Scottish National Party (SNP) leader, Donald Stewart, proposed a motion of no confidence. It was passed by one vote, the first such defeat since 1924. In the ensuing election Labour was driven from power and the Conservatives under Margaret Thatcher were returned to office.

Labour's record assessed

The Wilson and Callaghan governments largely failed. They failed to control inflation, the unions, unemployment, as well as in policies such as devolution, Northern Ireland and Rhodesia. In this period Britain was seen being 'ungovernable', its system of government suffering from 'overload', trying to do too much with limited resources and facing a 'revolt' by taxpayers which threatened the whole basis of the post-war consensus. Opinion surveys showed increasing rejection of some of the main planks of Butskellism. This applied specially to the unions, increasingly seen as too powerful and a danger to prosperity or even survival. The mood became increasingly hostile to aspects of the Welfare State, which was viewed by a growing number of commentators and a sizeable section of the Conservative Party, as well as by many electors, as rewarding idleness and fecklessness. Social welfare policies lost favour, as did Keynesian-style demand management. Labour lost one of its major advantages over the Tories when its relationship with the unions seemed to collapse during the 'Winter of Discontent'. From being the party which could work with the unions Labour appeared incapable of controlling organised labour.

Thus the view developed that the social democratic experiment of the post-war period had been tried and had failed. A new direction was needed. That new direction seemed to be the one offered by the Conservative Party under Thatcher. They offered a return to free market economics, involving a withdrawal of the state from economic management, a reduction of the money supply and public expenditure. Much influenced by the work of the economists Milton Friedman and Friedrich von Hayek, these ideas attracted considerable attention in the media, which gave them the name 'monetarism'.

In opposition after 1979 the Labour Party moved to the Left. The administrations of Wilson and Callaghan were blamed by many party members for 'betraying' socialism: they had behaved like a Conservative administration, cutting public expenditure and increasing unemployment in an attempt to reassure foreign speculators and central banks. Partly because of superior organisation and partly because of a reaction against the Right-wing leadership of the party, the Left managed over the next few years to gain control of the policy making organs of the party and commit Labour to a wide range of policies, such as unilateral nuclear disarmament, withdrawal from the EC, large-scale nationalisation and so on. Thus the 1979 election inaugurated a period of confrontation in British politics in which most if not all of the post-war consensus seemed either to have disappeared or to have undergone a basic reassesment.

Yet in some respects the record was not so bleak. If Callaghan had gone to the country in the autumn of 1978 he might have won a further term of office. The economy had recovered from the shocks of 1974–76, inflation had fallen and British industry, due in part to state intervention, could have taken advantage of the end of the recession. The contribution of oil revenues could have been to the advantage of the Labour Party instead of providing a cushion for Mrs Thatcher. The miscalculation of the attempt to impose a 5 per cent pay limit destroyed any hope of Labour weathering the storm and moving into calmer seas. The verdict of history on the Labour government will depend partly on the success or otherwise of the policies adopted by the Tories to reverse Britain's decline. Whether Labour's record will be re-appraised by the population at large and historians in general depends on the fate of the Thatcher experiment, and the degree to which it permanently changes the political landscape.

Summary

This chapter has traced the role of government in economic management during the post-war Butskellite consensus. For most of the period there was agreement about the generally beneficial nature of state intervention to correct deficiencies in the market system and to supplement capitalism in ways which suited the political objectives of successive governments. A 'mixed' economy, run on generally Keynesian lines, suited a reformist Labour Party and a paternalistic Conservative Party. For much of the period, debate about economic management was more about rival claims of competence than a clash of ideologies. However, with the oil price shock of the mid-1970s this consensus collapsed, to be replaced with polices which offered a change of direction. To some, this was to be a progression to a 'bright new world' of personal responsibility and limited government. To others, it marked a return to the failures of the past, where 'hands-off' government ignored its responsibility to society while a minority were enriched. The next chapter will examine this new (or rediscovered) direction.

Notes

1 Clive Ponting: *Breach of Promise. Labour in Power 1964–70*, Hamish Hamilton, 1989, p.64.

2 Ibid., p.66.

3 Ibid., p.72.

4 Dennis Healey: *The Time Of My Life, Michael Joseph, 1989*, p.334.

5 Ibid., p.345.

6 Dennis Kavanagh: The Heath Government, in Peter Hennessy and Anthony Seldon (eds.): *Ruling Performance. British Governments from Attlee to Thatcher*, Blackwell, 1989, p.216.

7 Michael A. Young: Controversy: Heath's Government Reassessed, *Contemporary Record*, Vol. 3, No. 2, November 1989, p.24.

8 Martin Holmes: Controversy: Heath's Government Reassessed, *Contemporary Record*, Vol. 3, No. 2, November 1989, p.27.

9 John Campbell: Edward Heath, *Contemporary Record*, Vol. 2, No. 2, Summer 1988.

10 Philip Norton and Arthur Aughey, *Conservatives and Conservatism*, Temple Smith, 1981, p.150.

11 Kavanagh, The Heath Government, p.234.

12 Campbell, Edward Heath, p.28.

13 Joel Barnett: *Inside the Treasury*, André Deutsch, 1982, p.49.

14 James Callaghan: *Time and Chance*, Fontana, 1988, p.426.

4

The Conservative record 1979–1990

This chapter examines the manner in which the Conservative government led by Mrs Thatcher undertook the management of the British economy. The course followed offered a drastic change of approach and promised an 'economic miracle'. This chapter and the next will attempt to assess the validity of the claim made by Mrs Thatcher and her ministers that there was a British 'economic miracle'. The conclusion will be that this claim is unsustainable.

Introduction

The 1979 general election presented the clearest choice since 1945. The Conservatives, with a manifesto similar that of 1970 and entitled 'Time for a Change', offered the most radical administration since the 1945–51 Labour government. The Tories challenged the three main planks of Butskellism: the mixed economy, the welfare state and full employment, identifying what Sir Keith Joseph had called the 'rachet' effect, whereby each Labour government in office had moved to the Left with the Conservatives following in a vain effort to court electoral popularity. Thus the country was moving towards a 'command' economy on the East European model. The 1979 election was portayed as the last chance to avoid sliding into authoritarian socialism and to restore the 'proper' balance between the individual and the state.

This interpretation of events was part of the growth of 'New Right' thinking in Britain, which closely mirrored that in the USA; in 1980 the Republican Party under Regan swept to power on the basis of a very similar critique. During the 1970s there had been a shift in a number of countries away from Keynesian theories and the social democratic consensus.

Monetarism

Monetarism, which briefly dominated the economic policies of the Conservative government, was basically the rediscovery or revival of pre-Keynesian ideas. 'The belief that controlling the rate at which prices rise in the economy lies in the control of the amount of money in circulation is based on one of the oldest ideas in economics.'[1] Monetarism is the quantity theory of money, resurrected by economists such as Milton Friedman.

Monetarism concentrates on the price level because it believes that a situation of non-inflation best creates the conditions in which the economy can flourish. Zero or near zero inflation will stimulate the private sector of the economy into growth. Demand management in order to stimulate economic growth along Keynesian lines is self-defeating, in that it will 'crowd out' private sector investment and generate inflation, the enemy of real economic improvement. The only way to control prices is through the money supply. Thus the growth of the money supply should be related to the expected growth rate of real output; in this way extra output can be purchased at existing prices. Balance of payments problems will be dealt with by allowing the exchange rate to float freely.

Governments should resist the temptation to create money by spending more than they receive, i.e. by borrowing (the PSBR) and should aim at balanced budgets. Public expenditure should be tightly controlled because individuals and markets are better than politicians and bureaucrats at deciding what should be consumed. Taxes can then be cut, leaving more money in people's pockets, increasing the incentive to work harder and more efficiently, leading to economic growth. This would be 'real' growth, as opposed to the 'artificial' growth of Keynesian-dominated governments, propping up 'lame duck' industries and subsidising inflationary wage demands by over-powerful unions.

In assuming that for non-inflationary growth to begin supply must be created *before* demand, this approach stressed 'supply-side' economics. The micro-economic effects were far-reaching. Market forces must be encouraged and the fortunes of individuals and firms allowed to succeed or fail only in so far as they served those markets, although there would be a safety-net of sorts for those individuals unable to cope with the demands of a market economy. In particular, the market for labour, rather than the activities of government, would determine whether a person had a job or not. The ability of unions (and of professional bodies) to resist market forces must be destroyed in the name of economic progress.

These ideas had enormous economic, social and political effects, marking a return to a society where the individual is held responsible for his own destiny and the role of government is limited. The post-war drive towards equality was reversed. To be rich became the social model to which the British were to aspire. Some proponents of this doctrine believed that poverty was unnecessary; thus the poor must in some way be responsible for their own condition and too much concern should no longer be shown for their situation.

Monetarism was based on the view that the money supply was the main determinant of inflation; by controlling the money supply the government could control inflation, thus restoring Britain's competitive position. Economic growth could recommence. Unemployment, which would of necessity rise considerably in the early stages as government ceased to prop up uncompetitive industries and took other corrective action, would begin to fall. However, there would be no return to the 'artificial' levels of full employment brought about by Keynesian techniques. From now on, the free market would fix the level of employment in the economy. The control of inflation was said to be the major governmental contribution to economic recovery. If mass unemployment resulted it was to be blamed on world economic conditions and the interference in market forces by trade unions and other groups. The government would accept no responsibility. 'The political significance of monetarism was that in placing sound money once more on a pedestal above all other objectives of economic policy it rejected Keynesian modes of intervention. The objectives of Keynesian policies were derided as far too ambitious. Governments could not choose how much unemployment or inflation or growth they wanted and then engineer it. In the monetarist world the only policy governments needed to have was a policy for controlling the money supply. If governments delivered sound money then the economy would be stabilised. The amount of employment and the rate of growth both depended on the conditions prevailing in particular markets. They could not be altered by injections of demand from the centre.'[2]

These theories were most closely identified with Milton Friedman, but F.A. von Hayek was another major influence on Mrs Thatcher and her wing of the Conservative Party. He believed that the role of government should be limited to creating the necessary conditions for a market economy to thrive. It should not attempt to redistribute wealth or to seek social justice. Market forces, individualism and sound money should be the values governments should subscribe to.

The initial diagnosis

The Conservatives identified the root cause of Britain's poor economic performance as lack of international competitiveness. Mrs Thatcher and her supporters concluded that no government could secure full employment. Previous efforts to boost the economy by injecting demand had led to higher inflation, not more jobs, while measures to protect employment had cushioned declining industries and hampered the drive for more efficiency by distorting 'market forces'. The result of previous policies was low growth, poor productivity and lack of competitiveness with steadily rising unemployment worsened by rigidities in the labour market caused by excessive union power.

The job of government was to reduce inflation, help remove market distortions and create the conditions for economic success. The tax system was seen as a major constraint on enterprise, because the 'burden' of direct taxation acted as a disincentive to entrepreneurs to create wealth for themselves and for the nation. The stated aim of the Tories was to release initiative and enterprise on a scale that would produce an economic 'miracle'. Thus the 1979 manifesto emphasised a number of themes.

1. The first priority was to be the control of inflation through the use of monetarist techniques, particularly the reduction of the money supply.
2. Government borrowing (the PSBR) was to be reduced and there was to be an assault on 'waste' in the public sector.
3. Privatisation, although mentioned, was a relatively minor

theme, although its importance, both economic and electoral, grew later.

4. Enterprise was to be promoted through cutting direct taxes and the deregulation of industry. A 'hands-off' approach to industry was promised along with a commitment to end the 'lame ducks' policies of previous governments.

5. There was a foretaste of the themes of 'a property and share-owning democracy'; legislation was promised to force local authorities to sell council houses to sitting tenants.

6. There was a promise that there would be no form of incomes policy; union power would be curbed and the law on trade unions altered to 'hand power back to the members'. There was a general assault on the 'corporatist' style of government–union relations, with a pledge that the power of the 'union barons' would be trimmed.

Though many Conservatives had doubts about this strategy, the most senior economic ministries were in the hands of the Prime Minister's supporters, who came to be known as the 'dries' (as opposed to her critics, who were dubbed 'wets'). Sir Geoffrey Howe became Chancellor of the Exchequer, Sir Keith Joseph was Secretary of State for Industry and John Nott Trade Secretary.

The economic policies of the Thatcher government fell into several phases which have been analysed by Paul Whiteley.[3] He saw little of the continuity of policy of which Thatcherites boasted. 'far from there being a well-defined economic strategy during the Thatcher years there have been inconsistent policies which have often ignored the underlying problems of deindustrialisation'.[4]

Phase One: early monetarism

In this period the government attempted to implement monetarist policies. 'Monetarism embraces fixed rules of monetary management and eschews counter-cyclical policies which argue that monetary policy should be relaxed in time of recession and tightened in time of boom.'[5]

Howe's first Budget established four principles on which the new strategy would rest.

1. A 'strengthening of initiative' to allow people to keep more of
   what they earned. The top rate of income tax was cut from 83
   per cent to 60 per cent and the standard rate from 33 per cent
   to 30 per cent plus other cuts in direct taxation. Partly to
   finance these tax cuts and partly to prevent an increase in the
   money supply there were substantial increases in indirect
   taxation; in particular the virtual doubling of VAT was attacked
   for its effects on inflation and the condition of the less well-off.
   The strategy of reducing direct and increasing indirect
   taxation also aimed to extend choice: with more of their
   earnings retained and increased taxes on consumption people
   could choose whether to spend or save instead of allowing the
   state to do it for them.
2. The enlargement of freedom by reducing the role of the state
   in the economy. This involved an end to the 'lame ducks'
   policy, ending controls on pay, prices and dividends, in-
   augurating an end to exchange controls and reducing the
   subsidies to nationalised industries.
3. Control of the money supply and a reduction in the PSBR from
   4.6 per cent of GDP in 1980–81 to 1.5 per cent by 1983–84.
   Public expenditure was to be cut by subjecting it to cash limits,
   with large sums to be raised from the sale of public assets.
   Targets were set for the growth of the money supply (defined
   as M3, i.e. cash plus current and deposit accounts in banks).
   This attempt to define the money supply soon ran into
   difficulties as it was realised that the money supply was impossible to define with accuracy and thus hard to control. For a few
   years Treasury ministers gave the impression that the sole
   guide to the success of the government's policies and hence of
   the economic health of the country was the monthly figures for
   the money supply. As time went on, political and academic
   support for the money supply as a weapon declined; other
   factors, most notably the exchange and interests rates, took its
   place as the bedrock of Thatcherite orthodoxy.
4. The link between inflation and pay was emphasised. Although
   there was no overt incomes policy, the government attempted
   to influence the level of pay settlements, indirectly in the
   private sector by urging that they reflect the money supply

targets and by increasing interest rates in order to prevent firms borrowing money to get out of difficulties, and directly in the public sector by attempting to contain wage increases by imposing cash limits. Although it would be an over-simplification to argue that the government intended to use unemployment to reduce wage rates and inflation, there is no doubt that this was partly the strategy. Mrs Thatcher and other ministers warned about workers 'pricing themselves out of a job' and for a while pay settlements reflected the very consider-able increase in unemployment of the first few years of Mrs Thatcher's premiership.

The results

Inflation rose rapidly and was further increased as oil prices rose following the overthrow of the Shah of Iran. Inflation reached 22 per cent in the second quarter of 1980, although it began to fall in the third quarter, reaching single figures by the time of the 1983 election. Bank lending went up as firms tried to get over what they hoped would be short-term difficulties. Government revenue fell leading to further cuts in public spending. The Minimum Lend-ing Rate (formerly called Bank Rate) rose to 17 per cent in the autumn of 1979; high interest rates were intended to reduce the demand for credit, partly as an anti-inflationary device and partly to prevent employers borrowing to finance 'excessive' pay rises.

The Medium Term Financial Strategy

The MTFS was introduced in the 1980 Budget. It aimed to establish clear targets for monetary growth over a number of years. This envisaged a planned growth of M3 of between 7 per cent and 11 per cent in 1980–1, falling to 4 per cent–8 per cent by 1983–4. Expectations of inflationary growth were to be reduced by convincing the market that the government would stick to its aim of reducing the growth in the money supply. In the event, these targets were not achieved and were gradually abandoned. Pressure from the strong pound and a deepening recession eventually forced a departure from strict monetary guidelines and despite targets for the growth of money supply not being reached, interest rates were reduced. Unemployment continued to grow although labour costs also increased.

This decision to abandon monetary targets gradually has been the source of much controversy. Monetarists criticise it as responsible for the inflation which returned following the 1987 election, the distortions caused by soaring house prices and then by the serious slump in the housing market when recession struck at the end of the decade, and the growing balance of payments deficit. This view was emphasised by Sir Alan Walters, who saw the need to raise interest rates nine times in the second half of 1988 as a belated attempt to correct past mistakes. Other critics argued that the government had been wrong in the first place to put such emphasis on monetary policy. Efforts should have been made to stabilise the exchange rate; failure to do so was at the root of the deindustrialisation so marked in the early Thatcher years.

The exchange rate

Another factor which helped push Britain into recession was a sharp rise in the exchange rate. 'Hot' money was attracted into Britain, which drove up the value of sterling at a time when North Sea oil was having the same effect. The price of exports was increased and the price of imports was reduced, worsening Britain's competitive position and adding to unemployment. Ministers and their advisers did not foresee the effects of high interest rates on the exchange rate. 'What the MTFS had failed to take account of was the crucial importance of the exchange rate. If the pound is too high, this has an adverse effect on the ability of British industry to compete against manufacturers from overseas, both in export markets and at home.'[6] The high interest rates hit industrial investment, and unemployment in the capital goods and construction industries grew rapidly. 'Distress' borrowing, in which companies borrowed simply to stay in business, grew, leading to increased pressure on the money supply, especially as public sector borrowing also rose under the pressure of the recession. Monetarist theory was failing to match reality.

No 'U-turn'

Amid fears of a major recession pressure grew for a change of policy, resisted by Mrs Thatcher in the phrase 'You turn if you like. The lady's not for turning', a reference to the 1972 'U-turn'. Heath had become increasingly critical of government economic management, in turn to be accused by 'dries' of a lack of 'intestinal fortitude'. This battle between the two wings of the Tory Party

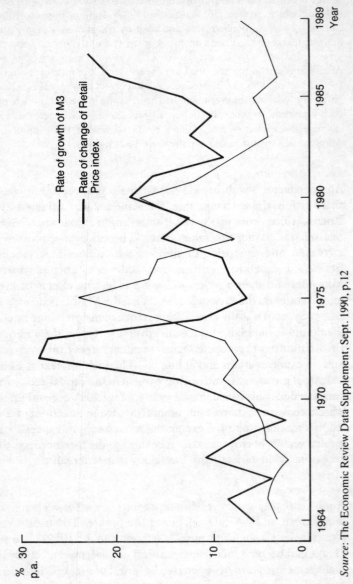

Figure 4: Monetary growth and inflation in the UK

— Rate of growth of M3

— Rate of change of Retail
Price index

% 30
p.a.

20

10

0

1964   1970   1975   1980   1985   1989
                                                              Year

Source: The Economic Review Data Supplement, Sept. 1990, p.12

rumbled on for the rest of the decade.

The 1981 Budget ignored the rise in unemployment and did not index tax thresholds and allowances, in effect raising taxes. This tightening of policy came when the economy was in deep recession and produced a sharp increase in unemployment. 'Contrary to all post-war conventional economic wisdom, fiscal policy was tightened substantially in face of sharply rising unemployment.'[7] Many critics saw parallels with the Depression of the 1930s, and in a letter to *The Times* 364 leading university economists, including four former chief economic advisers to various governments, warned that the policies being pursued would deepen the depression. The government, to demonstrate to the financial markets the seriousness of its anti-inflationary policy, refused to change course; Sir Alan Walters called the 1981 Budget a turning-point in establishing financial confidence, while Professor Patrick Minford, a noted monetarist, said that it 'brought inflation expectations down decisively'.[8] Some have seen the 1981 Budget as a turning-point. Others, however, see it in a much less favourable light; Jim Prior referred to it as a 'stinker' and in retrospect thought that he should have resigned in protest at the damage being done to industry. Initially public reaction was hostile.

Support for the government fell sharply. Ministers followed Mrs Thatcher's lead in arguing that the adverse economic indicators were either exaggerated by disgruntled Keynesians or were the necessary prelude to the creation of a 'leaner and fitter' British economy. Joseph later admitted that the government did not realise how far the exchange rate would rise and what pressures this would produce for business. But he claimed (perhaps with the benefit of hindsight) that *only* such pressures would have forced the management transformation and persuaded the unions to moderate their wage demands in order to avoid unemployment, key claims of the New Right, but both increasingly challenged by critics.

The consequences

The economic consequences of this experiment in monetarism were far-reaching. Supporters believe that the conditions were being created for a 'turn-round' in the economy. Professor Geoffrey Maynard, discussing the first few years of the Thatcher government, said 'there are . . . signs, particularly in the greatly improved productivity performance of British industry in recent years which suggest that a real and much needed transformation has taken place and can bode well for the future'.[9] Samuel Brittan said that the government deserves 'two cheers' for avoiding some of the traps that post-war governments have fallen into and for 'starting to reduce the difference in performance between Britain and her main trading partners'.[10]

Critics point to a significant weakening in Britain's economic position at this time. GDP fell sharply in 1980 from the level of the previous year and did not recover until 1983. Supporters made much of the rise in output as a key component in the 'economic miracle'. But although output per person employed, the key measure of productivity, did reach pre-Thatcher levels by 1982, it reflected a rapid rise in unemployment (since it is the ratio of output to employment) as much as a rise in competitiveness. Britain's competitive position continued to decline, largely because of the increased value of the pound.

The money economy was not performing as expected. It was increasingly difficult to control the money supply, both because of the unexpectedly high levels of pay settlements and of the distortions caused by the strong pound. Reducing the PSBR proved initially difficult; however it fell rapidly after 1985 and by the 1987 election Chancellor Nigel Lawson was boasting of his success in repaying part of the National Debt. In 1988 £11.6 billion was repaid. However, this policy of debt repayment coincided with the reappearance of a balance of payments deficit, despite the beneficial impact of North Sea Oil. After some years of surpluses deficits reappeared in the late 1980s, to reach £20 billion in 1989 and £15.5 billion (provisional) in 1990. Another worrying indicator was the decline in the savings ratio, the percentage of income which consumers save. By 1988 it had fallen to roughly one-third of its 1979 value, producing 'a veritable credit explosion in the run-up to the 1987 election which in turn produced a surge in imports, and balance of payments problems'.[11]

While supporters see this period as one which, at the cost of

Figure 5: Balance of payments: visible and invisible balance (current prices, £bn)

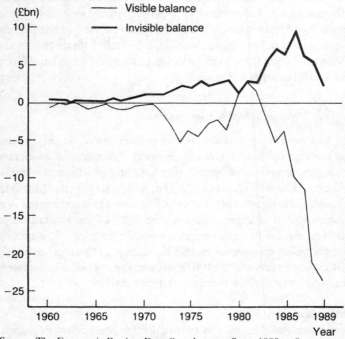

Source: The Economic Review Data Supplement, Sept. 1990, p.8

short-term pain, laid the foundations of future recovery, critics believe that great and unnecessary damage was done which could have been avoided by a more flexible response to economic problems. Far from creating the conditions for recovery, the policies adopted so damaged the British economy that it was *less* able to respond to the changes in policy which came after 1982.

Inflation began to fall. It had risen to 21.9 per cent in May 1980 but by April 1982 it had fallen to single figures. Although the government claimed that this was due to prudent and firm management of the economy, critics pointed to the effect of unemployment, which by the end of 1982 had climbed to over 3 million. Opponents claimed that the fall in inflation was due partly to the lack of purchasing power (partly borne out by the rapid rise in the number of bankruptcies) and the effect of the dole queues on wage bargainers. The handling of the economy led to a serious division in the Cabinet which was only partly resolved by the reshuffle of September 1981 which removed most of the prominent 'wets', and replaced them with Thatcher loyalists such as Norman Tebbit (Employment), Nigel Lawson (Energy) and Cecil Parkinson as Party Chairman.

Phase Two: pragmatic monetarism

In this period the government responded more flexibly to the increasing signs of recession. Several indicators of monetary policy were embraced, with a downgrading of M3 as *the* key to success. The MTFS was redrafted, with a larger target for M3 growth. In a significant shift of policy, the Treasury announced that it would change targets in the light of circumstances, a marked change from its previous intention to stick to the money supply policy come what may. This change of strategy, in which the exchange rate and the PSBR became the key policy guidelines, attracted much criticism from strict monetarists.

Policy changes

Electoral considerations increasingly influenced policy decisions. Interests rates were gradually reduced, with a consequent easing of monetary policy. National insurance payments by employers were cut and the abolition of hire purchase restrictions in July 1982 when interest rates were falling helped stimulate a consumer boom in time for the 1983 election. There were efforts to reduce the value of the pound and from then on control of the exchange rates replaced control of the money supply as the main mechanism of monetary policy. As export prices fell Britain's competitive position improved.

During 1982 there was a dramatic change in Tory fortunes. Signs of an improvement in the economy were slow to appear. In January 1982 Mrs Thatcher's poll rating at 25 per cent was the worst for any Prime Minister since the war. The Falklands War distracted attention from the economy, and the Tories, aided by a sustained fall in inflation and a weak and divided opposition, moved into a lead in the polls. Tax relief in the 1983 Budget provided hope of better things to come. The 1983 election produced a massive Conservative majority, and allowed Mrs Thatcher to remove more of her critics from the Cabinet, replacing them with her supporters.

Problems unsolved

Despite this stunning victory the economic indicators were very gloomy. The GDP had fallen, while unemployment (even on figures which underestimated the total) had risen to well over 3 million. Taxation had increased, mainly at the expense of those on average or lower than average incomes, while public spending had risen as a percentage of GDP. Most of the statistics mean that the aim of 'rolling back the frontiers of state' had not been achieved, and the relative decline of the last forty years had not been reversed; indeed, in some respects it had turned into an absolute decline. By 1983, for the first time since the Industrial Revolution, Britain became a net importer of manufactured goods. Though the government blamed the world recession, in international terms Britain was performing worse than most of her competitors.

However, as part of the changed national mood which had been so noticeable at the time of the 1979 election, there was a tendency to say that there was little that governments could do to improve the situation and that past errors of policy were responsible. A significant section of the electorate seemed to be prepared to give the Conservatives time to get the economy right, and Mrs Thatcher used her political skills to the full to build on this somewhat pessimistic (or, as she would say, realistic) appreciation of the power and responsibility of government.

Lawson as Chancellor

When Lawson was appointed Chancellor although the goal, that of fighting inflation as the prerequisite for sustained economic growth, remained, the method of implementation changed. The mixed approach, using a number of economic indicators, replaced the obsession with formal monetary targets. Lawson adopted yet another target measure of the money supply, M0, a measure of the cash base and the narrowest measure of all. However, as a measure of money it excluded credit and as such was never taken seriously by commentators. Yet it is clear that the new strategy signalled by Lawson's Mansion House speech of October 1983 marked a departure from the emphasis of 1979–80.

Apart from a package of spending cuts and asset sales designed to take back some of the pre-election generosity, Lawson faced a relatively stable economic environment until 1984. However, a sterling crisis led to the raising of interests rates to defend the value of sterling. The dilemma, familiar to most post-war Chancellors, 'was that a rapid devaluation of the currency would accelerate inflation by driving up the cost of imports, whereas a rapid rise in interest rates would undermine investment and ultimately slow economic growth'.[12] The aim of policy in this period was to keep interest rates as low as possible consistent with a slow devaluation of the currency. But the pound dropped to $1.12 in January 1985, and interest rates were raised by 4.5 per cent in the space of two weeks; foreign exchange uncertainty was worsened by apparent differences between the Prime Minister and the Chancellor. By this time monetarism had effectively been abandoned when the target range for M3, now growing at an annual rate far above the designated figure, was abandoned. It was at this time that Lawson gave a hostage to fortune, when he said 'the acid test of monetary policy is its record in reducing inflation ... The inflation rate is judge and jury.'[13]

Although a more flexible and realistic set of policies had been adopted, the traditional stop–go strategy had returned. The government was stimulating the economy to produce growth and reduce unemployment, followed by deflation to deal with the balance of payments and currency problems which resulted.

Political problems

The 1983–7 programme emphasised privatisation, trade union reform and the creation of the 'enterprise culture'. The changes to local government, amongst which was the abolition of the Greater London Council (GLC) and the six metropolitan county councils, had a number of aims, one of which was the curbing of public expenditure, a major theme of this period.

Although there were a number of 'banana-skins' in the path of the government (including the resignation of Cecil Parkinson after an affair with his secretary, the banning of trade unions at Government Communications Headquarters (GCHQ), Cheltenham, and then a series of highly publicised and sometimes unsuccessful prosecutions of civil servants for 'leaking' sensitive and embarrassing information, the government won back significant support by the way it handled the year-long miners' strike. The violence of the strike and the unpopularity of Arthur Scargill rebounded to the benefit of Mrs Thatcher. Support among the electorate, however, declined during 1985 because of the various policy errors and because of the failure to reduce unemployment, plus the consequences of efforts to reduce public expenditure. A poor performance in by-elections and local elections led to rumblings of discontent on the Tory backbenches; various dissident (though short-lived and generally ineffective) groups, such as Francis Pym's Centre Forward, sprang up with the aim of forcing some kind of change of tack (even if not a 'U-turn'). This reflected a deeper anxiety in the constituencies; the Liberal–SDP Alliance still seemed a threat in many Tory marginals, while Labour was slowly recovering. The Westland Affair, which caused a further fall in the government's popularity, nearly toppled Mrs Thatcher. It was partly caused by a row between the Prime Minister and Defence Secretary Michael Heseltine about the role of government in promoting industry – an issue at the heart of Thatcher's apparently hands-off approach.

Phase Three: reverse monetarism

The approach of the 1987 election inaugurated a third phase of policy. Westland led to a temporary change in style by Mrs Thatcher, and the Cabinet reshuffle brought in people who were less enamoured of her political beliefs. By January 1986 the Prime Minister's popularity stood at around 30 per cent and for the remainder of that Parliament the more moderate, consensual Thatcher was projected: the 'Iron Lady' with the 'caring face'. The aim was to engineer an economic recovery which would enable the Conservative Party to win a fresh term of office. In this period the improvement in the world economy and the absence of shocks such as the quadrupling of oil prices after the Yom Kippur War, worked to the government's benefit. The British economy had been growing, albeit slowly, since 1983, inflation had fallen to below 5 per cent and the standard of living of those in work had improved, in some cases dramatically. Unemployment still stood at above 3 million and there was a campaign to get this figure down before the next election. A programme of retraining and youth employment schemes was undertaken, masterminded by Lord Young, and, in conjunction with a judicious massaging of the figures, the total fell to below 3 million by the summer of 1987.

An improving outlook?

During 1986–87 there was a major expansion of the world economy, caused in part by a fall in oil prices. The value of sterling fell, boosting British exports. There were major adjustments to policies. Monetarism was finally abandoned; for a while the strict control of public expenditure took its place as the touchstone of fiscal probity. Battles in the Cabinet over spending became so fierce that the 'Star Chamber' of senior ministers, chaired by Lord Whitelaw, was convened to settle the disputes. The emphasis shifted to increasing revenue; indirect taxes and energy prices were raised and the programme of privatisation increased. Between 1979 and 1988 some £27 billion was raised from the sale of public assets. Added to the ideological pressures for privatisation was the need to raise large sums of money to finance the tax cuts which were a major feature of the 1987 Conservative manifesto. A programme of selling-off of profitable state enterprises was rushed through Parliament, often at the expense of the stated aim of encouraging greater competition. Critics of this policy included the former Prime Minister Harold Macmillan, who likened it to 'selling the silver to pay the servants'.

The pre-election boom

Economic indicators appeared favourable for the creation of a pre-election boom. Although the benefit of North Sea oil to the balance of payments was declining it was sufficient to stimulate the economy without risking a run on the pound. Inflation was below 5 per cent and as the electorate thought that unemployment

The Conservative record 1979–1990

was the biggest problem facing the government, 'a stimulus to the economy designed to bring down unemployment which would have only a small impact on inflation in the short run was an attractive political option'.[14] For some time, as monetary targets were relaxed and then abandoned, monetary policy concentrated on influencing the exchange rate. The reason for this shift in policy 'lay in an increasing concern that exchange rate volatility affected adversely the trade performance of UK industry, and an acceptance of the view that exchange rate depreciation was the main mechanism through which inflation was transmitted to the domestic economy'.[15] The Treasury increasingly came to the view that 'if the value of sterling could be tied to the currency of a stable, low inflation economy this would provide an "anchor" for the UK's inflation rate'.[16] Efforts were made to link sterling with the Deutschmark, a rather covert operation which became a source of friction between the Prime Minister and her Chancellor. The decision by Lawson to go for growth and to try to help the competitive position of industry led to higher inflation later.

This relaxation of monetary policy was the beginning of the 'Lawson Boom', with its overtones of the disastrous 'Barber Boom' of the early 1970s. A number of key indicators registered sharp increases. Real GDP grew from 2 per cent per annum in the first quarter of 1986 to 5.7 per cent in the same quarter of 1988. Inflation, which had fallen to 2.7 per cent per annum in the third quarter of 1986 rose to 6.5 per cent by the end of 1986. It reached 10 per cent during 1990. Average earnings, despite record levels of unemployment and increasingly anguished exhortations by ministers for restraint, remained high and consistently above the rate of inflation. Consumers' expenditure and consumer credit also rose sharply, as did the figure for M3. The current balance went from a surplus into a rapidly increasing deficit. The similarities between the Barber Boom and the Lawson dash for growth are marked: the reckless expansion of consumer credit, the short-lived boom in house prices, the rise in consumer spending and a sharp deterioration in Britain's balance of payments are features of both periods. Policy contradictions were becoming increasingly obvious. 'The unfolding of events at this time is instructive since it reveals the government's attempt to deal with a major policy dilemma and its abandonment of the pretence that it did not believe in demand management of a sort.'[17]

The stage was set for a pre-election boom. During 1986 there was a rapid rise in the money supply of a magnitude much greater than that required to support economic growth. In addition, there was a reversal of policy on public expenditure; in November the previous targets were scrapped and increases of around £7.5 billion were announced for 1987–88. This was widely seen as the prelude to an early election and critics from the Left *and* the Right said that the government was in the process of inducing a Keynesian-type consumer boom as a way of raising living standards in the short term. 'Stop–go' was back with a vengeance, and some economists referred to it as a 'U-turn'. Private consumer debt, what some have termed the 'Private Sector Borrowing Requirement', soared, largely as a result of the deregulation of the financial sector. This development considerably boosted the political fortunes of the Conservatives, since the consequences were not felt until after the election. In 1987 economic growth and consumer spending rose quickly, investment reached levels not achieved since the late 1970s, unemployment, while still very high began to fall, and the balance of payments deficit was not yet serious enough to worry speculators, anxious for a continuation of Mrs Thatcher in No. 10.

In a period of buoyant tax revenues and lower government borrowing economists and politicians continued to argue about the scope for tax cuts in the 1987 Budget. Lawson cut 2p from the standard rate of income tax and excise duties were pegged; the main emphasis, however, was on reduced borrowing which set the scene for interest and mortgage rate cuts. Living standards for many people rose sharply, boosted by an expansion of credit which the government had encouraged and facilitated by changes to the structure of financial institutions. The atmosphere of prosperity and the Chancellor's carefully fostered reputation for financial probity and expertise were major factors in the Conservative victory in the 1987 general election.

The consequences

The consequences of this crude electoral bribery were soon

Table 3: *The Lawson Boom – selected indicators 1985–1988*

		Real GDP growth % pa[1]	Inflation (% pa)	Average earnings (%) pa)	Real consumers' expenditure (%)	Consumer credit (%)	M3 (% pa)	Current balance £ mn
1986	I	2.0	5.0	8.3	4.5	43.0	16.9	763
	II	2.4	2.9	8.1	6.6	50.0	18.9	138
	III	3.5	2.7	7.4	5.2	43.1	19.1	−856
	IV	3.8	3.5	7.9	5.2	36.9	19.1	−898
1987	I	4.3	3.8	7.0	4.5	12.4	19.7	−872
	II	4.4	4.2	7.5	4.2	20.1	19.8	−388
	III	5.1	4.2	7.7	5.4	21.2	20.2	−1,205
	IV	5.1	3.8	8.4	6.4	29.2	22.8	−1,968
1988	I	5.7	3.4	8.9	6.8	30.4	21.0	−2,835
	II	5.0	4.3	8.2	5.4	25.0	20.1	−2,661
	III	4.3	5.6	8.7	6.0*	27.9	22.5	−3,724
	IV	3.8*	6.5	—	5.5*	18.4	20.3	−5,051

Notes:

* Estimates.

[1] All % changes are year on year.

Source: Peter Curwen (ed.): *Understanding the UK Economy*, Macmillan, 1990, see p.329 for full details of sources.

apparent. 'Instead of reining back the monetary and fiscal stimulus to the economy after the election, an essential tactic for operating a successful political business cycle, the government further stimulated an already overloaded economy.'[18] The money supply continued to expand, reaching a staggering 40 per cent per annum by 1988. The stimulus provided by the tax cuts of March 1988 was even more significant. The basic rate of income tax was cut to 25 per cent and the maximum to 40 per cent, personal allowances were raised by twice the rate of inflation and other taxes were also reduced. This gave a large boost to personal consumption and was defended by ministers as a supply-side stimulus which would reward initiative and enterprise, made possible by a surplus in revenue. In the event, aggregate demand grew rapidly, producing a balance of payments deficit of increasingly alarming proportions.

Phase Four: after Lawson

The fourth, post-election, period had begun. For a while after the 1987 general election the mood was one of optimism and expansion, with Lawson being described as the greatest Chancellor since Gladstone. However, the euphoria did not last long.

During 1987 interest rates had been cut in anticipation of the election and further cuts were made necessary by the Stock Exchange collapse of October 1987 and by the need to keep sterling to its Deutschmark target. By the autumn of 1988 criticisms of Lawson grew. The economy had overheated, inflation was rising rapidly and the balance of payments deficit was the worst in Britain's history. Interest rates were increased nine times before the year ended, and the government's handling of the economy increasingly was compared to the 'stop–go' years of the 1950s and 1960s. Critics from different schools argued forcibly that the 'economic miracle' was a mirage and that few if any of the basic problems of the British economy had been addressed, let alone solved. The accusation that Thatcher had frittered away the once and for all benefits of North Sea oil in tax cuts for the better-off at the cost of a major and perhaps irreversible erosion of the industrial base of the British economy was increasingly heard.

Fears were expressed that the consumer boom, financed by seem-ingly limitless credit, would worsen the balance of payments problem as imported goods flooded into the country. Domestic manufacturers, weakened by the earlier decline in Britain's manufacturing base, were unable to expand to meet the demand. Lawson was seen as a one-policy Chancellor, relying solely on interest rates as *the* weapon with which to control the economy.

Lawson's resignation

The Prime Minister and Chancellor increasingly disagreed about economic management, especially the role of exchange rates. Mrs Thatcher felt that the value of the pound should be set by market forces; with a strong demand for the pound the value should rise. She argued that 'you can't buck the market'. Lawson, however, wanted a more managed exchange rate. In particular, he wished to 'shadow' the German mark and in so doing ensure a more stable exchange rate for the pound which would aid British exporters. He also saw it as the first step towards taking Britain into the European Monetary System (EMS), another point of contention with the Premier. The dispute became more open, despite repeated assertions of mutual trust and respect. The views of Sir Alan Walters, the Prime Minister's personal economic adviser, were scarcely hidden; they were that the Chancellor's policies were 'misguided'.

The disagreement, now hardly disguised, rumbled on through-out 1989, and developed into a major struggle within the Cabinet about Britain's relations with the EC. Pressure was growing in the Community for closer integration, particularly economic, but also of social policy. Mrs Thatcher and her supporters were urging that the EC should remain a broadly free-trade concept, while others, who included such senior figures as Howe, Lawson and Hurd, came increasingly to accept the logic and inevitability of closer links and seemed less concerned about the loss of sovereignty than was the increasingly nationalistic Prime Minister. In July 1989 Thatcher reshuffled her Cabinet; Howe was shifted from the Foreign Office to become Leader of the House; he was replaced by John Major, thought to be a committed supporter of the Prime Minister.

But the real battle was over the economy, which was increasingly fragile with inflation at 8 per cent and rising (a particularly worrying figure for a government which had made the defeat of inflation its first priority), and the balance of payments deficit was £20 billion. Behind the scenes Lawson was trying to have Walters removed; he objected to his policies being 'shadowed' by this unelected adviser, responsible to no one but the Prime Minister. The opposition was having a field day, asking which was the real Chancellor; the increasingly shrill protestations of support by Mrs Thatcher somewhat lacked conviction. Critics pointed out that the uncertainty about British economic management was doing real damage on the foreign exchanges, with dealers increasingly unsure whether the policy was to support the pound (as Lawson favoured) or to let it float downward (as Walters, supported by Thatcher, clearly advocated). The crisis came to a head in a somewhat surprising manner. In an article in a little known journal, the *American Economist* Walters argued for freely floating exchange rates, and said that attempts to control them through the EMS were 'half baked' and ineffective. When the article was reported in the British media Lawson demanded that the PM should choose between him and Walters. When she refused Lawson resigned on 26 October. Some commentators speculated that the real reason was Lawson's recognition that the economy had got out of control.

Major as Chancellor

Following Lawson's departure, John Major was switched to the Treasury with Douglas Hurd becoming Foreign Secretary. As signs of economic troubles increased Major held out bright prospects for the British economy in the 1990s. In January 1990 he denied that a recession was in prospect, despite forecasting negligible economic growth, reduced consumer spending and industrial investment. He blamed the difficulties on high wage settlements, which he linked directly with threats of higher unemployment. He stressed his belief in membership of the EMS within what he termed a 'reasonable period of time', in the interests of exchange rate stability. He admitted past mistakes, saying that Lawson should have acted earlier to restrain excessive demand after the 1987 election. Similarly, the reduction of interest rates following the 1987 Stock Exchange crash was a mistake, further adding to inflationary pressures.

The 1990 Budget was widely criticised as inadequate to deal with the multiplying problems of the economy, and some critics felt that Major had put the electoral needs of the Conservative Party before the long-term requirements of the economy. Electoral opinion was not impressed; two days after the Budget the Conservatives lost the previously safe seat of Mid-Staffordshire to Labour.

The issue of Europe was again raised during the Budget debate when Lawson warned that the anti-inflationary strategy was being imperilled by the failure to enter the ERM. He said the government's timetable was 'too leisurely for the circumstances in which we find ourselves. In my judgement, it is a pity we did not join some time ago.'[19]

The Budget failed to halt the slide into what more and more commentators described as a recession. Inflation rose to around 10 per cent, industrial unrest grew, pay claims mounted despite an increase in unemployment and investment fell, while the balance of payments deficit continued to grow at a rate which increasingly alarmed the City.

Behind the scenes Major and other ministers urged closer links with Europe on a reluctant Thatcher. She seemed, however, to be conducting a battle against several possible lines of development in the EC in the interests of preserving as much 'independence' for Britain as possible. She attacked the plan put forward by Jacques Delors for a single European currency and central bank and stridently advocated the alternative suggestion of a 'hard' Ecu as an extra currency. To the alarm of Conservative MPs, once again the Prime Minister seemed at odds with her Chancellor, who seemed to favour an eventual single European currency. Increasingly the Prime Minister voiced doubts about the whole direction of the EC, even expressing reservations about the desirability of German unification. In July 1990 Nicholas Ridley, the Secretary of State for Trade and Industry, resigned after an outburst of anger at developments in Europe; he was widely seen as voicing the sentiments of his Prime Minister, albeit in rather colourful language.

Entry to the Exchange Rate Mechanism

Events moved quickly. Major, Hurd and Howe were instrumental in forcing British membership of the ERM on an unwilling Mrs Thatcher, whose authority was waning. On 5 October 1990 Britain joined the ERM and announced a 1 per cent cut in interests rates. The exchange rate for the pound was fixed at 2.95DM, with the possibility of fluctuating 6 per cent up or down before the Bank of England would have to step in by buying or selling pounds. The decision was defended on economic grounds by Major, who claimed that the decision to join would reinforce the government's framework of monetary discipline. Commentators saw the decision, taken just before the Tory Party Conference, as an effort to restore morale among the faithful. It was also seen as a sign that Britain could no longer go it alone in fighting inflation, a significant defeat for the Prime Minister's dream of 'sovereignty'. Putting a brave face on it, Mrs Thatcher said that the move would aid the fight against inflation, claiming that the rate would drop nearer the European average in the 'coming months'.

Proponents of membership hoped that it would help to reduce inflation to the level in Germany, the sheet-anchor of the system. They suggested that sterling would behave in a more stable manner, enabling exporters to plan with greater certainty since prices would not fluctuate as in the past. It was hoped also that membership would strengthen the pound, thus attracting foreigners to invest their money in Britain without the need for cripplingly high interest rates. Critics, including Sir Alan Walters, warned that Britain had entered at too high an exchange rate (a consequence of above-average inflation at the time of entry). The option of devaluation as a way of regaining competitiveness was now ruled out. Deflation of the domestic economy, with its consequences for unemployment, living standards and the public services, was the likely alternative.

Mrs Thatcher's resignation

Howe resigned on 2 November 1990, the culmination of an

increasingly bitter feud. His resignation speech on 13 November was devastating. Most of his attack was over Mrs Thatcher's attitude to Europe, and he made plain that he thought her resistance in 1989 to membership of the ERM had damaged the economy by making the fight against inflation more difficult. He ended by virtually inviting a challenge to her leadership.

Michael Heseltine's decision to stand against Thatcher in a leaderhip contest was based on a number of points of difference with the Prime Minister, including on Europe. However, underlying specific policy disagreements lay a basic philosophical difference about the role of government in a modern economy. Thatcher's policy of 'hands-off', no aid for 'lame ducks' was challenged by Heseltine, who believed that there was an active role for the state in creating the conditions in which economic growth could occur and which would enable British industry to compete on equal terms with nations such as Japan and Germany. His views were set out in an interview in which he stated: 'There is no advanced country – no capitalist country – in which there is not a continuing effort made to develop the closest relationship between Government and industry.'[20] Mrs Thatcher's response was to accuse her rival of 'Labour policies'. She said he risked pulling the country down and destroying all she stood for. Attacking what she saw as Heseltine's 'interventionism' and 'corporatism' she said 'There is a fundamental difference on economics and there's no point in trying to hide it.'[21]

John Major as Prime Minister

Much to the surprise of most commentators, John Major was elected leader on Mrs Thatcher's resignation. He had stressed his support for the policies associated with Mrs Thatcher. He claimed to have stood in order to continue the changes of the last ten years, particularly the creation of a more mobile society. He had emphasised this theme at the 1990 Tory Party Conference, and repeated it after he became Premier, when he pledged himself to develop a classless society. He stressed the need for caution on European monetary union, and reiterated his opposition to a European central bank or a single currency. The existing framework, in which Britain was a member of the EMS, was satisfactory. He also distanced himself from the monetarist experiment of the early Thatcher years. 'I believe it's extremely important to control the money supply as one of the mechanisms of managing the economy. But it's not the only means of managing the economy – I wouldn't have joined the Exchange Rate Mechanism if I thought that.'[22] He accepted that there had been policy misjudgements when interest rates were reduced after the Stock Market crash in October 1987 but claimed that it was impossible to foresee what he termed the continued growth in investment despite the shock. He asserted that with greater liberalisation of the economy Britain would move much more speedily out of what he called the 'slowdown' than critics anticipated. He predicted that inflation would come down 'sharply' in 1991, permitting a reduction in interest and mortgage rates, thus ensuring the resumption of steady growth. He repeatedly asserted his support for what he saw as the main themes of the Thatcher era: freedom, choice, opportunity, property and lower taxation. Privatization, the way to a capital-owning democracy, was lauded as the way to a society where there were more share owners than trade unionists. The aim was to bring greater social mobility, choice and freedom to every section of society.

Norman Lamont, who had been Chief Secretary to the Treasury under Major, was appointed Chancellor. He acted quickly to quash speculation that there would be any relaxation of government policy on the economy generally and on inflation specifically. In a debate in the Commons in December he warned that the severity of the recession, a term now openly used by ministers, required continued high interest rates. Unemployment was expected to rise sharply in 1991. There was no guarantee, he said, that the recession would be short-lived or relatively shallow, especially if wages continued to rise or if war began in the Gulf. These gloomy predictions were widely interpreted as a signal that there would not be a snap general election despite the Conservative lead in the polls following Major's succession, a lead which quickly declined.

Summary

By common consent, the outlook for the British economy at the end of 1990 was grim. If economic factors continue to dominate the voting intentions of the British electorate, the long reign of the Conservative Party will be in serious jeopardy. The next chapter will attempt to assess the nature of Mrs Thatcher's economic experiment.

Notes

1 David Smith: *Mrs Thatcher's Economics*, Heinemann, 1988, p.3.

2 Ruth Levitas (ed.): *The Ideology of the New Right*, Polity, 1986, p.35.

3 Paul Whiteley: Economic Policy, in Patrick Dunleavy et al. (eds.): *Developments in British Politics 3*, Macmillan, 1990, p.179.

4 Ibid., p.179.

5 Ibid., p.180.

6 William Keegan: *Mr Lawson's Gamble*, Hodder and Stoughton, 1989, p.71.

7 Peter Riddell, *The Thatcher Decade*, Blackwell, 1989, p.19.

8 Patrick Minford: Mrs Thatcher's Economic Reform Programme, in Robert Skidelsky (ed.): *Thatcherism*, Chatto and Windus, 1988, p.95.

9 Geoffrey Maynard: Britain's Economic Revival and the Balance of Payments, *Political Quarterly*, Vol. 60, No. 2, April–June 1989, pp.154–5.

10 Samuel Brittan: The Thatcher Government's Economic Policy, in Dennis Kavanagh and Anthony Seldon (eds.): *The Thatcher Effect*, OUP, 1989, pp.1–37.

11 Whiteley, Economic Policy, p.186.

12 Ibid.

13 Quoted in Riddell, *Thatcher Decade, p.21*.

14 Whiteley, Economic Policy, p.189.

15 Peter Curwen (ed.): *Understanding the U.K. Economy*, Macmillan, 1990, p.330.

16 Ibid.

17 Ibid., p.331.

18 Whiteley, Economic Policy, p.190.

19 *The Independent*, 27 March 1990.

20 The *Observer*, 18 November 1990.

21 *The Times*, 19 November 1990.

22 The *Sunday Times*, 25 November 1990.

5

Mrs Thatcher's economics:
an assessment

Introduction

Some kind of assessment of the economic legacy of Mrs Thatcher's eleven years as Prime Minister must be attempted, if only because she herself often seemed to invite comparison with Winston Churchill. To her admirers such an analogy truly reflected the scale of her achievements in almost single-handedly 'destroying socialism' (not just in Britain but throughout the civilised world). To her critics such claims smack of colossal and rather frightening vainglory. They see the boast of an 'economic miracle' as evidence of a politician increasingly out of touch with reality and increasingly inclined to believe the myth self-created (though with a little help from her friends).

Thatcher defended

Some believe that Mrs Thatcher succeeded in her crusade to 'turn Britain around'. Professor Patrick Minford, a noted monetarist, drew attention to her vision of the world as one 'in which small businesses could compete freely for the favours of the individual family consumer; in this world the state keeps law and order, including the elements of a moral order to protect family decency, and provides succour to the genuinely unfortunate who cannot help themselves'.[1] As Minford pointed out, this world view is based on the lessons learned in her father's shop in Grantham; happiness and self-respect depends on independence (particularly of the economic variety) and what charity could be spared for helping the (deserving) poor was to be 'wrung from the house-keeping budget'.[2] Minford, while concluding that mistakes had been made and too slow a pace adopted, believed that the omens were good for Mrs Thatcher to reach her goal.

Alan Budd saw the most important single principle of Thatcherism as the reduction of the government's direct economic role, progressively withdrawing from functions previously regarded as essential. Activities which Budd saw as no longer the business of government included short-term demand management, interference with private sector pay and prices, involvement in the structure and location of economic production, the direct production of goods and services and a reduction in the attempt to affect the distribution of income and wealth. Budd believed that the government had succeeded in directing its attention away from short-term demand management towards setting long-term objectives for the economy (an argument hard to square with the policies pursued around the time of the 1987 election). In common with other supporters of Mrs Thatcher's policies, Budd saw the 1981 Budget as a turning-point, and pointed to evidence of sustained growth in the years following, which he called a 'productivity miracle'. He saw the changes in policy, especially over control of the money supply, as evidence of pragmatism and denied that the Conservatives were ever 'recognisably monetarist'. While worried about inflation Budd believed that 'We are witnessing a remarkable transformation of our economy . . . If the hardships of 1979 to 1981 have produced a base from which our economy can grow steadily by 3 per cent or more a year, Thatcherism will have proved a success.'[3]

Professor Geoffrey Maynard pointed out that criticism of Mrs Thatcher's economic policies concentrates on a number of points: the high level of unemployment, 'the destruction of UK manufacturing industry', the 'waste of North Sea oil' and the 'attack on the welfare state'. Maynard believed that these attacks are all misguided: 'if attention is focused on the long term and underlying problems of the UK . . . it could well be argued that the Thatcher government's refusal to maintain full employment at any cost in terms of low productivity, low efficiency, high inflation;

its refusal to maintain the welfare state at any cost in terms of resource use; and its refusal to maintain uneconomic industry for the sake of maintaining employment in depressed areas of the economy do not per se constitute evidence of mistaken policy or policy failure: on the contrary, the evidence might indicate that the UK's long term economic problems were at last being tackled'.[4] Maynard's view, echoing other Thatcher supporters, was that the government should not be judged by the test of full employment, but instead by whether it had brought about or at least established the conditions for an improvement in Britain's longer-term economic prospects. Writing in 1988, Maynard suggested that, given the recent improvements in productivity, 'a real and much needed transformation has taken place and can bode well for the future'.[5]

Discussing the vexed question of labour productivity, Maynard concluded that its rise after the recession of 1979–80 probably exceeded that of the previous twenty years. He also believed that Britain's improvement relative to other major industrialised countries was striking. Thus a 'sea change' had taken place in the British economy, and was related to longer-term trends in improved management, including better working practices, better directed investment and greater readiness to innovate. Maynard attributed improvements in, for example, British Steel and the motor industry to better labour relations and improved technology.

Maynard claimed that a key element in these successes was the 'legislative attack on trade union power and privileges . . . and [the] willingness to stand up against crucial strikes . . . or to provide explicit or implicit support for others who have done so';[6] these were significant in reducing trade union opposition to new technology and new working practices. The government's willingness to accept mass unemployment through its fiscal and monetary policies also helped to break trade union resistance to change.

Maynard took issue with those critics of government macro-economic policies who said that the restraint of aggregate demand, high interest rates, an overvalued exchange rate and the abolition of exchange controls (which diverted capital away from investment in British industry) weakened rather than strengthened manufacturing industry and the British economy generally. He believed that the attempts of Thatcher's critics to suggest that Britain should have followed the example of Germany and Japan in pursuing an export-led strategy (based on an undervalued exchange rate and perhaps subsidised labour costs) were misguided: 'The bases of success in fact lay in these countries' superior productivity performance, which enabled competitiveness to be combined with a strong nominal exchange rate, low inflation and rising real wages, rather than the reverse.'[7] He agreed with Keith Joseph's judgement that the high exchange rate of the early 1980s imposed pressure on industry to raise productivity, lower costs and generally improve its products. The years 1979–81, generally regarded as disastrous for British manufacturing, will be seen as a period 'in which the essential basis for sustained long run improvement in economic performance was laid down'.[8] The costs in terms of unemployment and the heavy fall in UK manufacturing output were brushed aside as irrelevant in the long term, although failures in education, training, and research were acknowledged. Overall, his judgement was that the test of policy will come when North Sea oil runs out.

However, in a later article, Maynard, while remaining confident about the underlying supply-side performance of the UK economy, expressed alarm at the deteriorating balance of payments. He criticised government failure to stick to its monetary policies and targets, and his earlier optimism about the prospects for a long-term rejuvenation of the economy was more hesitant: 'convincing evidence of the success of the Government's strategy is not likely to be seen before the end of its third term in office and, given the deep-rooted nature of Britain's educational and training problems, perhaps not even then'.[9] To some, this seems to echo Keynes' comment that 'in the long run, we are all dead'.

Brittan argued that the successes in improving Britain's relative growth rate would not be negated even by the tighter policies pursued since 1988, even if they resulted in recession.[10] Though in his view economic growth is not something which can be achieved by governments, the Thatcher administration did do something to create the conditions for the catching-up process. Brittan drew attention to the international context, pointing to similar movements towards a more market-oriented economy in many Western nations. Though Brittan approved of the broad thrust of Mrs Thatcher's policies, he criticised the illiberal centralisation of power which accompanied economic change.

The record questioned

A commentator who assessed the pluses and minuses of Mrs Thatcher's economic record was Peter Riddell. He had 'sympathy with the redirection of economic and industrial policy which began in the mid-1970s and developed a new energy and momentum with the arrival of the Thatcher Government'.[11] However, while agreeing that there have been undoubted gains for the economy, they fall far short of an 'economic miracle'; in addition, the social costs were considerable, a point echoed by Brittan, who pointed out that 'it is worrying that the least well-off should have fared as badly as they did'.[12]

Riddell's view was that the figures represent a mixed record, which improved considerably in the second half of the 1980s. However he stressed that the overall performance was good only in comparison with the 1970s, not with the late 1960s.

Riddell echoed other commentators in asking two central questions.

1. Could these apparent gains could have been achieved without the severity of the initial squeeze?
2. Are they sustainable over the long term?

He saw no evidence that the government deliberately planned an economic shock to produce the squeeze on industry and rise in unemployment of the scale which occurred. Several crucial mistakes were made and the approach was too literal-minded; too much faith was placed in one indicator, sterling M3. Yet overall the government's view that a shock was necessary to force industry to end over-manning and to improve efficiency was justified by events, although some of the effects of the recession could have been mitigated, for example by an earlier introduction of work-experience and similar schemes.

On the second question Riddell believed that the evidence was mixed. Reviewing the arguments about productivity, he said that although Britain may have improved its position, both by its own standards and internationally, it still had a long way to go to catch up with overseas levels of productivity. He warned that labour costs were rising, thus undermining competitiveness. He drew attention to the reappearance of inflation and balance of payments deficits as evidence that the problems of the past had not disappeared, and echoed Brittan in awarding the Thatcher government at best 'two cheers' for solving those problems.

Some themes examined

In assessing the economic record a number of themes need to be examined. In May 1988 Mrs Thatcher spoke of the 'British miracle', the 'liberated energies of a free people'. She said that sound money, lower taxes and freedom for enterprise were the only solid foundations for growth without inflation. Thus the validity of the claim that an economic miracle has occurred needs to be assessed in the light of claims made by or on behalf of the chief architect and driving force, Mrs Thatcher herself.

Inflation

Nigel Lawson's statement that inflation is the 'judge and jury' of policy came back to haunt him. The twelve-month figure for retail prices rose sharply from 10.3 per cent in May 1979 to a peak of 21.9 per cent in August 1980, before falling to single figures in April 1982, where it stayed for some time. By May 1983 the rate had fallen to 3.7 per cent, its lowest point until 2.4 per cent was reached in the middle of 1986. It then began to rise, despite the 1987 election commitment that the target was zero inflation. In August 1990 the figure, at 10.6 per cent, was above that inherited by Mrs Thatcher; it rose to 10.9 per cent later in the year. The underlying inflation rate (excluding the influence of poll tax and mortgages) in May 1990 was 6.2 per cent, considerably above most major competitors. Samuel Brittan referred to the failure of the monetarist experiment to squeeze inflation out of the system as 'the god that failed'.[13] Most commentators are agreed that the expansion of the economy around the 1987 election, and especially the credit boom, was mainly to blame for the rise in inflation. However, while the 'judge and jury' test finds the government guilty of failure to solve the problem of inflation, for a while the Conservatives were undoubtedly able to project themselves as the party of 'sound money' and to paint Labour as the party of inflation.

Earnings
Despite repeated strictures from ministers about the dangers of workers pricing themselves out of jobs, earnings outpaced inflation; the annual rate of increase was around 7.5 to 8.5 per cent for most of the period before rising in the spring of 1989 to well over 9 per cent. Earnings continued to grow strongly in 1990, adding to inflationary pressures. Across the whole economy wages increased by an average of 9.75 per cent, while at the same time there was a fall in productivity. Unit labour costs rose by 10 per cent in 1990, while those of our major competitors were virtually static. Thus although real disposable income for those in work rose by around 25 per cent between 1981 and 1988, providing a rich harvest of votes for the Conservatives, this did not provide the basis for the promised sustainable inflation-free growth.

Unemployment
Both the scale of and the reasons for unemployment have been hotly contested since 1979. Ministers claimed that there was a sustained fall from the peak of 1986, which they attributed to the success of their policies, while critics concentrated on the many revisions to the way in which unemployment is calculated.

Adult unemployment rose sharply in the first half of the 1980s. If the definitions adopted when Labour was last in power are used, it rose from 1.09 million in May 1979 to a peak of 3.13 million in July 1986. By the spring of 1989 the total was below 2 million, a scale of decline surprising to many people.

However, there was much controversy about the frequently revised definitions of unemployment. To a monetarist like Minford, the argument is meaningless. In his view, much of the unemployment figures were phoney, 'swollen by those either not wanting a job on reasonable terms or actually doing a job while claiming'.[14] To redefine unemployment is perfectly acceptable: 'If a problem is defined by a statistic, then a legitimate part of its solution is the refinement of the statistic.'[15] However, there is wide disagreement about what is meant by 'reasonable terms' and critics see the problem not as a statistic, but as people wanting work and unable to find it; on this analysis, the redefinitions *do* matter.

In all there have been 28 changes of definition, all except one producing a reduction in the unemployment figures. Among the changes was a switch from counting people registered as unemployed to those claiming benefits, while at the same time changing the social security rules in order to virtually eliminate the under 18 year-olds. The treatment of those over 60 has also changed. In addition, since 1986 those unemployed for over one year have been called for an interview on the Restart Programme, while the 'availability for work' test has been applied more rigorously. This has led to a number of people ceasing to claim benefit. The government sees this as evidence that many of those working in the 'black economy' (that is, working at various jobs for cash) have been frightened off; 'scroungers' and 'cheats' have been flushed out, to the general public good. The Labour Party has attacked the moves towards an American-style 'workfare' system, whereby the unemployed are pressured to take *any* work, however low-paid, or lose benefits. Labour argues that Restart interviews are a way of exerting pressure on many people not to register; they are seen by unemployed people as a threat to their benefits. The 1989 Social Security Act requires claimants to prove that they have been actively seeking work each week with the result that 515, 000 have disappeared from the labour market. This puts them in a kind of employment limbo, not officially classed as unemployed because no longer claiming benefit, but neither employed nor self-employed. They have been classified as 'economically inactive and not seeking work'. Concern about the reliability of government statistics has been voiced by a number of leading statisticians.

Yet few would deny that in the second half of the 1980s there was a sustained fall in unemployment, especially in the southern half of the country. Employment was more responsive than expected to a growth in economic activity. Ministers boasted of the growth in the number of jobs in the economy, often as a way of diverting criticism from the unemployment figures. They also brushed aside criticism that a large proportion of the new jobs were part-time, and for women, rather than full-time for male heads of households. For a while, concern was being expressed by a number of people, including employers, that in some parts of the country skill shortages were a significant problem, especially in the prosperous south. Critics pointed to the failure of industry to invest in and encourage an adequately trained workforce. It was pointed out how far behind our competitors we were in fields such as education and training and in the vital areas of research and development. Yet the worry about a shortage of workers again faded as recession began to bite in 1989 and 1990. By the end of 1990 unemployment had reached 1.75 million and was predicted to rise to well over 2 million by the end of 1991. Although unemployment is a problem not confined to Britain, international comparisons show that our rate is above that of Japan, Germany and the USA.

The enterprise culture

Did the Thatcher government reverse Britain's decline by promoting the existence of an enterprise culture? A major theme was the revival of British enterprise, the restoration of the Victorian entrepreneurial spirit, which Thatcher and supporters such as Keith Joseph and Lord Young said had been blunted by Butskellism. Thatcherites believed that there was an urgent need to modernise the economy, with attention paid to the supply-side rather than to overall demand. 'High taxes and over-regulation by the state had discouraged effort, and, together with the growth of trade union power, had circumscribed and demoralized management.'[16]

This view influenced policy strongly, both towards economic management in general and in specific areas. Much of the impetus came from Lord Young, first as Employment Secretary and then as Secretary for Trade and Industry. His main aim was 'de-

Figure 6: Unemployment, Labour and Conservative, 1975–88

Million (seasonally adjusted, excluding school-leavers)

Source: Bill Jones (ed.): *Political Issues in Britain Today*, MUP, 1989, 3rd ed., p.161

regulation', the removal of barriers to enterprise; at the DTI (renamed the Department for Enterprise) the theme was that of creating the correct climate for enterprise to thrive.

Taxation

A major component of the stategy was concerned with taxation, both to cut the overall burden and to shift from direct to indirect taxes. Taxation of the rich was reduced to allow their revived spirit of enterprise to 'trickle down' to the less well-off (a modern version of Adam Smith's 'Invisible Hand'). Many state benefits were cut to encourage the less fortunate to 'stand on their own two feet' and to 'get on their bikes'. This led some observers to note that the rich need *more* money to encourage them to work harder, while the poor need *less*! Generally throughout the Thatcher years there was a policy of reducing the top marginal rate of tax (which fell from 83 to 40 per cent), while the standard rate fell from 33 to 25 per cent. Tax allowances were raised, sometimes by less than the rate of inflation, sometimes more; the reductions for standard rate taxpayers sometimes seemed to be related to the electoral cycle. Corporation tax and taxes on unearned income also fell.

Commentators differ as to the *scale* of the cuts; the government claim that what they see as the revived spirit of British enterprise has much to do with the incentive effect of reduced taxation. However, others point to the lop-sided nature of taxation policy since 1979. 'The average married couple with two children in 1978–79 paid 35.2 per cent of their income in tax; in 1989–90 the figure had increased to 37.6 per cent. The reduction of higher tax rates, however, from 83 per cent to 40 per cent in the 1988 budget has had a dramatically beneficial effect upon the bank balances of the higher paid.'[17]

There is also little agreement about the *effects* of tax cuts. Nigel Lawson defended the policy of cutting taxation by claiming that the sharply increased tax revenue, particularly from higher rate taxpayers, was evidence of the success of the strategy. However, there is disagreement about whether this reflects specific incentive effects as opposed to other factors, such as the rapid growth in earnings for the higher paid during the 1980s. Some economists believe that the incentive effect of tax cuts is cancelled out by the wealth effect, that is that higher incomes may lead to greater leisure (or perhaps to less tax avoidance). Though the arguments are finely balanced, the claim that people had been 'liberated' by tax cuts was taken up by the media and clearly helped to create a political climate favourable to the Conservatives.

Public expenditure

Closely allied to the strategy of cutting taxation was that of reducing public expenditure. In 1979 the Conservatives argued that excessive public spending leading to excessive borrowing and higher taxation was one of the root causes of the British economic malaise. 'The policy was based on the economic argument that excessive government spending can only be financed by borrowing or taxes. Since borrowing fuels inflation and taxation increases inflationary pressures and reduces the incentive to work, both are to be avoided. But underpinning the cool economics, there was a passion amounting almost to moral fervour about the iniquity of excessive government intervention through spending and the importance of tax levels low enough to encourage those who want to earn more to work harder and keep more of the fruits of their work.'[18] An important part of the analysis was also that public expenditure had crowded out private investment.

Despite an intention to reduce public expenditure so that by 1983–84 the total would be about 4 per cent less than in 1979–80, it rose sharply, partly because of the effects of the recession, with the consequent rise in unemployment, but also because of the expansion of spending on law and order and defence. Central government also tried to reduce local government expenditure, leading to the introduction of the Community Charge (poll tax).

Riddell believed that although the government failed to cut the total of public expenditure, given the scale of the problems caused by the recession and by the built-in pressures caused by demographic changes (plus the immense political pressures inherent in the scale of government responsibilities), 'the Government did remarkably well . . . to limit the overall level of growth and overall spending as much as it did in the first half of the 1980s'.[19] Others were not so sure. Brittan pointed out that because the government had failed to reduce its responsibilities for any of the large spending areas such as social security or health, 'it had to be as tight-fisted as possible simply to contain spending increases. Thus the defenders of the Welfare State saw meanness and cheese-paring all round, while the Radical Right felt it had been betrayed.'[20]

In the second half of the decade the recovery of the economy enabled the government to spend more. Increased tax revenues, decreased borrowing and the proceeds of privatisation meant that, although total public expenditure fell as a percentage of national income the total amount actually spent rose rapidly from 1986 onwards. Ministers were able to boast on the one hand that public expenditure was accounting for a declining share of national wealth while on the other to claim that more was being spent on politically popular areas such as the NHS.

By the 1987 election the government presented itself as having efficiently managed the nation's affairs by tax and interest rate cuts with a reduction of borrowing and public expenditure as a percentage of national wealth, while increases in spending protected vital services. However, critics from the Left complained about the damage to the infrastructure and to the quality of life by

'Scrooge' Thatcher, while the Right argued that failure to cut public expenditure in real rather than percentage terms was a major cause of the reappearance of inflation.

Table 4: *Public spending 1963–1989 (general government expenditure excluding privatisation proceeds)*

	Real terms (£ bn)	*% of GDP*
1963–64 (last Tory year)	87.9	36.2
1969–70 (last Labour year)	115.6	40.2
1973–74 (last Tory year)	140.6	42.8
1975–76 (pre-IMF crisis)	157.5	48.5
1978–79 (last Labour year)	153.8	43.2
1982–83 (pre-election spending)	167.6	46.8
1988–89 (lowest ratio since 1967)	173.5	39.5

Note: The table shows real-term figures in constant 1987–88 prices.

Source: Peter Riddell: *The Thatcher Decade*, Blackwell, 1989, see p.34 for full details of sources.

In his autumn 1990 Statement, John Major announced a large increase in public spending. Some of the increases were largely outside the government's control; social security increased by 12 per cent, partly due to the growing number of pensioners, partly to the expected rise in unemployment. Other increases were related to more political considerations, such as the need to cushion the poll tax and to spend more on areas, such as education and the NHS, where the opposition had scored hits and where the government was feeling increasingly vulnerable. The approaching general election was a significant factor. Early in 1991 Norman Lamont announced that the Gulf War would be financed by borrowing rather than by tax increases, making it virtually certain that the government would need to borrow again. Clearly, the government's record in this area was mixed.

Privatisation

A central aim of the Thatcher government was simultaneously to reduce its economic role and to improve public sector efficiency. Privatisation was part of the drive to 'roll back the frontiers'; to the economic arguments about efficiency and competition were added the more political aims of raising large sums of money to finance tax cuts and to spread share ownership. 'Popular capitalism' would have the benefit of increasing the number of people who would have an interest in the return of a Conservative administration. Another very significant reason for privatisation was the hope that it would reduce the power of public sector unions.

Privatisation has been seen as the most important policy of the Thatcher administration and perhaps her most enduring monument. The boundary between the public and the private sectors has clearly been shifted fundamentally and may be difficult or even impossible to alter in any significant way. The Labour Party's policy review document 'Meet the Challenge, Make the Change', while asserting the need for 'natural monopolies' such as water and electricity, to remain in social ownership and control (the word 'nationalisation' is avoided) accepts that the debate about the boundaries between the public and private sectors is an arid one. By accepting that it is no longer as possible or necessary as it used to be to draw strict dividing lines between 'public' and 'private', Labour have signalled their acceptance that most if not all of the privatised industries will remain in the private sector; supporters and critics of Kinnock see this as a successful attempt to bury Clause Four.

By 1979 nationalised industries accounted for 10 per cent of GDP and 7 per cent of employment. Several of these industries had very poor industrial relations, low productivity and massive losses. There was considerable public dislike of these concerns, which were widely seen as favouring the producers (more specifically the unions) at the expense of the consumer. The 'Winter of Discontent', which saw a wave of strikes mainly in the public sector, added to public disillusion. Yet the short-lived Heath experiment seemed to show the difficulty of reversing the process of nationalisation. However, after 1979 the Conservatives began an assault on the concept of public ownership.

They had become convinced of the merits of a market-oriented economy but what has turned into a crusade had a very muted beginning. The 1979 manifesto merely committed the Con-

Table 5: *The major nationalised industries*

Industry	First nationalised	Subsequent reorganisations
Electricity	1926	1926 Central Electricity Board 1948 Area Electricity Boards added 1958 Reorganised into Electricity Council, Central Electricity Generating Board (CEGB) and Area Electricity Boards 1990–91 Privatised
Coal	1947	1947 National Coal Board (now called British Coal)
Gas	1949	1949 Gas Council and Area Boards 1973 Re-established as British Gas Corporation (later called British Gas) 1986 Privatised
Water	1972	1973 Regional Water Authorities (10) took over from local government 1989 Privatised as 10 separate companies
Oil	1976	1976 British National Oil Corporation (BNOC) (part of industry only) 1982 Privatised as Britoil
Posts and tele-communications	1961	Previously a government department 1981 Split into the Post Office and British Telecom (BT) 1984 BT privatised
Railways, etc.	1948	1948 British Transport Commission 1963 Split into British Railways, London Transport (and also British Transport Docks Board, British Waterways Board, Transport Holding Company)
Buses	1969	1969 National Bus Company 1986 Privatised
Road haulage	1947	1953 Privatised Re-nationalised as National Freight Corporation 1982 Privatised (management and worker buyout)
Car manufac-turing	1976	1976 British Leyland 1984 Jaguar privatised 1988 Rover Group privatised
Shipbuilding	1977	1977 British Shipbuilders 1985–86 Privatised
Areo engines	1971	1971 Rolls-Royce 1987 Privatised
Airways	1940	1940 British Overseas Airways Corporation (non-European) 1946 British European Airways (European) 1974 BOAC and BEA combined to form British Airways 1987 Privatised
Airports	1966	1966 British Airports Authority 1987 Privatised
Aerospace	1977	1977 British Aerospace (part of industry only) 1981 Privatised
Steel	1951	1951 Iron and Steel Corporation 1953 Privatised 1967 Re-nationalised as British Steel Corporation 1988 Privatised

Source: John Sloman: *Economics*, Harvester Wheatsheaf, 1991, p.449.

servatives to reversing the nationalisation measures of the 1974–9 Labour government. The privatisation programme of the 1979–83 government was modest and without a clear rationale. 'Although general economic benefits were expected to flow from the programme, it was viewed neither as a political crusade nor as a way of changing the patterns of ownership in the United Kingdom other than by involving employees both at the time of the initial sale and through future profit-sharing schemes. Within a space of five years, privatisation was to become one of the most successful polices of the Government.'[21]

The arguments for privatisation

These can be grouped into two basic ideas.

1. Political

Conservative hostility to the economic role of the state has again become marked with particular dislike of public sector industries. In 1979 the 18 largest employed 1.6 million workers in what were alleged to be protected or monopoly markets. The workforces were strong and heavily unionised (the role of the NUM in 1973–74 was an especially sore point). Many had large debts. The nationalised industries were blamed for the rate of public borrowing, the high level of taxation and unemployment. The Prime Minister and her leading colleagues spoke of them as 'horrific, poisonous, debilitating, voracious and a haemorrhage.'

There was no radical programme of privatisation before 1979. But after the election pressure grew; it became one of Mrs. Thatcher's major preoccupations and Joseph's main priority. Several Right-wing pressure groups, such as the Institute of Economic Affairs, the Centre for Policy Studies and the Adam Smith Institute, added to the clamour. By 1981 Howe had produced a list of industries which were candidates for sale to the private sector and after the 1983 election privatisation became a central and distinguishing feature of the Thatcher government. The 1983 manifesto contained a detailed commitment to privatisation and the process was stimulated by the appointment of Nigel Lawson as Chancellor of the Exchequer.

A major aspect of the policy was to strengthen property by extending share-ownership to new sectors of the population, especially the more affluent of the working class. This is the counterpart of the sale of council houses to tenants; the 'share-holding democracy' was to be added to the 'property-owning' democracy to create a 'peoples' capitalism'. Thus small shareholders were favoured in some of the privatisations while employee buy-outs were also a feature. Beside the ideological imperative of spreading the benefits of capitalism there were political objectives. It was hoped to increase the percentage of the population, many of them former Labour voters, who would have a vested interest in capitalism and who would oppose the return of a Labour government. However, a large number of small shareholders quickly sold their shares for a speculative gain and the big financial institutions continue to dominate the newly created companies. Despite this, there was considerable popular support for this aspect of Thatcherism.

2. Economic

Supporters believe that private sector companies *per se* are more efficient than those in the public sector, that competition and the free operation of market forces produce more consumer choice. Privatised companies would invest more so expanding and providing more 'real' jobs and be in a better position to meet foreign competition. This would contribute to Britain's economic revitalisation and reverse the cycle of economic decline. There is an emphasis on freedom of choice for the consumer.

Another aim was to increase government revenue through the sale of public assets, which by 1989 had reached around £20 billion and which reduced the PSBR. Ministers claimed that this would simultaneously lessen the pressure of inflation and allow additional expenditure in areas such as road building, the NHS and so on. Critics saw this as a form of economic conjuring-trick which enabled the goverment to claim that public expenditure was under control while continuing to spend with a large deficit and expressed concern that this process of raising large amounts of money could not continue indefinitely as there was a limit to what could be sold. They pointed to the long-term economic consequences of selling off public assets, often for less than their market value. A number of share flotations were fixed at levels far less than could have been achieved. Thus not only had the government failed to realise the true value of these assets but had also lost the future profits from their activities. Many of the industries sold were not loss-making utilities but highly successful commercial operations. Some critics felt that the real aim was less to do with the promotion of competition and efficiency than with the political pressure to raise revenue with which to cut taxes before the 1987 election. The government answered this by saying that tax revenues would expand as the economy prospered and that this would more than compensate for the decline in one-off receipts from privatisation.

Other aspects of the economic case for privatisation stress the advantages of involving workers through selling shares to the workforce, thus making them into 'mini-capitalists'. Beside the political advantages, the intention was to reduce the power of the unions (especially in the public sector) to resist the process of privatisation. In the long term the motivation and efficiency of the workers would be improved by giving them the incentive to share in the increased profits that privatisation was expected to achieve. Privatisation would free industries from control by Whitehall, removing the restrictions imposed by successive governments as well as making clearer who was actually responsible for performance, profitability and so on.

Critics attacked the policy on several grounds, pointing out that the arguments in favour of selling private assets have changed and no coherent strategy can be seen; in particular, there is an inconsistency between the ideological drive for liberalisation and competition and Treasury demands for maximum revenue from sales. What determines which industries will be privatised is not whether they would benefit from greater commercial freedom but how much money the sale would realise. The criticism is that the real motive is not the regeneration of the British economy but the need to finance tax cuts. The privatisation of British Telecom was an example, as the sale would not benefit the consumer through increased competition, since BT was changed from being a public monopoly to being a private monopoly. Similar criticisms were made of the sale of British Gas, British Airways and so on. In several cases the government resisted pressure from free-market enthusiasts because revenues from sales would be reduced if the concerns were broken up in the interests of competition.

It was also argued that a change of ownership does not necessarily improve performance. Accountability to the public would be reduced when anonymous boards representing large institutions such as pension funds and insurance companies take control. Critics argued that enterprises such as BP, Cable and Wireless and British Gas were public sector successes. Considerable indignation was felt when the government, perhaps sensitive to criticisms that loss-making concerns such as British Rail were not being considered for privatisation, began a policy of massive investment after years of neglect as a prelude to sale to the private sector. Such sales were accompanied by massive write-offs of accumulated debts; the criticism was that the public, having made the investment, was being deprived of its benefits, which would be reaped by shareholders.

It was also argued that some industries need to be organised on a national scale and competition, far from bringing benefits, causes duplication and waste. Strategically vital industries, either for defence or national self-sufficiency, including the oil and the nuclear industries and some parts of the defence industry, are too important to allow into the hands of private enterprise dominated by the search for profits. There is particular anxiety that these concerns might be dominated by foreign investors and in some instances foreign holdings in sensitive firms have been limited.

However, public support for privatisation was widespread. Share-ownership (much of it the result of the purchase of former state assets) has tripled since 1979; over 9 million people now own shares, around one quarter of the adult population, with shareholding going beyond the middle class into social groups C1, C2 and even DE. The performance of nationalised industries remains unsatisfactory. Despite promises (or threats) in the 1983 manifesto of wide-spread re-nationalisation, the increasingly dominant Right in the Labour Party became convinced that this was a vote-loser and efforts were made to find a new formula to express the commitment to some form of common ownership. 'Social ownership' was stressed and various forms were suggested, such as companies being owned by the employees and managed as workers' co-operatives; local authorities might have a role in the running of enterprises. The 1989 policy review left vague the precise degree of commitment to public ownership; instead protection for the consumer was stressed.

By 1989 the Tories were coming under considerable pressure over the privatisation of the water industry; public opinion was hostile and the government was accused of ideological obstinacy in seeking to sell a natural asset which even a majority of Conservative voters thought should be publicly owned rather than being an asset run for profit. The impending sale of water, plus the reforms in the NHS (itself widely seen as the prelude to privatisation) were held by many commentators to have contributed to the disasterous Tory showing in the 1989 Euro-elections and to the surge of Labour in the polls. The government, however, showed no signs of a 'U-turn', and the privatisation of water was successfully completed in December 1989. Electricity followed in December 1990; it was the most popular privatisation ever. Share applications were received from 12.75 million people, and the issue was 10.7 times over-subscribed. Should the Conservatives win the next election, it is likely that British Rail and British Coal will be next in line for privatisation.

Other policies
Other initiatives accompanied these general strategies. There was an emphasis on *deregulation*. Price, dividend, private sector pay and foreign exchange controls were abolished. In particular, the abolition of foreign exchange controls was hotly contested. It was claimed that it released market forces and enabled British investors to build up overseas portfolios, the income from which would help cushion the blow when the revenues from North Sea oil began to decline. Critics lamented the failure to invest in British industry and saw the benefits of overseas investment going not to the 'real' economy but to the City, generating huge windfalls for a few rather than ensuring an adequate supply of investment income for the manufacturing sector. Deregulation also extended to banks and building societies; here again, the beneficial effects are a matter of controversy, with supporters seeing the benefits of competition as self-evident, while critics point to the unsustainable credit explosion as a major reason for the return of inflation and balance of payments difficulties. *Competition* was promoted and an attempt made to break down the privileged position of opticians and solicitors. *Liberalisation* meant the ending of controls over bus routes, the licensing of Mercury as a competitor for British Telecom and so on. There was a bewildering range of initiatives to help *small businesses*, with claims that the considerable growth was a sign of the revitalisation of a previously oppressed sector of British business. The government's role in *industrial aid* in switching from support for regional policies to a variety of advisory services, often of a highly public-relations-conscious nature, was criticised. There was also an

emphasis on improving *education and training*, although there was less than unanimity on its success.

The 'enterprise culture' has had mixed success. There is evidence of a revival of entrepreneurial activity, especially in the service sectors and in small businesses and of a recovery of managerial self-confidence in much of manufacturing industry. On the other hand, this does not indicate that all of Britain's industrial problems have been solved. In many internationally competitive sectors, especially those with a high technological content, Britain still lags and there is a growing trade deficit in high-technology products. Problems of inadequate training (plus growing criticism of Britain's record in vital areas of research and design) are still unsolved. Yet many feel that the early 1980s were an important turning-point for British management as a whole; it may be that the injunction to 'get on your bike' has produced a real shift in attitudes.

Mrs Thatcher's decade[22]

Examining the Thatcher years Curwen found a policy vacuum. While Keynesianism dominated British economic policy making from the Second World War to 1970 before going into a steady decline, the reign of monetarism was short. 'Monetarism . . . hardly had the chance to evolve at all before significant aspects were consigned to virtual oblivion, leaving the UK in a kind of policy limbo – part-monetarist, part-Keynesian, and with a heavy dose of what might best be called "pragmatism" thrown in for good measure.'[23] Curwen believed that this more pragmatic approach may be the only way forward.

David Gowland and Stephen James looked at two contrasting analyses of the Thatcher years:

1. Because of the initial shake up, followed by prudent fiscal policies and the supply-side encouragement to the free market, the economy has emerged as more robust and flexible with more sustainable economic growth.
2. A much more pessimistic analysis sees the improvements in the economy as a catching-up process after the severe

recession of the early 1980s. Many inherent weaknesses remain and will resurface given the right conditions.

In the view of Gowland and James, 'both these two views are too extreme. The period has produced some positive benefits – for example in the marked improvement in the trend growth of productivity and the competitiveness of the manufacturing sector. On the other hand, such achievements have been obtained at the cost of heavy unemployment and lost output. As is the case with all economic adjustments, the costs have not been shared equally. In addition, there is ample evidence of the resurgence of some of the underlying problems of the UK economy – the current account deterioration, rising inflation and the behaviour of earnings.'[24]

Others remain deeply unimpressed with the claims of Mrs Thatcher and her supporters to have 'turned Britain around'. Some have seen it as a series of flawed experiments, of missed opportunities; at best a patchy record of achievement. Fiercer critics see Mrs Thatcher's time in office as a virtually unmitigated disaster, a period which did little or nothing to solve the underlying problems of the economy and in which real and lasting damage was done to Britain's manufacturing base. They point to the vast wealth produced by North Sea oil which Mrs Thatcher's government had the good fortune to inherit but which was used either to sustain the huge growth of unemployment, itself a product of errors of policy, or to produce the increase in living standards for those fortunate enough to remain in work, to the detriment of Britain's long-term prospects but to the electoral advantage of the Conservatives.

Some have asked whether the economy has been fundamentally transformed as Mrs Thatcher and others have claimed. Whiteley pointed out that most commentators are now agreed that disastrous mistakes were made in the first period when manufacturing industry was badly damaged by the excessive recession. A more successful period followed from 1982 to 1986 when 'the government did as well as any government could do in the circumstances in promoting growth without inflation. Real gains in productivity and the profitability of industry were made in these years, but in the entire Thatcher period investment was

significantly below rates achieved in the late 1970s'.[25] Whiteley
was highly critical of economic policy in the approach to the 1987
election, in which prudence was abandoned in the desire to
stimulate the economy for electoral purposes. He picked up the
point made by other observers, namely that in this period
ministers appeared to have actually *believed* the claims they were
making about the British economy: 'seduced by its own rhetoric
and apparent success the government continued the reflationary
policy long after the election was over'.[26]

Economic policy should be judged by the long-run performance of the 'real' economy, i.e. of productivity and growth. Productivity was stimulated but at great cost in terms of unemployment. Growth rates were lower than in previous periods,
inadequacies in education and training showed in skill shortages
in key industries and rising wage inflation at a time of high
unemployment. Echoing an increasing volume of anxieties,
Whiteley pointed out that commercial research and development
was low compared with competitor nations. He summed up the
Thatcher years thus: 'At the end of the day perhaps the most
telling fact of the Thatcher era is that for the first time in two
centuries, Britain has become a net importer of manufactured
goods. Since production volumes of North Sea oil have already
peaked, and are now on a declining trend, the supply-side
weaknesses of the British economy will become more and more
apparent as time goes on in terms of balance of payments and
currency problems. That is the most telling legacy of the 1980s.'[27]

In a survey of the British economy under Mrs Thatcher, Ken
Coutts and Wynne Godley examined the main economic
indicators since 1979. They showed that growth was distinctly
lower than in the 1950s, 1960s and 1970s; from the second
quarter of 1979 to the fourth quarter of 1988 growth averaged 1.9
per cent, while growth in the 1950s never fell below 2.4 per cent,
and the comparable figures for the 1960s and the 1970s were 3.1
per cent and 2.4 per cent respectively, although this does not
invalidate the claim that after 1980 there was an unusually long
period of sustained growth. In terms of international comparisons,
Coutts and Godley showed that the growth rate in the UK from
1979 to 1988 was much less than in Japan, rather less than in the

US and Italy, about the same as in France and greater than in Germany. This point was taken up by Whiteley. 'In the 1980s Britain did some modest catching-up with the growth rates of other countries, such as France and West Germany, though not relative to Japan and the United States. If Britain was doing better relative to some other countries during the Thatcher years, that might be described as an improvement, but it is hardly an economic miracle.'[28]

Coutts and Godley then turned their attention to productivity, showing that, taking the economy as a whole, the growth of labour productivity (output per member of the employed workforce) was lower than in the two previous periods of equal length, although labour productivity in manufacturing industry rose significantly faster than in the earlier periods (reflecting the growth of unemployment). However, the growth rate of manufacturing production was relatively low. They went on to show the deterioration in the balance of trade in manufactures (a point already remarked on by Whiteley), a fact masked for some years by a large improvement in the balance on oil. However, production of oil has started to deteriorate and the balance of trade in services, which ministers said would replace manufactures, has also started to decline. Thus 'our current balance of payments (as a percentage of national income) is far worse than those of all the larger European countries and of Japan, though much the same as in the US'.[29]

Coutts and Godley reviewed other indicators, such as unemployment, inflation, the growth of personal consumption, the money supply and so on before assessing the validity of Lawson's claim of an 'economic miracle'. Their conclusion was: 'It is not easy to write temperately about Mr Lawson's claim; it is quite simply preposterous, as the evidence in this paper clearly shows.'[30] The performance of all the indicators has been poor in relation either to the past or to other countries, or in many cases, to both. This point was taken up by Whiteley, who said that any apparent improvement in the economy would be short-lived: 'to claim economic success, and a break with 'stop–go' policies it is necessary to show that higher growth rates are sustainable over time. There have been periods when UK growth rates were high in relation to competitors, but unfortunately these were short-lived.'[31] Coutts and Godley wrote that 'What distinguishes the UK most sharply from other countries (and indeed from previous periods in the UK) is that, despite its relatively slow rate of growth, total demand has run beyond our capacity to produce.'[32] Hence the rapid deterioration in the current balance of payments, which is no 'blip' as Lawson called it. At the same time, inflation was increasing despite heavy (and currently rising) unemployment.

They concluded that an enormous strategic predicament faced policy makers. The balance of payments would continue to deteriorate unless action was taken to prevent it, in which case it was likely that there would 'be a virtual stop to growth or even an absolute decline in total demand and output, with a renewed rise in unemployment and the blighting of business confidence just as this seems to have recovered'.[33]

By the end of 1990 even ministers could not disguise the depth of the recession. Evidence had been growing of first a slowing and then a halt to economic growth. The housing market went into a nose-dive, followed by retailing, the motor trade and then virtually the whole of the economy. Unemployment began to rise and by the end of the year the figure was accelerating. The Treasury predicted that the economy would grow in 1991 by a paltry 0.5 per cent. The CBI repeatedly warned about declining business confidence and called for interest rate cuts, a call ignored by the government, fearful above all of an inability to bring down inflation before the next election. Indications grew that the recession in Britain was considerably worse than in most competitor countries; in December Oxford Economic Forecasting Ltd issued a report which showed that the USA and the UK were deeply in recession, while the rest of the OECD countries were slowing down but avoiding the problems of the Anglo–Saxon economies. The report predicted a contraction in the UK economy, with most of the fall concentrated in the last quarter of 1990 and the first quarter of 1991; it predicted that although growth would recommence in 1992 and continue in 1993, it would be at a sharply lower rate than that of competitor nations. The report stressed that 'To blame much of this on oil prices would be superficial . . . More pertinent is the existence of large external imbalances and unacceptable rates of inflation, forcing policy makers to retrench after the boom years of 1987 and 1988.'[34]

Summary

The claim of Mrs Thatcher, Nigel Lawson and others that an 'economic miracle' has transformed the British economy now seems like a sick joke. The verdict of Edward Pearce 'that Margaret Thatcher was dismissed by her party for a compounded failure, long postponed by oil, opposition division and big loyal headlines, but coming at last as a judgement on a career falling so short of greatness as to miss mediocrity'[35] is perhaps harsh. But only 'perhaps'.

Notes

1   Patrick Minford, Mrs Thatcher's Economic Reform Programme, in Robert Skidelsky (ed.): *Thatcherism*, Chatto and Windus, 1988, p.94.

2   Ibid., p.95.

3   Alan Budd: Thatcher's Economic Performance, *Contemporary Record*, Vol. 2, No. 2, Summer 1988, p.32.

4   Geoffrey Maynard: *The Economy Under Mrs Thatcher*, Blackwell, 1988, p.148. See also Kent Mathews and Peter Stoney Explaining Mrs Thatcher's Success, *Economic Affairs*, Vol. 10, No. 2, December/January 1990.

5   Ibid., p.149.

6   Ibid., p.156.

7   Ibid., p.157.

8   Ibid., p.159.

9   Geoffrey Maynard: Britain's Economic Revival and the Balance of Payments, *Political Quarterly*, Vol. 60, No.2, April–June 1989.

10   Samuel Brittan: The Thatcher Government's Economic Policy, in Dennis Kavanagh and Anthony Seldon (ed.): *The Thatcher Effect*, OUP, 1989.

11   Peter Riddell, *The Thatcher Decade*, Blackwell, 1989, p.viii.

12   Brittan, The Thatcher Government, p.34.

13   Ibid., p.32.

14   Minford, Thatcher's Economic Reform Programme, p.102.

15   Ibid.

16   Riddell, *The Thatcher Decade*, p.71.

17 Bill Jones and Dennis Kavanagh: *British Politics Today*, MUP, 4th edn, 1991, p.180.

18 Andrew Likierman: Public Expenditure, *Contemporary Record*, Vol. 4, No. 3, February 1991.

19 Riddell, *The Thatcher Decade*, p.33.

20 Brittan, The Thatcher Government, p.25.

21 Gerry Grimstone: Privatisation. The Unexpected Crusade, *Contemporary Record*, Vol. 1, No. 1, Spring 1987.

22 See articles in *Economic Affairs*, Vol. 10, No. 2, December/January 1990.

23 Peter Curwen (ed.): *Understanding the UK Economy*, Macmillan, 1990, p.2.

24 David Gowland and Stephen James: Macroeconomic Policy, in Curwen (ed.): *Understanding the UK Economy*, p.332.

25 Paul Whiteley, Economic Policy, in Patrick Dunleavy et al. (eds.): *Developments in British Politics 3*, Macmillan, 1990, p.195.

26 Ibid.

27 Ibid.

28 Ibid., p.194.

29 Ken Coutts and Wynne Godley: The British Economy under Mrs Thatcher, *Political Quarterly*, Vol. 60, No. 2, April–June 1989, p.140.

30 Ibid., p.150.

31 Whiteley, Economic Policy, p.194.

32 Coutts and Godley, British Economy under Mrs Thatcher, p.150.

33 Ibid., p.151.

34 OEF Press Notice, 27 December 1990.

35 The *Guardian*, 28 November 1990.

Part Three

The making of economic policy

6

The machinery of economic policy making

This chapter examines the machinery of economic policy making in Britain. It considers the nature of the official policy making bodies and processes, such as the Treasury, the Budget, the NEDC and so on, and the impact of pressure groups, 'think-tanks' and similar organisations. It starts with an examination of the major policy preoccupations of successive post-war governments.

The aims of economic policy

The aim of economic management is to enable the government of the day to control and influence the economy in ways that it considers beneficial.

This generalisation begs the question of precisely whom the policy is benefiting. The *intentions* of politicians and policy makers may differ from the *outcomes* of their policies. 'In their approach to economic policy, successive governments have resembled children who think they will not make the mistakes of their parents, only to find that life is more complicated than they thought. To change the metaphor, the economic policy machine of ministers and officials has given the impression of permanently trying to run up the downward escalator.'[1]

British governments have pursued policies which they thought would benefit the 'national interest'. Yet in addition to realising that they have often made major policy errors, it is necessary to analyse what is meant by this concept. Governments have interpreted it in terms of their own philosophical beliefs and in the interests of those they represent: for example, Tory governments in the eighteenth century interpreted the national interest largely as that of the landed interest, while nineteenth century Liberal administrations believed that it was best served by encouraging manufacturers and traders. Yet governments have often been forced to compromise their ideological positions; 'reality' has intervened. Post-war Labour governments sought to improve the economic and social position of the working class but often found that the problems posed by Britain's weak economic base meant that cherished plans had to be postponed or abandoned. Similarly Mrs Thatcher found that the apparent simplicity of the monetarist analysis was illusory and was forced to abandon many cherished hopes.

For around thirty years after 1945 there was broad and general agreement about the aims of economic management, and argument was partly about priorities and methods and partly about competence. Underlying all these aims was the more general concept of 'social justice'. This was an explicit goal for Labour and the post-war government emphasised the improvement of the conditions of the working class. Subsequent Labour administrations found it harder to achieve egalitarianism as economic weakness became more apparent and as ideological doubt and division set in. The Tory version was less clear; it combined rewards for 'enterprise' with a paternalistic concern for the working class. This latter impetus, which Mrs Thatcher termed 'bourgeois guilt', was not a feature of her policy; her priorities were different.

For much of the post-war period these aims were seen as complementary; all were important, all were thought to be within the power of governments to achieve, and all should be pursued simultaneously although with policy adjustments to reflect particular problems or priorities. 'Fine tuning' the economy by use of various Keynesian techniques was a feature of the period. However, these assumptions broke down in the 1970s, especially after the IMF loan.

The making of economic policy

Economic policy results from the interaction of a diverse range of pressures from a variety of sources. The degree of influence of the various groups varies over time. Often at the beginning of a government the party manifesto provides the main impetus for policy making; commitments have to be honoured, governments and their supporters need to feel that their efforts will at last succeed in 'setting the people free', or 'creating an enterprise economy' or whatever is the current slogan. Later, as economic policies run into difficulties, the influence of institutions such as the Treasury and the Bank of England becomes stronger; civil servants may 'educate' politicians about the limits of their power. Governments may become more dependent on the international financial system; ultimately the IMF may be called in.

In a representative democracy economic policy making is in theory the result of a general election in which the victorious party, having put its programme to the voters and having won a majority of seats in Parliament, implements its policies with the aid of the Civil Service and other expert advice. The voters' wishes determine policy. But clearly the reality is different. The preferences of politicians and bureaucrats are a factor; they will crucially affect which policies are implemented and how. Policy making takes place in an historical, legal, institutional and cultural setting; all these factors influence what happens, although they can be modified to reflect and permit change. An example is the changing role played by pressure groups, many of whom will play a part in the formulation of policy while others will be of vital significance in its implementation. The corporatist-type policy making of the 1960s and 1970s, whereby employers' organisations and trade unions were intimately involved in policy making, was not a feature of the Thatcher era while groups such as the various free-market think-tanks and City institutions were very influential after 1979.

The influence of the international financial and political systems is ever-present as a major constraint on domestic policy. The weaker the British economy, as in 1976, the greater the influence of international opinion; the need to reassure foreign holders of sterling has played a significant part in policy making since 1945. The dramatic events in Eastern Europe caused talk of a 'peace dividend'; it was hoped that very significant resources could be shifted from defence into electorally more appealing areas, such as tax cuts or increases in infrastructure or social spending, depending on one's political preferences. However, tension in various parts of the world, allied to fears of growing unemployment at home, may affect decisions about defence spending, showing that the room for manoeuvre of British policy makers is limited.

Economic policy making is the outcome of a process of political bargaining in which rational decision making has a secondary role. There are two stages to the process. The first is formulation, where the views of voters are influential and politicians have great significance. The second is implementation, where public sector bureacrats dominate. The role played by various groups must be considered.

1. The voters

Britain is a representative democracy with a tenuous link between voter preferences and government action. Countries such as Switzerland use referenda to connect the two, but this is not so here. The 1975 EEC referendum was unique (and in any case, given that Parliament is sovereign, could only have been advisory not binding). The policies set out in election manifestos are often vague and give the party concerned much leeway in their interpretation. A commitment to 'tackle' inflation or to 'deal with' unemployment can lead to debate about what precisely was meant at the time and the extent to which such promises have been kept. Voters have to choose between competing policy packages and cannot discriminate or choose parts of one and parts of another. In the 1987 election opinion polls reported that many voters who expressed grave reservations about government policies on health, education and welfare and who preferred Labour's alternatives still voted Conservative because they believed that the government was more capable of producing or safeguarding economic prosperity than was the opposition.

Similarly, there is no guarantee that the winning party will implement all the policies mentioned in the manifesto, though it is a myth that parties promise anything in order to get elected and then cynically ignore their commitments. The government can adopt new policies once in power; indeed, all governments *have* to adapt their campaign promises during their time in office. Not to do so would be both unrealistic and irresponsible. It is an over-simplification to think that voters decide how to cast their votes after a process of analysing the relative merits of the various policy packages on offer. Voters are swayed by a variety of factors and are affected by the image of politicians and the programmes of the parties as conveyed by the media, although the extent to which this affects voters' perceptions of policy issues is uncertain. In Britain, the first-past-the-post electoral system distorts the relationship between votes and seats and should, in theory, make it difficult for politicians to claim majority support for their policies, although few in government can resist the opportunity.

Sometimes voters have a direct impact. 'Perhaps the best recent example of voters' influence on economic policy during an administration was the experience in 1975–6: Denis Healey's acceptance that voters in his constituency were turning against ever-rising public expenditure (because of the implications for the average man's taxes) was a major factor behind the Labour Party's more rigid approach to public spending.'[2] This does not mean that governments are obliged to follow the wishes of voters, or even of party members; it does however show that electoral opinion may significantly shape politicians' actions.

Economic issues are regarded as important by voters. In recent elections there has been a conflict in voters' minds between giving priority to reducing unemployment or keeping inflation down. Other examples include the pressure to spend more on social services as opposed to the desire for lower taxation. There is much evidence that the popularity of a goverment is closely linked to voter satisfaction with its economic performance. The main indicator is real income per head; unemployment and inflation have also been important but have varied in impact over the post-war period. Contrary to received wisdom, the Conservatives did not suffer a political backlash from unemployment in 1983.

Voters consider the present position of the economy and their hopes for the future; they also evaluate past performances in deciding which party is best able to keep its promises.

2. Parliament

The power of Parliament increased in the seventeenth and eighteenth centuries because it controlled the flow of money to the Crown; the power to grant or refuse 'supply' (i.e. funds) was an important factor in asserting its predominance. However, with the rise of disciplined parliamentary parties in the nineteenth century, and especially after 1867, this power declined. Although Parliament's permission is still required for the raising and spending of most public money, it is virtually a rubber-stamp exercise. Parliament can only refuse to approve public spending; it cannot vote to *increase* expenditure. Decisions about public expenditure are taken by the executive. This is also true of taxation matters. Parliament has only the most indirect role in the discussions leading to the preparation of the Budget. Tax changes are embodied in the Finance Bill which is normally passed by Parliament with little discussion, although the experience of the minority Labour government of the mid-1970s was somewhat different. An amendment to Healey's 1977 Budget, proposed by two Labour backbenchers, Jeff Rooker and Audrey Wise, related income tax reliefs to the cost of living, much to the fury of ministers concerned to limit public expenditure.

Parliament *does* have an important part to play in the political process which shapes all aspects of policy. Parliament is the forum within which the political battle is fought out. Government and opposition are engaged in a debate, not to convince each other but to bolster support on their own side of the House, and more importantly to appeal, via the media, to the electorate. In addition, Parliament does act as a constraint on the executive. Governments, however large their majority and however self-confident their leaders, do pay attention to the opinion of Parliament as a whole; in this respect the Commons is the predominant Chamber, given the limited role played by the Lords in the process of raising and spending public money. Particularly important is the attitude of the government's own supporters; the whips play a major role in canvassing views and ensuring support. The ultimate sanction of backbenchers is to refuse to vote in support of their leaders. Unlikely as this is (the defeat on the Second Reading of the Shops Bill, designed to legalise Sunday trading, was virtually unprecedented in this century), pressure can be brought during debate or, more effectively, in private party meetings. It was a row in the the 1922 Committee which forced the then Education Secretary, Sir Keith Joseph, to withdraw a plan to compel better-off parents to pay for their children's university tuition fees.

Supply procedure in the House of Commons
The House of Commons formally controls supply; to simplify the position somewhat, the Lords has little or no control over finance. 'The ancient rights and privileges' of the Commons means that all

Table 6: *The House of Commons financial year*

Date	Information and estimates presented to the Commons, etc.	Voting timetable
November to February	(1) Autumn financial statement (2) Winter supplementary estimates (3) Votes on account (4) Consolidated Fund Bill	Voted on not later than 6 February
January to March	(5) Public Expenditure White Paper (6) Main estimates (7) Spring supplementary estimates (8) Excess votes (9) Consolidated Fund Bill (10) Budget statement (11) Finance Bill	Items 7 and 8 voted on not later than 18 March; bills (9, 11, 13) enacted March–July
April to August	(12) Summer supplementary estimates (extra sums needed for current year) (13) Consolidated Fund (Appropriation) Bill	Voted on not later than 5 August

Source: Andrew Adonis: *Parliament Today*, MUP, 1990, p.117.

proposals dealing with 'aids and supplies' must originate from that House and once approved cannot be altered by the Lords.

Today 'aids and supplies' are brought together in Finance Bills which deal with taxation and Consolidated Fund Bills which authorise expenditure. Together they are known as Supply Bills. They must be passed by the Lords before they can become law, even though the powers of the Lords are extremely limited. The annual Finance Bill, embodying the Chancellor's Budget proposals, is debated in general terms on Second Reading, although subsequent stages are formal. In debating bills not connected with supply the Lords may make proposals which involve expenditure; in such cases, the Commons may agree. However, if the Commons does assert its financial privileges the Lords will give way. There is a specific category of financial legislation, known as Money Bills, first introduced by the Parliament Act 1911, passed to overcome the Lords' veto of the 1909 Budget. A Money Bill is certified by the Speaker of the Commons to concern only taxation or public expenditure. Though such bills *are* debated in the Lords they can only be delayed for one month and are cautiously handled. In return, the Speaker will be scrupulous in giving his certificate to a Money Bill.[3]

A basic outline of supply procedure in the Commons is as follows.

1. The government presents estimates requesting money and explaining how it will be spent.
2. The Commons votes on the estimates.
3. Parliament passes an Act which authorises the Bank of England to make the money available.
4. After the money is spent there is an audit.

This complex procedure, despite dealing with some £200 billion of public money, is largely formal; little is debated in detail and much goes through 'on the nod' completely undiscussed. Parliament's control is partial. It does have the ultimate deterrent; it can reject the estimates as a whole or vote against a Consolidated Fund Bill. In such a case, the government would have to resign and face a general election, something which has not occurred in the twentieth century.

In the nineteenth century a number of Supply Days were allocated to the examination of the estimates. In this century the figure was fixed at 26. It became the practice to allow the opposition to choose the subjects for debate, which usually turned into a general discussion of government policy rather than actual scrutiny of expenditure. So in 1982 the 26 Supply Days were replaced by 19 Opposition Days, with the opposition parties determining the subjects to be debated, and three Estimate Days set aside to examine specific details of the estimates, although even these days tend to become general debates rather than detailed scrutiny of spending plans. While this provides the House as a whole with an opportunity to examine the government's spending proposals, it is clearly of little value.

Parliament also plays a vital scrutinising role. This is mainly carried out in the departmental select committees, established in 1979. These bodies have the power to investigate the expenditure, administration and policies of the principal government departments, as well as public bodies such as nationalized industries. They have powers to call people to give evidence and can request the presence of ministers. The committees issue reports, though the government decides whether they are debated; similarly, whether the recommendations are implemented is largely a matter for the executive.

In terms of scrutinizing the estimates (i.e. the government's spending plans) the most significant of these departmental select committees is the Treasury and Civil Service Committee. This has eleven members, most of them experienced in financial and economic affairs and often former Treasury ministers. There is a sub-committee which deals with taxation and Civil Service matters, while the main committee deals with broader policy questions and can appoint specialist advisers. Its reports are often highly critical of government policy (even though it contains a majority of members from the government side, as do all the select committees). However, its value as a watchdog is limited in that it is concerned more with broad policy and departmental organisation and methods than with detailed scrutiny of particular estimates.

The Public Accounts Committee (PAC), established in 1861,

the oldest and most prestigious of the investigatory select committees, scrutinises public expenditure to ensure value for money, although its main role is to ensure that public money is spent as intended by Parliament 'rather than assessing whether the objectives of economic policy have been adequately secured'.[5] It is chaired by a senior opposition MP, currently (1991) Robert Sheldon, Financial Secretary to the Treasury in the last Labour government. It is treated with great respect by the Civil Service (something not always accorded to select committees). The PAC is aided by the Comptroller and Auditor General who heads a staff of around 900 in the National Audit Office and is responsible for auditing the accounts of all government departments as well as other public sector bodies. His value-for-money audits, which have include topics such as the De Lorean car project in Northern Ireland, are of great value and the fact that he can choose which topics to investigate means he can make suggestions for the future rather than just examining past errors. He reports to the PAC, which in turn mounts investigations with the department concerned. He is an Officer of the House of Commons and so is independent of the government of the day.

The Budget

The House of Commons also exercises a formal control over taxation, which is the principal way in which the government raises money. Government borrowing, another important source of finance, is not subject to parliamentary scrutiny.

The Budget is presented to the Commons in March or April; it is prepared in great secrecy, and is not normally discussed in Cabinet beforehand. The Chancellor works closely with the Prime Minister and ministers will probably be consulted about those aspects which apply to their own departments. The whole package is revealed to the Cabinet shortly before being presented to the Commons, but there is little or no opportunity to press for changes, except of the most marginal nature. The Budget speech reviews the general economic situation and makes detailed proposals about changes in taxation. Its original purpose was primarily to raise the revenue needed to finance the operation of government, but it has become, particularly in the post-war period, an economic and political instrument of the greatest significance. Since 1941, the first Keynesian Budget, it has been a major factor in shaping the national economic situation. However, in recent years the annual Budget has somewhat lost its pre-eminence in terms of economic policy; Chancellors often make an Autumn Statement, in effect a mini-budget. In addition, there are often adjustments to economic policy at various times of the year. This additional flexibility in economic management has been generally welcomed as a sign of greater realism in a rapidly changing world.

The Chancellor's statement is followed by a general debate lasting some four days which begins with a speech by the Leader of the Opposition, setting out his party's criticisms of the Budget and of the government's economic policy generally and outlining the opposition's alternative. The taxation proposals embodied in the Budget come into effect immediately the Chancellor sits down provided the Commons agrees the necessary resolution (under the Provisional Collection of Taxes Act, originally passed to deal with the problems created by the Lords' rejection of the 1909 Budget); the Commons then confirms these charges by a Ways and Means resolution within ten days. Briefly, Ways and Means resolutions are those which permit the imposition of new taxes or an increase in the rate of existing ones. Final confirmation comes when the Budget is passed into law.

At the end of the four-day general debate the Budget proposals are embodied into a Finance Bill. There is a one day Second Reading debate, after which the Bill goes to Committee. The main principles are discussed in the Commons itself, in what is called the Committee of the Whole House, while the more detail-ed and technical parts are discussed in a standing committee. The Report Stage and Third Reading usually last two days. Finally the bill goes to the Lords which restricts itself to a brief Second Reading debate. The Finance Bill receives the Royal Assent, usually in the early summer unless the Budget is an emergency measure introduced at a time other than March or April (for example, following a general election).

It is an important convention that the details of the Budget are kept a closely guarded secret so that the Commons will be the first to hear the full statement by the Chancellor. Dalton resigned in 1947 because of an injudicious word to a journalist immediately before delivering his speech. But increasingly the Budget is subject to a spate of officially inspired 'leaks' so that the main outline and often much of the detail is known in advance. A large number of groups and organisations, many of whom 'lobby' the Chancellor and the Treasury in order to put their views across, will brief MPs collectively as well as individually in the hope that MPs will be convinced of the justice of their case and put down amendments at the Committee Stage.

Most are resisted unless there is evidence of widespread disquiet among government backbenchers, usually reflecting a wider discontent. Such changes are usually marginal; the passage of the Budget in more or less the form proposed by the Chancellor is an important matter of prestige; any substantial changes forced upon it would not only distort the economic strategy, it would also reflect upon the government's political competence and suggest divisions in the party. Defeat on the Finance Bill as a whole would mean the resignation of the government and a general election. Thus government backbenchers usually vote for most if not all of its proposals, whatever their reservations. This was demonstrated clearly in 1981; a significant number of Tory MPs were known to have had doubts about the Budget's deflationary nature but swallowed their anxieties in defence of party unity. In addition MPs lack the expertise and resources necessary to present alternatives to government proposals; the Commons is at a disadvantage compared to the executive in a way which is not true of the much more powerful US Congress.

3. Central government

In Britain central government is mainly responsible for formulating economic policy; this may be compared to the USA, where Congress is a much more significant actor in the process than Parliament is here and where various financial institutions have considerable independence of the executive. The term central government in the British context embraces a variety of centres of power and decision making, including the Cabinet, various parts of the government machine, particularly the Treasury but also including economics ministries such as Employment and Trade and Industry, plus the Bank of England and so on.

Central government is crucially concerned in macro-economic policy, policies concerned with the economy as a whole such as the levels of demand, inflation, unemployment and so on. Ajustment of these variables was the main concern of Keynesians. In the formulation and implementation of macro-economic policies the Treasury and the Bank of England play the major role. The government is also concerned with micro-economic policy, which concerns the behaviour of individual consumers, groups or firms. The responsibility for micro-economic policy is very diffuse and affects the work of most government departments as well as a host of other public sector bodies, including local authorities. The two types of policy are not separate; each will affect the other, sometimes in ways which make a co-ordinated strategy difficult if not impossible.

Another important factor is that central government is not a single entity, seeking the same ends. There will be both institutional and personal rivalries and differing perspectives, making the achievement of a co-ordinated policy difficult. These rivalries begin at the top. A successful economic policy depends crucially on a relationship of trust between the Prime Minister and the Chancellor. Dennis Healey paid tribute to Callaghan's support, both in general and particularly in the Cabinet battles over the IMF application in 1976. This generally harmonious picture can be contrasted with the bitter battles between Mrs Thatcher and Chancellor Lawson over exchange rate policy; Lawson resigned because Sir Alan Walters, the Prime Minister's unofficial adviser, was shadowing his policies and publicly criticising them. In his letter of resignation Lawson wrote:

The successful conduct of economic policy is possible only if there is – and is seen to be – full agreement between the Prime Minister and the Chancellor of the Exchequer.

Recent events have confirmed that this essential requirement cannot be satisfied so long as Alan Walters remains your personal policy adviser.

Of course, Mrs Thatcher was not alone in using other sources to second-guess the Chancellor. Harold Lever, a member of the Cabinet, played such a role, first for Wilson between 1974–1976 and then for Callaghan. At first Healey found it irksome, but after a while Lever's advice became a source of strength. Bernard Donoughue, Head of the No. 10 Policy Unit, also acted as a source of outside advice for both Prime Ministers. However, the Lawson episode illustrates the danger of a Prime Minster and a Chancellor having different policy agendas. Lawson's replacement, John Major, had a different perspective from that of Mrs Thatcher on European monetary union and there were rumours of a triumvirate of Major, Hurd and Howe putting pressure on the Premier.

There will be other sources of disunity in a government. Ministers will have their own personal and policy interests to pursue. Departments often have their own policies; there are many accounts of fierce behind-the-scenes battles and bitter intrigues in Whitehall. Then there is the vexed question of Civil Service power; politicians as far apart as Tony Benn and Richard Crossman on the Left to Thatcher on the Right have felt unease about the extent to which civil servants will, given the opportunity, impose their wishes on reluctant politicians. Benn and others tend to see a powerful bureaucracy trying to stifle political initiatives in the name of continuity and consensus. While this is an over-simplification the role of the Civil Service in general and of the Treasury in particular needs to be examined. In the end, however, much comes down to personality. 'Such basic but often forgotten points as the sheer strength of intellect or character of particular ministers or civil servants can be as important in explaining a particular act of policy as ten volumes on the theory of their constitutional relationship.'[5]

There are several centres of power and influence in the machinery of central government which affect economic policy making and they need to be examined in some detail.

a.   *The Cabinet*
There is considerable controversy about the role of the Cabinet and the extent to which decisions are made by that body. Some commentators see the Cabinet as the place where all the 'impor-

tant' decisions are taken, while others see it more as a 'rubber stamp', giving formal approval to decisions taken by the Prime Minister and a small group of colleagues and advisers, often in secret Cabinet Commitees or even less formal groupings.

In many respects the precise role of the Cabinet is a matter for the Prime Minister, and they have varied considerably in the extent to which the Cabinet has been allowed to discuss major questions of policy, including the management of the economy. The usual practice seems to be that Prime Ministers consult whom they choose; there is usually some kind of inner group of senior ministers, supplemented by advisers, both official and unofficial. Generally, economic policy is conducted from Downing Street. The Prime Minister is chair of the Cabinet Committee on economic policy. Harold Wilson, especially in the early years of his premiership, was a major influence on economic policy, in particular over the decision not to devalue the pound. Heath was a very important influence on the policies associated with his Chancellor, Anthony Barber, and took direct charge of the negotiations with the unions over pay policy in 1973–74. Callaghan, as an ex-Chancellor, was deeply involved in all aspects of economic policy, sometimes virtually taking control from Dennis Healey and the Treasury. However, on occasions the Cabinet comes into its own as a policy making body. One such example was the handling by Jim Callaghan of the discussions leading up to the IMF loan in 1976.[6]

Mrs Thatcher was also reluctant, except on rare occasions, to permit a general debate on economic policy. The 1981 Budget, which resulted in a sharp increase in the tax burden, led to a row in the Cabinet, with 'wets' like Gilmour, Prior and Walker considering resignation because of fears of a deepening recession. This resulted in an agreement to hold regular Cabinet debates on the economic strategy. But following the reshuffle in September 1981, which removed a number of critics, the experiment was abandoned. The significance of the Cabinet as a decision making body declined and much economic policy was made in Mrs Thatcher's version of the 'Economic Seminar'. It handled similar subjects, such as monetary policy and delicate matters affecting the money markets. Its composition varied according to circumstances and the issue being discussed. Yet Mrs Thatcher's preference for working with small groups of ministers, civil servants and advisers did not mean that there was an absence of discussion about the policies to be adopted. 'Mrs Thatcher, and the Treasury . . . generally had their way in the end, though with arguments along familiar inter-departmental lines.'[7]

Public expenditure is an aspect of economic policy in which the Cabinet may well have a vital role. Whatever their view in opposition or when making a speech at a party conference, ministers 'soon tend to adopt their departmental view that spending in their department – education, housing, defence, social security – has a pristine sanctity of its own. They tend to fight for their departmental rights in Cabinet: if the general proposal under discussion be the apportionment of an increase or a cut in general resources available for public expenditure, then each individual minister usually wants to gain more or lose less than his colleagues; at the very least he does not want to be worse off than they are.'[8] In this annual battle the crucial role is played by the Chancellor and by the Chief Secretary to the Treasury, who has special responsibility for trying to get the total of departmental estimates to match the figure set by the Chancellor for public expenditure in the coming year. The Chief Secretary, from 1968 to 1970 and since 1977 a full member of the Cabinet, has responsibility for the annual Public Expenditure Survey Committee (PESC). This consists of senior departmental civil servants and is chaired by a senior figure from the Treasury. Its task is to conduct a review of public expenditure over a rolling five-year programme. The Chief Secretary's responsibility is performed primarily in bilateral negotiations with the departmental ministers concerned; only if these bilaterals fail to bring the total of estimates down to the Chancellor's figure will the matter be referred upward. This may necessitate a hearing of the dispute by the full Cabinet, which then makes the final decision. A departure of recent years has been the establishment of what is known as the 'Star Chamber', a group of senior, mainly non-departmental ministers, whose task is to adjudicate between the Treasury and the spending ministers and which for some years was headed by Lord Whitelaw.

b. *The Cabinet Office*

The Cabinet Office is the link between the Cabinet and the Civil Service. It serves the Cabinet generally, but is primarily at the disposal of the Prime Minister. Relatively small, it has many tasks, including a major role in economic affairs. This is partly because successive Prime Ministers have felt they needed a source of advice and support to counter the power of the Treasury and the Bank of England and partly because of the increased importance of economic affairs generally. The Cabinet Office is headed by the Secretary to the Cabinet who is also the Head of the Home Civil Service; this powerful figure is in effect the Prime Minister's chief policy adviser.

The Secretary to the Cabinet heads a small unit which services the Cabinet and its committees. Under the direction of the Prime Minister he draws up the agenda, circulates papers and ensures that action is taken throughout Whitehall in accordance with the wishes of the Cabinet. The Cabinet Office has an important role in dealing with departmental disputes, in which the struggle for resources plays a significant part. It was closely involved in the running of the Central Policy Review Staff (CPRS, known as the 'Think Tank') set up by Edward Heath in 1970 to help formulate an overall strategy for the government and to think long term about problems. The CPRS played an important role in advising successive Prime Ministers about economic issues but was abolished by Mrs Thatcher following the 1983 election.

The Prime Minister's Office in No. 10 Downing Street is divided into a number of sections. One of its tasks is to assist the Prime Minister in formulating economic policy. Of particular importance is the Policy Unit, set up by Harold Wilson following the February 1974 election to provide him with medium-to-long-term policy analysis as an alternative to that coming from the official machinery of government; in particular, its members will normally be in sympathy with the political aims of the party in power. Mrs Thatcher expanded its size and scope and used policy advisers such as Sir Alan Walters; some of its most influential members have come from business.

c.   *The Civil Service*

Ministers are extremely busy and face an almost impossible range of responsibilities and burdens to an extent rare among their counterparts in other countries. Much of the work of a minister must, in reality, be undertaken by civil servants.

The structure of Cabinet Committees is shadowed by a network of interdepartmental committees manned by civil servants. In addition to the Treasury and other departments the Bank of England is represented on many of these official committees, and it is here that some of the fiercest battles in Whitehall go on. Civil servants try to resolve their own departmental disputes in order to present coherent options for consideration by the Cabinet or Cabinet Committees. In addition, departmental civil servants play crucial role in advising their ministers about policy options. Thus the Civil Service plays a much more significant role than that of policy *advice*, which is the constitutional theory of its place in the British system of government.

Among the many criticisms of the British Civil Service is the belief that there is a common Whitehall view, a preference for a certain type of approach to policy making and problem-solving. While the question of Civil Service power, of whether civil servants *make* policy and whether ministers are in some way prisoners of their civil servants is beyond the scope of this book, it is clear that officials *do* play a major role in the formulation of economic policy as they do in all other areas. Partly this is related with factors such as permanence and expertise, as well as with skills in presenting a case, where, by leaving out some options or downgrading others, 'the paper they present comes down subtly in favour of their preferred approach, while of course giving the appearance of fairness to all sides'.[9]

Joel Barnett made a number of references to the role of Treasury officials in policy making. He pointed out that most officials, because they felt that they were working for what they saw as the national interest, would come to their own conclusion about policy and seek by every means to carry their ministers with them. This would not usually be a problem; however 'It is in the small, but vitally important, number of cases where the decision is a very difficult one that a Minister can have major problems with his officials'.[10] Though in general he admired the officials, Barnett echoed other politicians in expressing concern about their methods. Dealing with the last days of the Labour government, Barnett commented that Treasury officials tried to get a package of public expenditure cuts, more likely to be acceptable to a Conservative government. In his view, Permanent Secretaries plan how to get 'their' policies through Cabinet 'along paths Ministers might not have originally intended'.[11] Yet his conclusion, like that of most other commentators, is that Treasury civil servants are the cream of the bunch, devoted to the public service, even if their interpretation sometimes differs from that of the elected politicians who are, at least temporarily, set above them.

d. *The Treasury*

The Chancellor of the Exchequer, whose official title is Second Lord of the Treasury (the Prime Minister being the First Lord) heads the Treasury. He not only presides over one of the oldest offices of state but is usually (although not invariably) the most influential member of the Cabinet after the Prime Minister. There are around twelve ministers in the Treasury, although a number of these function as whips. The responsibilities of the Chancellor are virtually limitless, in that few if any of the tasks of government do not involve financial and economic considerations. His functions include fiscal and monetary policy, the control of public expenditure, economic forecasting, the efficient use of public resource, and so on. He is above all the man charged with responsibilty for ensuring the economic health of the nation. These tasks have to be undertaken in a political context. The Chancellor does not apply economic theory but pursues a set of political objectives in an environment where he is constrained by the nature of the British economy, and the fact that much (the employers, the workers, the consumers of British goods and so on) is largely outside his control. Because Britain operates in a competitive international environment the Chancellor's freedom of action is limited. He is under pressure from his colleagues to achieve the sort of success that will simultaneously improve the prospects for the British economy *and* ensure electoral success;

Figure 7: Ministerial responsibilities

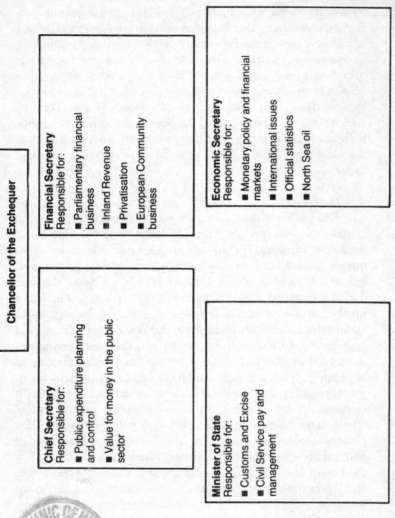

Chancellor of the Exchequer

Chief Secretary
Responsible for:
- Public expenditure planning and control
- Value for money in the public sector

Financial Secretary
Responsible for:
- Parliamentary financial business
- Inland Revenue
- Privatisation
- European Community business

Minister of State
Responsible for:
- Customs and Excise
- Civil Service pay and management

Economic Secretary
Responsible for:
- Monetary policy and financial markets
- International issues
- Official statistics
- North Sea oil

Source: HM Treasury: Economic Briefing, No.1, Dec. 1990, p.2

these are by no means identical. At the same time, he must try to keep his party happy, especially as his own chance of achieving even higher office may depend on the approval of the faithful.

The Treasury has most influence on the Prime Minister and Chancellor, who in turn generally dominate the Cabinet on economic matters. In addition, the Bank of England plays a vital role in many aspects of policy. The Treasury's role is to manage the economy in accordance with government policy as approved by Parliament. There has been considerable suspicion of Treasury power in both parties, especially since 1945, and various attempts have been made to diminish its predominance, usually by attempting to hive parts off, as in the creation of the DEA in 1964. The short-lived experiment with the Civil Service Department seemed for a while to threaten the Treasury's monopoly of control over that body. However, its abolition by Mrs Thatcher saw the return of most if not all of its functions to the Treasury. The CPRS, intended by Heath in part to act as a counterweight to the Chancellor and the Treasury, failed and it was also swept away by Mrs Thatcher. She was said to share the distrust of Treasury power, but rather than establish institutions to shadow it, she used unofficial advisers such as Sir Alan Walters.

The Treasury dominates the interdepartmental committees which deliver policy options to the Prime Minister and Cabinet. The Chancellor and his senior officials are the main influence on economic decision making by the Cabinet, and on those decisions made by the Prime Minister and Chancellor without reference to the full Cabinet.

The role of the Treasury

The Treasury has a wider role than simply managing the nation's finances. It has a central place in the machinery of government, despite its small size. About 2, 500 civil servants work in the Treasury; these include some of the most able recruits to the Higher Civil Service. One of the features of the Civil Service is the 'Treasury ethos', a set of attitudes and assumptions about the nature of the Service and its role in the British system of government. This is said to permeate Whitehall because many top officials spend at least part of their working life in the Treasury,

Figure 8: HM Treasury
Source: Peter Hennessy, *Whitehall.*
Fontana, 1990, p.393

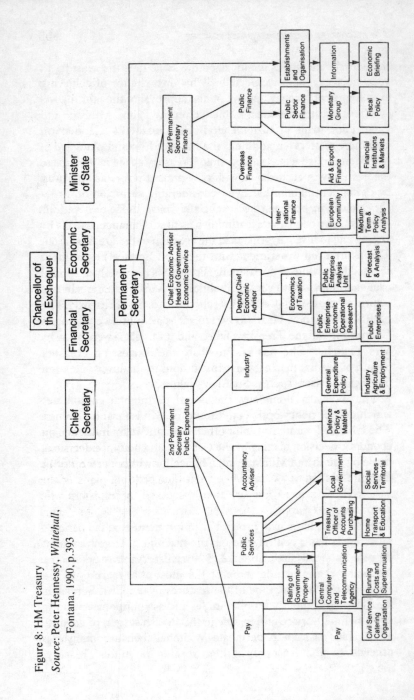

thus spreading similar attitudes and assumptions throughout the machinery of government. About one quarter of the Higher Civil Service (i.e. Permanent Secretaries and Deputy and Under Secretaries) have had Treasury experience.

The Treasury is organised on a 'functional' basis in that it is organised in sections covering groups of functions. It is headed by the Permanent Secretary. Under him comes the Chief Economic Adviser, responsible for economic forecasts and for continual analysis of policy options and of the likely effects of changes proposed by the Treasury. The Second Permanent Secretary is in charge of public expenditure and another Second Permanent Secretary in charge of finance. Treasury functions can be summed up as the raising of revenue, the control of expenditure and the management of the Civil Service, although in the last case control is shared with the Cabinet Office, which is responsible for recruitment and promotion. The Treasury is also responsible for other bodies, including the Board of Inland Revenue and the Customs and Excise Department.

Treasury functions
The major responsibilities of the Treasury are as follows.

i. *The scrutiny of departmental estimates* Annually, usually in January, the government issues a White Paper which announces spending plans for the coming year and, in less definite form, for the next three years. These figures are prepared by the Public Expenditure Survey Committee from the spending plans of the various departments, and are then discussed by ministers who make the final decisions about the contents of the White Paper. The Chief Secretary then undertakes bilateral negotiations with spending ministers; if no agreement can be reached the Chancellor may attempt to resolve the matter. If all else fails the dispute may reach the Cabinet, perhaps via the 'Star Chamber'. The expenditure plans are then submitted to Parliament in the form of Estimates. However, throughout the year departments have to seek Treasury approval for any major policies they may wish to adopt, so Treasury scrutiny of public expenditure is a continuous process.

Figure 9: The planning total and general government expenditure: how it is planned and spent, 1990–91

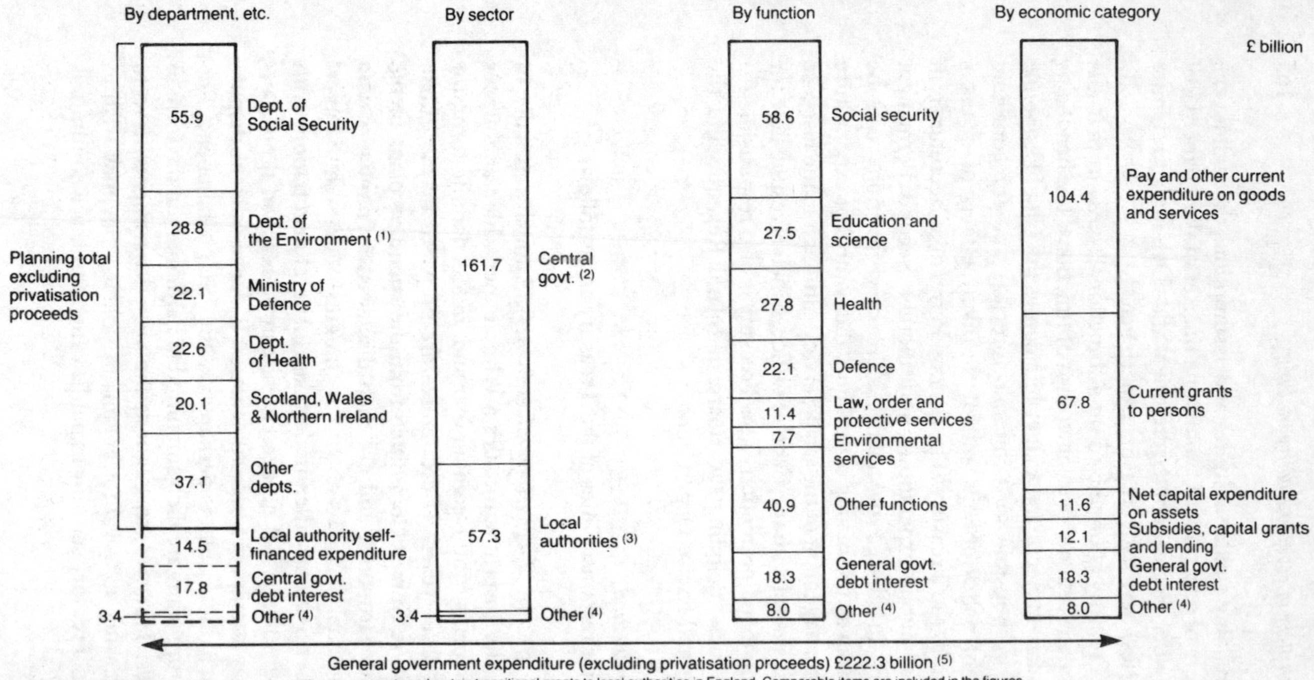

General government expenditure (excluding privatisation proceeds) £222.3 billion [5]

(1) Includes revenue support grant and non-domestic rate payments and certain transitional grants to local authorities in England. Comparable items are included in the figures for Scotland and Wales

(2) Includes grants, subsidies and net lending to public corporations, including nationalised industries. It also includes central government debt interest (£17.8 billion)

(3) The total is made up of £42.7 billion financed by support from central government and £14.5 billion financed from local authorities' own resources. It includes local authority debt interest (£5.2 billion)

(4) Includes the national accounts adjustments. The differences in these figures reflect the different treatment of local authority debt interest and market and overseas borrowing of public corporations in the analyses of GGE by function and economic category

(5) The figures in this table are based on detailed estimates of spending in 1990-91 published in February 1991

Source: HM Treasury: Economic Briefing, No.2, May 1991, p.5

Treasury attempts to control public expenditure are supplemented by departmental controls. The Permanent Secretary of each department is also the Accounting Officer, which means that he presents the accounts to the relevant select committee and explains and defends his department's spending policies. If the Permanent Secretary disagrees with his minister over spending policies he must draw the matter to the attention of the select committee. Governments attempt to keep public expenditure under some sort of control, if only for electoral reasons; government profligacy, especially if it results in higher taxes or inflation, may be punished by loss of office. However, pressures to increase public expenditure are constantly faced by governments. Dennis Healey spent much of his time at the Treasury trying to undo the effects of a rapid rise in expenditure after Labour regained power in 1974. Although the Conservative government elected in 1979 committed itself to reducing public expenditure, political and other pressures prevented this happening, although public expenditure as a percentage of GNP declined. So successive governments have instituted various procedures for containing and scrutinising public spending, with the additional aim of eliminating inefficient spending.

Between 1970 and 1979 Programme Analysis and Review (PAR) was in operation. Departmental proposals were examined with the aim of relating objectives and priorities to available resources. Though this achieved some success in containing expenditure it was abolished by the Conservatives in 1979. An Efficiency Unit was then established, initially under Sir Derek (now Lord) Rayner, and answerable directly to the Prime Minister. This small group, composed partly of civil servants and partly of businessmen, examines the activities of the various departments with the aim of achieving better value for money. The Unit has on occasions complained of obstruction by departments, and although it has achieved some valuable savings it has done little to contain public expenditure, the bulk of which relates to the scale of government activity rather than to waste and inefficiency in its spending. However, in its first six years savings of approximately £750 million were achieved.

In 1980 the Management Information System for Ministers

(MINIS) was introduced. This brainchild of Michael Heseltine in the Department of the Environment aimed to improve managerial efficiency and thus ensure greater economy in expenditure. It has spread to other departments and was supplemented by an expanded version of the Financial Management Initiative in 1982, supervised by the Efficiency Unit.

ii. *Raising revenue* The bulk of revenue comes from direct taxes such as income tax and indirect taxes such as VAT. The balance between direct and indirect taxation is partly decided on economic grounds; for example, would raising the rate of VAT result in more revenue for the Treasury or would it have such a depressing effect on expenditure that receipts would fall? Would reducing income tax result in more resources being freed for investment by the private sector or would it result in a spending spree which would add to inflationary pressures? These questions are in part technical and in their resolution the expertise of Treasury officials, particularly those who are trained economists, will be of great significance. But this is also an area where ideological and electoral pressures are often paramount. Labour governments tend to favour higher direct taxation than Tory administrations on the grounds that the better-off should bear a higher burden than the less well-off; the electoral significance of this policy is obvious. Similarly, the Tories, for a mixture of ideological and electoral reasons favour rewards for the enterprising; those who create wealth should be encouraged to create more by keeping more of what they create. Thus for Conservative governments, particularly since 1979, the emphasis is likely to be on indirect taxation. The relationship between direct and indirect taxation is a shifting one. Governments also borrow to make up any difference between income and expenditure, and again the policy on borrowing varies according to the needs of the economy and the ideology of the party in power. In all of these areas of policy the role of the Treasury is crucial.

The Budget proposals for raising revenue through taxation are presented by the Chancellor in the spring of each year, although additional mini-budgets can come at other times. In preparing his Budget the Chancellor is assisted by the Budget Committee of the

Treasury, consisting of senior officials, including representatives from the Inland Revenue and Customs and Excise. The main work starts in November and involves a consideration of the departmental estimates. The economic situation is reviewed and statistical information examined. The Budget is prepared in great secrecy; ministers and others regularly complain about being kept in the dark, although light *is* shone on the process through the 'system' of leaks! During the passage of the Finance Bill through Parliament, the Treasury advises the Chancellor about the effects of any suggested changes.

There are both political and economic constraints on taxation. So governments also need to borrow money, both long term and short term. The amount of money owed by the government is called the National Debt, which has grown enormously this century, partly because of the two world wars, although the biggest increase has come since 1945. The National Debt currently totals some £100 billion. Governments also use short-term borrowing to smooth out fluctuations in receipts. The Bank of England, under the direction of the Treasury, plays a vital role in managing both forms of borrowing.

iii. *The co-ordination of economic policy* There have been various attempts to control economic policy. Before 1914 the Treasury was primarily responsible for guiding the British economy. During the inter-war years several advisory committees were set up on aspects of economic management and during the Second World War the Treasury was downgraded in significance because of the primary importance attached to defeating Germany. For the first two years of the Labour government the emphasis on physical controls also reduced Treasury influence, but in 1947 Cripps restored its primacy in economic policy. This marked the start of a period of Treasury predominance, despite the attempts at more direct intervention with the creation of the NEDC and other bodies towards the end of the Conservative's period in office from 1951 to 1964.

The establishment of the DEA was partly the result of fears about Treasury power. However, criticism grew about Wilson's experiment in 'creative tension'. Because the Budget was retained as the major weapon of economic policy it did not make sense to weaken the Treasury as the main economic ministry. Since the Treasury retained major responsibilities for the machinery of government its power could not be matched by any other department, even one headed by a personality as expansive as that of George Brown. In the event sceptics were proved correct. The DEA operated against a background of almost continuous economic crisis, it failed to find a convincing role for itself, and the Treasury reasserted its position. The DEA was abolished in 1969.

Since then the Treasury has dominated both short-term and long-term economic planning. It has two ministers in the Cabinet who are also members of the Cabinet Committees and other less official bodies concerned with economic policy making. The Treasury continues to play a central role in all matters of policy, and although other departments, such as Trade and Industry and Employment, have important economic responsibilities they are subordinate to Treasury power. The crucial nature of economic management in the process of government, together with the influence that goes with the management of the Civil Service, means that the Chancellor of the Exchequer and the other Treasury ministers have a special place in government, and Treasury officials are regarded as the cream of the Civil Service. To an extent, the Treasury provides a central directing force within British goverment.

The Treasury since 1979

There has been some continuity in policy. The Treasury remains concerned to achieve economic growth and high employment without inflation, even though, as inflation is the main priority, the emphasis differs from that of the last Labour government. The changes, however, are more striking. If the 1970s marked a low point in the standing of the Treasury because of its association with failure, at least for a while the Treasury achieved a reputation in the 1980s for successful policies which were in tune with the ideological aims of the government. Inflation fell, the level of public expenditure as a percentage of GDP declined, largely by the use of cash limits on programmes, and borrowing was controlled. However, critics have drawn attention to what they see as errors in Treasury policy in the early years of the Thatcher government, when a depressed economy was pushed into recession by a combination of an overvalued pound and high interest rates, which led to the collapse of much of British manufacturing capacity. More recently, the over-expansion of the economy before and after the 1987 election has aroused much criticism.

The Treasury was also concerned with a range of policies central to government aims. Privatisation was very much the policy of Treasury ministers, both in terms of a belief in the market and as a way of raising large sums of money to be used either as a disguised form of public expenditure or as a way of financing tax cuts. The Treasury has also been at the forefront of supply-side changes and with the removal of restraints on the operations of markets. There has been a concentration on 'value for money' in assessing public expenditure; departments are under constant pressure to justify expenditure plans in economic terms, something which was not previously the case. The Treasury has taken a leading role in improving management techniques throughout Whitehall; initiatives such as FMI have been encouraged. Control of local authority finance, the NHS and the nationalised industries have all come from Treasury activities, although the political motivation is that of the government. The Treasury has buried the CPRS and the Civil Service Department, reasserting its predominance throughout the machinery of government. The leading figures in the Treasury reflected the views of Mrs Thatcher; the Permanent Secretary for most of the 1980s, Sir Peter Middleton, was an early convert to monetarism and was appointed by the Prime Minister over the heads of more senior colleagues. The former Chief Economic Adviser, Sir Terry Burns, 'has been an effective developer of the government's economic beliefs'.[12]

Yet at the same time as the Treasury has been reasserting its position, it has been in the forefront of 'rolling back the frontiers of the state' in terms of managing the economy. The Medium-Term Financial Strategy was a major shift in economic policy, a turning away from demand management as a way of ensuring full employment in favour of policies to contain inflation and emphasise the market. Privatisation was to be pursued as part of a disengagement policy in a wider context of emphasising the role of the market. The Treasury has regained its position as the centre of the government machine. 'Defeating the Treasury in Cabinet, never easy, has now become much harder. The Treasury as a whole, never a negligible quantity in Whitehall, is now a leading performer in the maintenance and development of government policy.'[13]

e. *The Bank of England*

Britain's central bank was established in 1694 as a private company, formed to lend money to the government and to manage the National Debt. In 1946 it was nationalised, although in reality it had been largely under government control for many years.

The Bank of England is the government's banker and handles its borrowing requirements. It is the principal organ for implementing financial and monetary policy. The Bank 'presides over the banking system as a whole, manages the nation's currency, administers the government's funds and accounts, domestic and external, and advises the government on financial affairs generally and financial markets in particular'.[14]

It is managed by the Governor (currently Robin Leigh-Pemberton), a Deputy Governor and a board of sixteen directors (four of them full-time executive directors). The Bank is obliged to follow directives issued by the Treasury, although the Governor has a statutory right to be consulted and acts as the channel of communication between the government and private financial institutions. It has wide statutory power to supervise and control the banking system. The Bank Charter Act of 1844 divided the Bank of England into an issue department and a banking department. The issue department is responsible for the issue of banknotes and coins, while the banking department deals with government departments and bodies such as the Post Office. It has a few private customers, although private banking is a tiny part of the Bank's responsibilities.

As well as being concerned in monetary policy the Bank also supervises the activities of the commercial banks and other financial institutions and on occasions supports them if their failure would damage the financial system as a whole. The failure of the Bank of Credit and Commerce International in 1991 caused problems for the Bank and for the government. It manages the National Debt and conducts transactions between Britain and the rest of the world.

The Bank's influence comes from its central place in the management of the British economy. It possesses information vital to any government and it has, over the years, built up a network of connections both internally and externally. Its influence varies over time and depending on the issues, and much depends on the personal relationships between the Prime Minister, the Chancellor and the Governor.

Besides supervising the banking system the Bank has a number of crucial roles in the management of the economy. It services the borrowing requirement of the government by selling bonds on behalf of the Treasury as a way of attracting savings rather than simply printing money. It manages the exchange rate by buying and selling reserves of sterling and foreign exchange. Finally it has a crucial role in determining interest rates.

The Bank of England has a great deal of influence over economic policy, although of a subtle kind. It has a degree of freedom in its public statements (in a way which would be impossible for the Treasury), but its pronouncements are submitted in advance to the Treasury and it is clear that the Bank takes careful note of any comments made. Some Governors have been rather outspoken; in the 1960s Lord Cromer made little effort to disguise his hostility to Labour's economic policies and more recently Leigh-Pemberton has been forthright in his criticisms.

The Bank's influence really comes to the fore during an exchange rate crisis. It is then that it plays a crucial role in determining how to deal with the problem; in practice, this usually revolves round cuts in public expenditure and rises in interest rates. It was very heavily criticised for mistakes in exchange rate management in 1976 which was an important factor in forcing the government to seek aid from the IMF. In the mid-1970s the Bank began to put rather more emphasis on keeping the growth of the money supply under tight control.

The relationship of the Bank of England with the Thatcher

government was not easy. There was tension at the start as the new administration, embarking on a policy of tight control over the money supply, began asserting its authority over the Bank. The Governor, Lord Richardson, who had worked with both the Heath government and its Labour successor, was not regarded as 'one of us' and was replaced by Robin Leigh-Pemberton who was faced with an immediate crisis in the secondary banking sector in which the Bank's role was publicly criticised by the government. However, this crisis soon passed and relations improved. The Bank's importance in policy matters has steadily become more obvious, to the point that its point of view was expressed by Mrs Thatcher's comment on Nigel Lawson's efforts to regulate the exchange rate that 'you can't buck the market'. Leigh-Pemberton's reappointment for a second term reinforced his authority, as seen by his public criticisms of government economic policy.

f. *The National Economic Development Council*

The NEDC (known as 'Neddy') was established in 1962 to bring together representatives of organised business, the unions, nationalised industries and government for regular exchanges of views. The aim was to improve the performance of industry and to achieve a higher rate of economic growth. Originally it was to be chaired either by the Prime Minister or the Chancellor, but Mrs Thatcher, who disliked such 'corporatist' relics, rarely attended. Its membership changes over time, but currently consists of the Chancellor, who normally chairs, various Secretaries of State (depending on the subject matter of the meeting), employers' representatives from the CBI and some large companies, representatives of nationalised industries such as British Rail and British Coal, trade unionists (from the TUC and some of the larger unions), and miscellaneous members (for example, from the Consumers' Association). The Director-General of the National Economic Development Office, the secretariat of the NEDC, also attends. A number of committees of the NEDC consider the specific problems of sectors of the economy, although these have been 'more talking shops dominated by industry spokesmen than genuine policy instruments designed to fix targets and then set about meeting them'.[15]

The NEDC's role is unclear. Both employers and the unions support it. At one stage there was a union boycott as a result of the ban on trade union membership at GCHQ, Cheltenham, but union representatives rejoined the NEDC as it is virtually the only place where unions can engage in a dialogue with ministers. But government hostility has been marked and the NEDC has had little influence on economic policy. It 'has come to represent a distinct brand of economic policy, one that lobbies for protection from foreign competition and for intervention on behalf of industry by government. It has been distinctly out of tune with the Thatcher government's economic policy and has had little influence, apart from detailed work to improve the performance of individual sectors.'[16]

4. Pressure groups

Especially since 1945 governments have consulted widely in policy making. What are loosely called pressure groups, which may be actual organisations such as the TUC or the CBI or less formally organised interests, such as the City of London, play a vital role in the process of economic policy making. They can supply specialist information, second expert staff for particular tasks within government, help to create a favourable climate in order to secure the success of a policy (or threaten to mobilise their resources to create an unfavourable situation in order to frustrate a policy of which they disapprove) and so on. Some government departments have a more or less permanent relationship with specific pressure groups, and some writers have drawn attention to the potential disadvantages for the public interest. Examples include the close relationship between the National Farmers Union and the Ministry of Agriculture and that between the Ministry of Transport and the roads lobby. Civil servants have close links with pressure groups; some are *members* of particular groups, which gives those groups advantages in terms of information, contacts and so on. Civil servants commonly meet delegations from pressure groups in the course of their work. Ministers are also involved in dealings with groups, although to some extent this is conditioned by the political or other acceptability of the group concerned.

It is customary to distinguish between sectional interest groups and cause or promotional groups. Sectional groups, such as trade unions and employers' organisations, are primarily concerned with the material interests of their members, while cause or promotional groups seek to ensure the success of an issue such as prison reform, environmentalism and so on, or to advance the interests of groups such as handicapped children, old people and others. Both kinds of groups have an impact on economic policy. The first category has an obvious and immediate interest in economic matters; trade unions bargain about wages, job security and similar matters, while employers are concerned about interest and exchange rates, state aid to industry, policies to promote competition and so on more. All of these things affect national economic policy and thus involve government. But cause and promotional groups also have an interest in economic policy. They may press for a different distribution of available resources; Age Concern campaigns for higher retirement pensions, while housing groups such as Shelter urge the government to spend more on public housing. However, sectional groups do not simply look after the interests of their members. Trade unions and employers' organisations both press government to spend more money on education, health and so on. Groups of every description, pursuing a host of often conflicting and incompatible aims, affect economic policy making.

The role of pressure groups

Pressure groups have several significant roles in the making of economic as well as in other types of policy. Whether a group is influential in policy making depends largely on how legitimate its operations are considered by government. Such groups have close relationships with the executive, both political and bureaucratic. Leading figures in a group, who may be volunteers or paid officials, have close and regular contacts with policy makers. Sometimes they may actually take part in the policy making process. In this sense, commentators speak of a policy making community, consisting of politicians, civil servants and representatives of those pressure groups referred to as 'insider' groups.[17] Members of this community often share common interests, such as the successful solution of the problem; but tensions may appear. Ministers and civil servants, under pressure, say, to limit public expenditure, may resist calls for additional resources from a group with whom they may have great sympathy. Groups favouring free-market solutions to problems had close relations with the Thatcher government; but on several issues they accused the administration of not going far enough, for example in failing to introduce market forces into education or in failing to privatise coal and the railways.

Nevertheless, the relationship is generally harmonious. Government and groups need each other. The government needs the co-operation of groups both in formulating and implementing policy which is often effected, not by government directly, but by groups. For example, the extensive regulation of the financial markets is carried out by a self-regulatory body, the Security and Investments Board (SIB). The power of financial interests was shown when the legislation establishing the SIB was amended, against the wishes of the government, to grant it various legal immunities.

Groups use a variety of methods to pursue their objectives. Outsider groups (those which find access to the executive difficult or impossible) may mount a public campaign which, on occasions, may spill over into disruption or violence, as in the campaign against the poll tax. Groups may target Parliament, either in the form of a campaign aimed at the legislature generally or by attempting to influence groups of MPs or peers or individual legislators. Coalitions of groups may appear; an example was that which emerged in opposition to the legislation to liberalise the law on Sunday trading. Trade unions joined with religious groups and groups mainly representing small shopkeepers to counter the efforts of large retailers to get the law changed. Groups will try to get an MP to represent them. The Member may have sympathy with the aims of the group or there may be a more direct financial relationship, perhaps in the form of a retainer to work of their behalf. Many Labour MPs are sponsored by trade unions, while most Conservative MPs have business connections. The growth of specialised public relations firms (known as lobbyists, or more formally as Parliamentary Agents) is increasingly significant. They act as go-betweens for clients (often large companies or financial conglomerates) wishing to establish a suitable climate for the protection of their interests.

The role of pressure groups in the policy making process reached its peak in the 1960s and 1970s. The establishment of the NEDC, bringing together government, unions and employers, marked what some have referred to as the "*corporatist*" experiment in British politics. 'In a 'corporatist' system government makes economic policy by bargaining with management and labour organisations to secure their agreement. This process of consultation and agreement bypasses the legislative assembly.'[18] Corporatism was not favoured by the Thatcher government, which asserted its responsibility for economic policy and publicly kept pressure groups at arms length. The role of pressure groups has changed since 1979 and in some respects their significance in the policy making process has declined. The influence on government of groups such as trade unions and welfare organisations has significantly declined, while business groups 'have enjoyed considerably more influence in view of their compatibility with government policy and in some cases the government's dependence on them to implement policy'.[19] Pressure groups remain very important in policy making; it is those free-market groups which reflect and supplement government thinking which are given access to the policy making process.

Dennis Kavanagh examined the way in which these groups and organisation have permeated the policy making process and how the media, both serious and popular, has publicised the ideas of the New Right. Although groups such as the Adam Smith Institute do not have formal links with the Conservative Party, a number of prominent members are involved in its work. Some have been concerned with the writing of recent election manifestos and with the formulation of party policy on a whole range of economic and non-economic issues. Others have more directly influenced policy making, either as advisers to ministers or as temporary civil servants. 'The groups and individuals represent different aspects of New Right issues. But the personal and institutional links between them constitute a network. Their personal contacts with Mrs. Thatcher or her Policy Unit or others to whom she and ministers may listen and their appointments to official bodies and access to the media are methods of permeation.'[20] Though competing with other pressure groups and facing scepticism from some ministers and civil servants, they led the way in the radical, market-orientated policies of the Thatcher years.

5. Other domestic pressures

The media plays a significant role in economic matters. In the latter part of the 1970s journalists such as Samuel Brittan of the *Financial Times* and Peter Jay then Economics Editor of *The Times* (and son-in-law of Jim Callaghan), strongly supported the doctrine of monetarism. The bulk of the press gave increasingly strident support to the Conservative Party, significantly aiding the spread of free-market ideas. Serious newspapers and journals such as *The Economist*, *The Daily Telegraph*, the *Spectator* and *The Times* enthusiastically supported the ideas of the New Right and provided a platform for writers such as Paul Johnson, Walter Goldsmith and John Hoskyns. Tabloids such as the *Sun* produced a less intellectual version of these ideas, with attacks on many aspects of the Welfare State, the education system and other targets of free-market enthusiasts.

The influence of television, which has a statutory duty to avoid party political partiality, is far greater than that of the newspapers. Yet newspapers clearly have a considerable impact on the policy makers and opinion-formers who do much to create the climate of opinion in which the electorate forms its views. Economic journalists thus play a significant role, both in terms of what they discuss and what they do not discuss. This can be seen in the failure of the press to deal with the devaluation issue between 1964 and 1967. 'The establishment managed to persuade the serious press that mere discussion of the issue would be harmful to the national interest, one argument being that, through the effect on the financial markets, ventilating the subject would force the issue.'[21]

6. International opinion

The reaction of the rest of the world to the strength or weakness of the British economy has been a major constraint on policy making, especially since 1945. As a major trading nation dependent on her ability to compete internationally Britain is part of the world economic system, something which the Labour Left failed adequately to take into account in their calls for an 'alternative economic strategy'. Increasingly British membership of the EC limits the autonomy of policy makers. This is a major factor in the increasing divisions in the Conservative Party over developments towards closer ties with Europe.

This integration of the British with the world economy influences policy making in two ways.

1. What happens in the world affects the British economy. Britain cannot isolate herself from world recession. An example is the shock given to the British economy by the oil price rise of the early 1970s.
2. British economic policy making is affected by foreign reactions. If Britain tries to pursue policies which are disliked by domestic and foreign financial markets this may cause such adverse reactions that policy changes are virtually inevitable. Chancellors may have to pursue policies which are the reverse of those on which their governments were elected.

Dennis Healey pointed to the strength of financial markets. When Treasury and Bank of England miscalculations led to a dramatic fall in the value of sterling in March 1976 (the event which forced the application to the IMF), it took eighteen months to restore confidence. British governments are also affected by the reactions of foreign governments to policy, both economic and non-economic. American hostility to the Suez invasion led to a run on the pound, which was a major factor in the decision to withdraw. The imposition by the Labour government of a temporary imports surcharge in October 1964 as an emergency measure to deal with a balance of payments deficit caused an international outcry and was soon abandoned in the face of threats of retaliation. The impact of external factors on the British economy can be seen in the support given to American policy in Vietnam in the early 1960s. In return for American help for the troubled pound, Wilson agreed to support (or at least not to criticise) the American involvement. This caused outrage in the Labour Party and was a significant factor both in the loss of membership, especially of young, more educated people, and in the shift to the Left among many who stayed. The more 'open' an economy is, the harder it is to plan and to control the pace and direction of economic change.

Ever since the eighteenth century Britain has been a major international trading nation. This takes the form both of the export and import of goods and services and of capital transactions; Britain is one of the world's most important financial centres. This central fact about the economy affects the balance of payments and the exchange rate. The reactions of both domestic and foreign holders of sterling are an important factor in policy making. This is particularly true when foreign holders of sterling, perhaps fearing the effect of inflation in Britain, sell their holdings. This causes sterling to depreciate in value. Both Labour and Conservative governments have been forced to cut planned public expenditure or refrain from tax reductions in order to prevent the exchange rate from further depreciation, which would have raised import prices and so fuelled inflation.

7. The European Community

On joining the EC, Britain accepted certain common European policies with defined procedures for reaching decisions and for enforcing them. Though it is difficult to state precisely the areas in which the independence of member states has been limited, virtually every aspect of the British economy is now increasingly affected by EC policy. The aim is to create a common market in goods and services (including capital and labour). The aim by 1992 is to remove all internal barriers, while maintaining common external barriers in the form of tariffs, quotas and regulations.

The EC has been most successful in the creation of a customs union. Member states have ceded authority in the setting of quotas or taxes on imported goods and the subsidising of exports.

However, progress has not been so rapid in the building of a common market, which involves the free movement of labour and capital and the elimination of barriers to competition. There has been a somewhat haphazard movement towards the creation of the kind of common market envisaged by the Treaty of Rome, which has been heavily influenced by the different policies of the member states.

It is in the agricultural sector that the EC has made the greatest progress, with a price support system covering most agricultural products. The Common Agricultural Policy (CAP) represents one of the few instances of the successful harmonisation of national policies at the European level so far. It has been bitterly criticised in Britain because of its effects on food prices and its creation of 'wine lakes' and 'butter mountains'. The aim was to raise the incomes of large numbers of poor agricultural producers in Europe and Ireland. There are few very small, relatively inefficient farms in Britain, so British farmers and consumers gain little from the redistributive effects of the CAP.

Other redistributive policies in the social field have had little impact. There have been some attempts to restructure industry and to regenerate some of the poorer areas of the EC, but with little success. The Single European Act (SEA) was intended to advance the social policies of the Community. It involves heavy cuts in farm subsidies, with diversion of revenue to the social programmes and the promotion of new technology. The SEA was intended as a step towards a more efficient Community. It gave slightly increased powers to the Commission and to the European Parliament, provided for more majority voting on the European Council, made a formal commitment to abolition of trade barriers by 1992, and increased the role of the EC in foreign relations. This hesitant groping towards a more federalist structure aroused Mrs Thatcher's ire.

Mrs Thatcher clearly expressed a positive attitude towards ties with the USA rather than with the EC, where her aim was to get what she saw as a fair budgetary deal for Britain rather than to advance the interests of the Community as a whole. She constantly expressed irritation with the bureaucratic aspects of the EC and resisted what she saw as threats to British sovereignty.

She saw the EC purely in economic terms and became increasingly distrustful of moves to greater integration. Yet 'her toughness, irritating though it has often been to other European leaders and to the Foreign Office, ensured that the question of whether or not Britain should be a member of the community disappeared from the domestic political agenda after the 1983 general election'.[22] The Labour Party gradually moved to a position of acceptance of membership and indeed to one of apparent enthusiasm for at least some aspects of the EC.

Mrs Thatcher's premiership was marked by a series of bitter battles over Britain's contributions to the EC budget and over the question of how much of the Community's resources should be devoted to the CAP. At one time as much as three-quarters of the total spending was devoted to agriculture. However, the problem gradually receded, and British policy shifted from a preoccupation with budgetary matters to a seemingly more positive attitude. In December 1985 Britain agreed to a series of far-reaching objectives which were embodied in the SEA. This extended qualified majority voting on decisions except where vital national interests were involved. Though it was attacked by some opponents as a further erosion of sovereignty, the government saw it as progress to a single common internal market for goods and services by 1992 and to enhanced co-operation in technical and foreign policy areas, though critics wondered whether enough was being done to ensure that Britain would be in a position to compete.

In the late 1980s the activities of the EC became particularly controversial in ways which led to some surprising political realignments. The debate about the implications of the single European market in 1992 highlighted growing differences of view about the direction the Community was taking. The suggestion by Jacques Delors, the French President of the Commission, that there was a kind of embryonic European government, with national governments playing an increasingly subordinate role, infuriated Mrs Thatcher. She stressed that her idea was that the EC was made up of separate states 'working together'; increasingly there were disputes about the practical working out of the SEA, with Mrs Thatcher seeming to be determined to emphasise British autonomy within the Community. Her constant reiteration of the need to preserve British sovereignty in the face of 'encroachment' by the EC bureaucracy reached what critics saw as hysteria when she hinted that the monarchy was in some way threatened. Commentators saw her suggestion that British sovereignty was in danger as a disguise for her ideological hostility to many of the aims of the Community. She clearly saw the SEA and the Social Charter as threatening to introduce 'Socialism by the backdoor'. 'The British government vehemently opposed the Social Charter not because this meant a further erosion of national sovereignty but because its goals conflicted with Mrs Thatcher's ideal of the EC as a maxi-free trade area devoid of protection and common rights for EC citizens.'[23] This led Mrs Thatcher and her supporters into increasingly harsh condemnations of Delors, and semi-public rifts with the governments of other member states. It also isolated the British Conservative Party from Christian Democratic Parties on the Continent, who 'accept the case for social partnership to go hand in hand with sound economic policies'.[24]

The argument was symbolised by the wrangle over the EMS, widely seen as a major step to full economic and monetary union. Despite Mrs Thatcher's repeated promises to join at the 'proper time', critics, many of them within her own party, accused her having no intention to join. The arguments of ministers such as Howe and Lawson, as well as much of the business and financial establishment, that Britain should enter the system seemed to be at odds with Mrs Thatcher, who appeared to see when 'the time was ripe' as a date to be postponed indefinitely. Pressure from colleagues persuaded the Prime Minister to moderate her hostility to EC plans for further discussion of a European central bank. The humiliating removal of Howe from his post of Foreign Secretary was evidence of Thatcher's anger at being forced into this concession. This attitude increasingly concerned the other members of the Community, and confirmed their suspicions that Thatcher was half-hearted in her commitment to Europe. This dispute was, at least in part, responsible for the resignation of Nigel Lawson in October 1989. Another blow to Mrs Thatcher was the loss of Nicholas Ridley, Secretary of State for Trade and Industry, following his outburst over European unity and what he saw as

German domination of the process. 'As the pound sterling began to falter in exchange markets in summer 1989 and the government's economic policy became exposed to increasing criticism at home, the interaction of EC and British levels of politics became acutely visible.'[25]

Mrs Thatcher's growing anger at developments in Europe were expressed in a speech in Bruges in September 1988, in which she outlined her 'minimalist' approach. She urged that the SEA was about 'encouraging enterprise'; 'Europe without frontiers' would continue to maintain national sovereignty. She attacked what she saw at attempts to fit the various nations into some sort of 'identikit' European personality. She went on to express sentiments which seemed to run counter to the aims of the SEA and to attack plans to eliminate frontiers in the EC. Clearly her view of the Single European Market was that it would create an opportunity for virtually unfettered capitalism. In this she ran counter to the aims, not just of Delors but of other member-states. A theme of her speech, a bitter attack on the Social Charter, an idea promoted by Delors for improving workers' rights, intensified after Bruges. She claimed that her government had not 'destroyed socialism' in Britain only to have it reimposed through the back door from Brussels; her attacks on 'over-regulation' by Euro-bureaucrats reached an increasing volume.

At the same time, the Labour Party was discovering an enthusiasm for closer ties which commentators had previously found hard to discern. Labour, apart from some elements on the Left, ceased to see the EC as a threat to socialism (a word increasingly avoided) and as a barrier to the achievement of Labour's domestic goals. Kinnock and his allies saw the opportunities offered by the strength of socialist parties in the European Parliament and by the Social Charter to achieve the kind of reforms denied by a decade of Thatcherism. It was also a way of drawing attention to what was seen as the low level of infrastructure and social spending by the British government and the extent to which Britain was lagging behind her EC partners in areas such as transport, pensions, education and so on. Labour accused the Tories of a doctrinaire objection to public expenditure, an attitude which it saw as harming Britain's ability to compete. The Delors plan even led Labour to abandon its support for the closed shop; the Charter, while calling for enhanced trade union rights also emphasised the right not to belong to a union. Labour also saw the opportunity to exploit the growing divisions in the Tory Party. Edward Heath led the assault on Thatcher's hostility to the EC in which he was joined by Michael Heseltine and others, including, in coded terms, several of her ministers. Labour's Policy Review, issued in 1989, drew attention to the party's commitment to Europe and called for a Community which would have social as well as economic objectives, attacking what it saw as Thatcher's view of the EC as simply a market with unfettered opportunities for big business and finance.

In the aftermath of the European Parliament election of June 1989, in which the Conservatives suffered a resounding defeat, the struggle in the Tory Party over the EC intensified, with Britain increasingly isolated in its opposition to the Social Charter and closer monetary and political integration. Conservative MEPs became vocal in their condemnation of Mrs Thatcher, whom they blamed for their isolation in the European Parliament. Leon Brittan, appointed as one of the British Commissioners by Mrs Thatcher, joined in the criticism of her attitude; some saw this as at least in part his delayed revenge over her part in his departure from the government over the Westland Affair. More problems were caused for the government when Brittan complained about 'sweeteners' and other benefits alleged to have been given to British companies during various privatisation transactions. The resignation of Howe sparked off the train of events which led to Mrs Thatcher's downfall; her hostility to Europe was a major aspect of the controversy.

Thus, the impact of the EC on British policy has been steadily growing since 1972, and virtually 'any field of policy with international ramifications automatically includes a European dimension and EC activities then begin to shape the parameters of British policy, as well as allow scope for British influence to be brought to bear on EC partners'.[26] This can be seen in the field of environmental policy; Mrs Thatcher's neglect was reversed partly because of increasing pressure from EC countries, who dubbed

Britain 'the dirty man of Europe' over acid rain and sewage-polluted beaches, and partly because the strength of the Green vote in the 1989 Euro-election began to convince ministers that there were domestic political advantages in emphasising European concerns. The adaptation of Britain to the requirements of membership of the EC is increasing in scale and scope; local authorities, public and private enterprises have all been increasingly affected. The arguments about sovereignty are beginning to seem irrelevant to the realities of the situation. The major political parties are engaged in a debate with each other and within themselves about policies for Europe. Clearly Europe is once again in the forefront of British politics.

8. The International Monetary Fund

The IMF was established in 1944 to operate the system of fixed exchange rates established by the Bretton Woods Agreement. Its most important function has been to lend to countries with balance of payments deficits so that they could take the necessary corrective action while maintaining their exchange rate, although countries with a 'fundamental disequilibrium' could adjust to a new fixed value, as Britain did in 1967. Britain made a number of drawings from the IMF, though the floating of the pound in 1972 reduced her dependence on the Fund. The last such drawing was in 1976, when the monetarist views of the IMF had a major impact on policy. The Fund has made loans to a number of developing countries, and its monetarist stance, involving severe cuts in public expenditure, has attracted criticism from a number of aid agencies and others, for inflicting hardship on the most vulnerable sections of society.

9. The role of economists in economic policy making

Economists act as advisers to policy makers, rather than being policy makers themselves. Some economists are employed as civil servants, mainly but not exclusively in the Treasury, to give policy advice to ministers, while many more are employed outside the government machine, in academic institutions, research bodies of all kinds, financial organisations and companies.

The ideal model of economic policy making goes as follows. The objectives of policy are clearly established and then the means which best achieve these ends are discovered and applied. The role of the economist is to advise on the means whereby the objectives desired by the politicians will be achieved; he will not allow his personal preferences to influence his judgement or advice.

However, the real world is clearly rather different. For one thing, it is rare that the objectives of policy are clearly stated. Policy is made by groups within government who often have diverging, sometimes contradictory, aims. The stated objective may not be the one actually being pursued; most governments have some kind of 'hidden agenda'. Objectives may be inconsistent; efforts to reduce inflation may conflict with the desire to keep unemployment in check. This dichotomy was a basic cause of the confusion in policy between 1979 and 1981. Most economists will admit that theirs is an inexact science; they may lack the knowledge of what is required to achieve particular objectives. 'Even if a high degree of probability can be attached to the direction in which an economic relationship is expected to work – say we know that reducing the rate of growth of the money supply will bring down inflation – there is greater uncertainty about the magnitude of the relationship: how much the rate of growth of money supply needs to be contracted to reduce inflation by one per cent still has to be determined.'[27]

Economists' advice is not value free. Like other experts, they bring their own value judgements with them. Their work is informed by reference to the sort of society they favour and the purposes they believe government action (or inaction) should fulfil. To some extent, whether one is a Keynesian or a monetarist depends on one's view of society and the purpose of government. The way economic evidence is used is partly determined by the perspectives of those producing and using it. 'It is impossible to construct for an economic adviser a role which is almost wholly detached from the political realities which dominate politicians' calculations.'[28] Healey drew attention to the perils of economic analysis. 'Economics is not a science. It is a branch of social psychology, which makes the absurd assumption that you can understand how people behave when they are making, buying, and selling things, without studying the society in which they live, and all the other ways in which they spend their time.'[29] He pointed out that: 'while economic theory can give you valuable insights into what is happening, it can rarely offer clear pre-scriptions for government action, since economic behaviour can change from year to year and is different in one country from another'.[30]

Healey and others have pointed to another important limitation on the efficacy of economic advice. This is the incomplete know-ledge at the disposal of policy makers and their advisers. Treasury forecasting is notoriously inaccurate. The Treasury estimate of the PSBR in 1974/75 was seriously incorrect, leading the Chan-cellor to apply to the IMF on defective figures. More recently, Treasury forecasts of inflation and the balance of payments deficit have been considerably understated.

Yet the model of economic policy making described above is not totally irrelevant. Models provide some kind of guide to action, some way of assessing likely outcomes. 'Faith and ideology are not sufficient guides to achieving economic policy objec-tives.'[31] Economic theory has a twofold role in helping to formulate policy: on the one hand, it offers some evaluation of goals and methods, while on the other it provides ammunition for politicians and others in the political battle. Keynes summed up the influence of economists. 'The ideas of economists and politi-cal philosophers both when they are right and when they are wrong are more powerful than is commonly understood. Indeed the world is ruled by little else. Practical men, who believe them-selves to be quite exempt from any intellectual influences, are usually the slaves of some defunct economist. Madmen in authority, who hear voices in the air, are distilling their frenzy from some academic scribbler of a few years back.'[32]

Summary

This chapter has considered to what extent economic theory, political ideologies, the various groups and institutions within the political and economic systems and the pressure of events interact in economic policy making. The conclusion is that since 1945 governments of both parties have attempted to direct the economy in the hope of achieving certain more or less explicit aims. The outcomes of such aspirations have varied, in ways difficult to predict, but the ability of British governments to control events has progressively declined as the domestic economy has weakened. Thus the significance of international bodies and of the world economy has increased. This does not mean that party ideologies have not been an important factor in economic policy making, and the next chapter considers the changing perspectives of the parties on the nature and extent of the state's role in the economy.

Notes

1 William Keegan and R. Pennant-Rea: *Who Runs The Economy?*, Temple Smith, 1979, p.9.

2 Ibid., p.113–14.

3 For more details, see Donald Shell: *The House of Lords*, Philip Allan/Barnes and Noble, 1988, pp.107–10.

4 Rosalind Levacic: *Economic Policy-Making. Its Theory and Practice*, Wheatsheaf, 1987, p.29.

5 Keegan and Pennant-Rea, *Who Runs The Economy?*, p.63.

6 For more details, see Bernard Donoughue: *Prime Minister. The Conduct of Policy under Harold Wilson and James Callaghan*, Cape, 1987, Chapter 4.

7 Peter Riddell: Cabinet and Parliament, in Dennis Kavanagh and Anthony Seldon (eds.): *The Thatcher Effect*, OUP, 1989, p.104.

8 Keegan and Pennant-Rea, *Who Runs The Economy?*, pp.66–7.

9 Ibid., p.76.

10 Joel Barnett: *Inside the Treasury*, André Deutsch, 1982, p.19.

11 Ibid., p.188.

12 William Plowden: The Treasury, *Contemporary Record*, Vol. 2, No. 3, Autumn 1988, p.26.

13 Ibid. See also Colin Thain: The Treasury, *Contemporary Record*, Vol. 3, No. 4, April 1990, pp.17ff.

14 Sir Leo Pliatzky: *The Treasury Under Mrs. Thatcher*, Blackwell, 1989, p.4.

15 Ian Budge, David McKay, et al.: *The Changing British Political*

System: Into the 1990s, Longman, 1988, 2nd edn, p.7.

16 Levacic, *Economic Policy-Making*, p.32.

17 See Wyn Grant: *Pressure Groups, Politics and Democracy in Britain*, Philip Allan, 1989.

18 Levacic, *Economic Policy-Making*, p.32.

19 Rob Baggott: Pressure Group Politics in Britain: Change and Decline?, *Talking Politics*, Vol. 1, No. 1, Autumn 1988, p.30.

20 Dennis Kavanagh: *Thatcherism and British Politics. The End of Consensus?*, OUP, 1990, 2nd edn, pp.95–6.

21 Keegan and Pennant-Rea, *Who Runs The Economy?*, p.139.

22 Peter Riddell: *The Thatcher Decade*, Blackwell, 1989, p.192.

23 Juliet Lodge: Europe, in William Wale (ed.): *Developments in Politics. An Annual Review*, Vol. 1, Causeway Press, 1990, p.143.

24 Helen Wallace: Britain and Europe, in Patrick Dunleavy et al. (eds.): *Developments in British Politics 3*, Macmillan, 1990, p.166.

25 Ibid.

26 Ibid., p.168.

27 Levacic, *Economic Policy-Making*, pp.36–7.

28 Keegan and Pennant-Rea, *Who Runs The Economy?*, p.56.

29 Dennis Healey: *The Time Of My Life*, Michael Joseph, 1989, p.377.

30 Ibid., p.383.

31 Levacic, *Economic Policy-Making*, p.37.

32 J.M. Keynes: *The General Theory of Employment, Interest and Money*, 1936, p.383, quoted in Keegan and Pennant-Rea, *Who Runs The Economy?*, p.51.

7

Economic policy and the political parties since 1945: the Conservative Party

This chapter and the next examine the interaction between party ideologies and economic policy making since 1945. The period is one in which both parties accepted major responsibilites for economic management and tried, with varying degrees of success, to impose *their* competing visions of economic 'reality' on an increasingly uncooperative world. This chapter examines the Conservatives, the agenda setters for the 1980s.

The Conservative Party

By 1945 government responsibility for economic and social well-being had gained much acceptance in the Conservative Party. A section led by Harold Macmillan argued that pre-war Conservative governments had done too little to deal with the Depression; capitalism should be regulated so that private enterprise would live alongside a significant extention of the state. R.A. Butler urged the Conservatives to develop an alternative to Labour's policies but which would reject *laissez-faire* in favour of a major economic role for the state. A committee under Butler produced the *Industrial Charter* which, while expressing support for free enterprise, committed the party to greater central direction of the economy as well as to acceptance of other parts of Labour's reforms. 'Tory collectivism', though it stressed different ends from that of Labour, was to dominate the party for almost a generation.

The years from 1951–1964 were generally marked by rising living standards and the Tories made much of the contrast with Labour austerity and gloom. Pragmatism marked the Conservative Party; most members saw themselves as practical people, uninterested in ideology. 'Conservatism was an ideology of adaptation, and the tasks of each generation of leaders was to adapt the party to changing circumstances. It was certainly non-socialist or even anti-socialist in that no one believed in equality or in the further expansion of collectivism. But what had been done was accomplished fact, part of historical evolution. It was the role of Conservatives to curtail socialist excesses, to abandon foolish dreams, and to run the system in a sensible businesslike fashion.'[1] They drew a contrast with Labour, divided over Clause Four and other doctrinal issues.

Economic growth became the main preoccupation of Conservative governments which lacked the inclination to appeal to abstract concepts such as social justice. Towards the end international comparisons of growth rates worked to their disadvantage, when it became apparent that Britain was falling behind. For most of the period, however, there was a general acceptance that growth could be achieved through Keynesian techniques. Just as Keynesianism was acceptable to Labour Party revisionism because of the role of the state in economic management, so its attractions for 'One Nation' Toryism were obvious. The use of state power to deal with unemployment, which could potentially destabilise the social order, without threatening business enterprise was attractive to the branch of Toryism then dominant.

Yet the unanimity was not complete; issues such as the Empire angered some on the Right, who saw decolonisation as a symbol of the loss of direction. Economic liberalism, in which the state's role would be much reduced, still had its adherents; although they were a small minority, the resignation of Thorneycroft in 1958 was a sign that they had not disappeared. On the Left, the Bow Group called for even more state involvement in economic management on the lines of the currently highly successful French model. Departures such as the establishment of the NEDC (as well as the unpopular 'pay-pause') marked moves in this direction. The new system of planning was to be indicative in which plans were drawn up and both sides of industry invited to take part. This move towards planning produced tensions in the Cabinet, foreshadowing later divisions in the party. Even more significant was the decision to apply for entry to the EEC, marking the hope that increased competition would force British manufacturers to respond. However, the Conservatives by the early 1960s had lost direction and could not resist Labour's onslaught.

The election of Heath to the leadership produced a new set of policies. His perspective was that too many concessions had been made to the unions and that the growth of the public sector was threatening national prosperity. These were the views of the progressive Right, not of a set of ideologues. He lacked the thorough going analysis of his successor and her supporters. The new policies were to assist economic growth; if they worked, they should be pursued, if not, something else should be tried. Heath broadly accepted Keynesianism and full employment whereas for Mrs Thatcher and her supporters economic liberalism was not just about economic efficiency; it was about freedom and much more.

This lack of a coherent ideology is part of the explanation for the failure of Heath's government, although he did not have the advantage of the profound shift in the climate of opinion which was to benefit Thatcher a decade later. 'The outlook of commentators, economists, intellectuals, journalists – the opinion formers in general – was anti-Conservative. The accepted philosophy was still *dirigiste* ... There was no serious challenge in intellectual circles to this orthodoxy.'[2] Heath was later blamed by many Conservatives for betraying the policies and principles on which he was elected, and for slipping back into an unprincipled collectivism. In many ways this is unfair. The 'dash for growth' was above all intended to create the economic climate in which British business could compete without the balance of payments constraints which had bedevilled previous attempts to achieve self-sustained economic growth. However, in the Conservative Party as elsewhere, history is written by the victors.

In the late 1960s and early 1970s, partly stimulated by disappointment with Heath's leadership, there developed a diverse set of ideas which have come to be known as the New Right. In so far as these ideas had a spokesman in this earlier period it was Enoch Powell. One of his themes (somewhat overshadowed by his more highly publicised views on immigration) was that of the defence of capitalism. Capitalism was to be admired partly because of its material achievements but more particularly because it produced the 'good society'; economic freedom meant political and social freedom, something later taken up with fervour by Mrs Thatcher and her supporters.

Following the two defeats of 1974 the conviction grew, mainly on the Right of the party, that a new leader was required. Margaret Thatcher, a relatively junior member of Heath's Cabinet who had impressed the parliamentary party as a Shadow Treasury minister during 1974–75, emerged as the standard-bearer for the New Right.

Thatcher's success in 1975 and her election victory in 1979 was part of a major shift in the intellectual climate to the Right. A significant number of commentators and academics produced alarming (or alarmist) studies of the 'decline' of Britain and pointed to what they saw as its growing 'ungovernability'. Some members of the Labour Party defected to the Conservatives; their prominence in the media and in academic life meant that their conversion was highly publicised. Yet the success of Thatcherism was not based simply on the conversion of intellectual opinion, important though that was in establishing the climate of ideas. It also reflected, as well as led, a significant movement in popular opinion away from the 'collectivist trinity' associated with the Labour Party which Callaghan referred to as a 'sea change' towards Mrs Thatcher.

Thatcherism

From one perspective, Thatcherism is synonymous with economic liberalism of the kind propounded by Hayek, Friedman and bodies such as the Institute for Economic Affairs. They argued that the free market guarantees liberty, while planning means the absence of freedom. The role of the state should be to ensure the conditions under which markets can operate freely; it can rightfully perform a limited range of other tasks, such as guaranteeing law and order and national defence, as well as providing a basic welfare safety net.

However, more is involved than simply a defence of the market. Thatcherism combines neo-conservative themes such as the nation and the family (explicitly linked together), the revival of authority and duty, with neo-liberal concerns such as the primacy of the acquisitive, self-interested individual and opposition to the economic role of the state. This mixture of ideas, in many ways contradictory, has been given the shorthand label of 'The Free Economy and the Strong State'.

Yet it is possible to overstress the ideological aspect of Thatcherism. The replacement of Heath by Thatcher in 1975 was not a search for a more coherent ideology, nor a move away from consensus to conviction politics. Thatcherism was very much a matter of instinct: a series of moral values and an attitude to leadership, deeply related to her upbringing. Hugo Young referred to her Grantham childhood as the daughter of a grocer who was also a local politician of deep convictions. Clearly her origins, which were far from affluent (but also not directly affected by the unemployment and poverty of the 1930s) influenced her greatly as when she compared the nation's finances to the domestic budget: 'the Grantham grocer's daughter, the prime minister who really does believe that the thrifty principles of home management are a perfectly sufficient guide to the management of the national economy'.[3]

Certain themes regarding the economy and the role of the state recurred. In 1968 she called for greater personal responsibility in life, with a consequent reduction in the role of government. The state must be rolled back so the right to property can be ensured against socialism, which she believed threatened to deprive people of the power to achieve success to the best of their abilities. 'If people could be sure that we would never have another socialist government, increasing control of the state, increasing control of ownership, then I think the prospects for this country would be really bright. If only we could get rid of socialism as a second force and have two parties which fundamentally believed that political freedom had to be backed by economic freedom and that you can get the best out of people when you delegate power down.'[4] She often boasted about altering the relationship between the people and the state and claimed to have reduced the state to a proper role in which 'personal responsibility' was paramount.

In her economic thinking the free market in goods and services was central. The economy operates by a system of laws, such as supply and demand, which are too complicated to be understood; attempts to regulate it in the interests of some abstract concept of 'social justice', 'fairness' or 'equality', will not only fail but will be damaging to the efficient operation of the capitalist system, which is the surest guarantor both of economic prosperity and freedom. The link between liberal democracy and the capitalist mode of production was explicit in Mrs Thatcher's thinking. But this does not mean that men are helpless and at the mercy of forces they cannot control. Though it is not possible to 'buck' the market, men can motivate themselves to discover alternatives when the market turns against them. They can, after all, 'get on their bikes' and look for work as Norman Tebbit suggested. The responsibility for prosperity is that of the individual, not the state, though it continues to provide a minimal welfare safety net.

The various economic strategies followed by the Thatcher government reflected ideological preferences. Monetarism was a reaction against the kind of state control and 'interference' implicit in Keynesianism, and at least for a while gave a core to all the resentments and fears of the New Right about the growth of collectivism. The effort to curtail the rise in public expenditure, which is implicit in monetarism and which has survived its demise, was justified partly in terms of the battle against inflation, but also in terms of 'freedom' and 'choice', as was the reduction in direct taxation, with the consequent increase in indirect taxation. Privatisation, originally seen as a way of bringing greater competition to state monopolies, soon took on the nature of a crusade with strong political overtones. If the aim came to be that of creating a 'share-owning democracy' and thus a society in which people had a vested interest in the success of capitalism, it was also noted that shareholders are more likely to vote Conservative than to support Labour. Sophisticated techniques of mail-order persuasion were used to remind share-holders, many of them first-time buyers, that the Tories had been responsible for the largesse. The offensive against trade unions was partly a reaction, shared by many non-Conservatives, against the abuses of power of the previous twenty years. Because the unions were seen as one of the major props of the system, it was also an aspect of the movement away from collectivism and part of the effort to re-establish 'rightful' authority; the unions had shifted power from management towards what were considered to be irresponsible and unrepresentative shop stewards and other union 'bully boys'.

Above all, inflation was identified as *the* enemy, and its defeat as the key to economic progress and social stability, a far cry from Macmillan's belief that 'a little inflation does no harm'. Inflation threatened the value of the currency and of the country's ability to compete, both of which in turn diminished Britain's standing in the world. This addressed itself to another of Thatcher's themes, that of the renewal of national greatness after a generation of retreat. Inflation threatened the savings of the middle class, making thrift decidedly out of fashion. Memories of inflation in post-1918 Germany were invoked as a way of demonstrating the danger of a debased currency, brought about by feckless governments and reckless experiments in economic management. In the face of the need to defeat inflation, a concern shared by many who were hostile to the actual methods used, both full employment *and* economic growth were downgraded. The prospect of growth was weighed against the need for a high exchange rate for the pound (with the consequence of high domestic interest rates); the collapse of a large sector of British manufacturing was partly the result of this policy. The consequent high unemployment was not allowed to deflect the government from its course, thereby destroying one of the great myths of British politics, that governments presiding over significantly increasing unemployment face electoral disaster.

The tensions implicit in the neo-liberal aims of reducing the role of the state and unleashing market forces and the neo-conservative emphasis on the restoration of 'authority' (which implies an active role for government in a range of policies aimed at 'remoralising' a 'permissive' society) caused ideological dilemmas. A number of Conservative critics, from both the 'One

Nation' and the neo-conservative wings, expressed fears that the pursuit of economic liberalism would produce social strains (for example through rising unemployment, homelessness and so on) which would endanger the social harmony which is the basis of Conservatism. In the 1980s some Conservative critics of Mrs Thatcher pointed to the inner-city riots as evidence that the pace of economic change had led to an increasingly alienated population. Such anxieties led Michael Heseltine, briefly 'Minister for Merseyside', to produce a report, 'It Took a Riot' calling for remedial action in Britain's increasingly derelict cities. The report was not published; Mrs Thatcher's response to the riots was to blame them on individual wickedness and the actions of Left-wing councils rather than on government policies. Her reaction to the 1981 riots was to sympathise with those whose property had been destroyed, saying 'Oh, those poor shopkeepers'. In this she reflected the views of the authoritarian Right, calling for action against 'the enemy within'.

On the neo-liberal wing, groups such as the Adam Smith Institute criticised what they saw as the timidity and half-measures of the government. It was asked why only nationalised industries which were profitable or which could quickly be made so were privatised and why, given the belief in the ethic of competition, British Rail and British Coal were not returned to the private sector. From this source came demands for the replacement of the NHS by an insurance-based system, the privatisation of prisons and the issuing of educational vouchers, all in the name of greater efficiency and choice.

Thatcher largely ignored these cries because of electoral considerations; her assurance that 'the NHS is safe in our hands' was designed to head off Labour criticisms which might have been politically damaging. But in addition she was keenly aware that too much choice. particularly in the wrong hands, might endanger her other aims. For example, the reforms to the NHS announced in 1989 were designed partly to bring 'market forces' more centrally into play. But calls for more consultation, perhaps through local referenda, were rejected, a rejection later repeated by John Major. Similarly, the Community Charge was defended on the grounds that, by making everyone pay something towards the provision of local services, greater accountability of local government to the electors would be ensured. The widespread charge capping after the introduction of the charge in England in 1990 seemed to negate this aim and increasingly the Thatcher government faced criticism of expanding the 'nanny state' it had so criticised.

The attempt to marry the neo-liberal and the neo-conservative strands in Thatcherism continued in the third term of government. Market liberalism continued with the privatisation of water and electricity, although it was conceded that British Rail and the coal industry would not be returned to the private sector during that Parliament. Mrs Thatcher and a number of her ministers announced policies aimed at restoring the social cohesion which they believed had been damaged by the 'permissiveness' of the sixties. 'The family', with its implicit relationship to private property, became *the* theme of the authoritarian Right, though in apparent conflict with Mrs.Thatcher's statement that 'there is no such thing as society', only individuals and their families. 'Thatcherism combines contradictory ideological elements and that Thatcher can deny the existence of society while at the same time trying to restore it is testimony to how difficult the holding together of such a contradictory yet potent doctrine can be.'[5]

The Thatcher governments were ideological in a degree unmatched since the post-war Labour administration. Slogans such as the 'property and share-owning society', 'the enterprise economy' and so on had an impact on policy. The repeated emphasis on 'Victorian values' and the need to return to sound finance and balanced budgets emphasised the attempts to cut the PSBR and reduce public expenditure. Clearly it would be a mistake to over-emphasise the ideological consistency; privatisation, for example, emerged gradually and was related to the desire to reduce public expenditure and raise large sums of money to finance tax cuts, while there was slower progress than many Thatcherites would have liked in altering the basis of the Welfare State. In many ways Mrs Thatcher was a pragmatic leader, with a keen sense of what Tory voters and the parliamentary party would accept.

That said, however, the ideological zeal with which Thatcher and her supporters went about their mission to 'turn round'

Britain and rid it of socialism cannot be denied. A number of commentators, from a variety of perspectives, have debated whether Mrs Thatcher was a Conservative at all. While it is outside the purpose of this book to enter that argument it is important to note the extent to which she was influenced by the dual legacy of Conservatism: the Tory tradition which sees a major role for the state, both in terms of providing at least a minimal safety net and in terms of ensuring social harmony and order, and the liberal tradition of individualism and the minimal state. The comment of John Nott, a former member of Mrs Thatcher's Cabinet that she was a 'nineteenth-century liberal' contained much truth. It is not surprising that Nott later became very critical of the centralisation and authoritarianism which increasingly marked her style.

Both Thatcherism and 'One Nation' Conservatism are but forms of Conservatism. At least since Disraeli, there has been a shifting balance between those who emphasised a positive role for the state and those who asserted the values of individualism and minimal government. The predominant message of Thatcherism was economic liberalism. She and her supporters argued that the battle was won; collectivism was dead, and with it socialism. But the truth is more complex and since the coming to power of John Major there are signs of a change of direction. Just as Wilson tried to deflect attention from economic setbacks by a Cabinet reshuffle or a visit to Washington or Moscow, perhaps the attention directed by Major early in his premiership to non-economic themes such as the quality of the public services indicates a growing realisation that many of Britain's problems defy the ministrations of *any* government, however zealous.

The New Right

In the 1960s Enoch Powell had attempted to revive a more market-oriented Conservatism. After the Tories were defeated in 1964 he criticised incomes and regional policies, economic planning and above all 'excessive' public expenditure and an over-expansion of the money supply (which he held responsible for inflation), all of which had been as much a feature of past Conservative administrations as of Labour ones. He linked the free market and the free society; the market distributed power as widely as possible by making economic decisions the outcome of an uncountable number of transactions by individuals seeking their own good without central interference. Powell's highly publicised views on immigration overshadowed what he had to say on the running of the economy. His dismissal from the Shadow Cabinet in 1968, his exclusion from office by Heath and his subsequent breach with the party over Europe all served to marginalise Powell's contribution to the re-emergence of free-market ideas.

These ideas gained ground following Heath's 'U-turn' and the double defeat of 1974. Opinion shifted considerably, at first among intellectuals and commentators and then among the public. The ideas were taken up by an important section of the Conservative leadership as a way for Thatcher and her supporters to distance themselves, not only from Labour governments but also from previous post-war Tory administrations. At first, these views were spread by sources other than the official policy-advising bodies in the Conservative Party. The Conservative Political Centre was thought too 'wet', so Sir Keith Joseph founded the Centre for Policy Studies as the vehicle for his vision of Conservatism. Other important think-tanks included the Institute of Economic Affairs (IEA) and the Adam Smith Institute. Thatcher and Joseph often expressed their admiration for and reliance on the work of two economists. The first was Friedrich von Hayek, the second, now somewhat less often quoted, was Milton Friedman.

Friedrich von Hayek
Kavanagh[6] pointed out that there are four main themes to Hayek's work.

1. *Opposition to central economic planning, which is described as 'evil'.* A central economic plan is politically dangerous and economically inefficient. It reduces liberty and gives too much power to government, leading to increasing pressure for controls of all kinds. Competition is reduced and monopolies flourish. The market increases the opportunities for experiment, while planning

stifles creativity. There could be no 'middle way', as Macmillan had supposed; freedom and planning cannot be combined, and no compromise is possible.

2. *The complexity of society:* 'there is a spontaneous natural order which is the outcome not of a plan or of design, but of human action'.[7] Hayek emphasises the complexity of the economic system and the impossibility of controlling these variables by some kind of government dictat. These views were shared by Mrs Thatcher, although, paradoxically, commentators pointed to her passionate concern to produce deep and permanent change to the character of the British people by a combination of legislation, moralising and what can only be called 'social engineering'.

3. *The importance of markets and prices in allocating resources, rather than government intervention.* The 'laws' of supply and demand will allocate resources efficiently, provided governments do not 'interfere'. Trade unions distort market forces and feed inflation by encouraging growth in the money supply; their power must be limited.

4. *The limited but important role of government.* Its job is not to promote social justice (a term having little or no meaning for Hayek) or to try to remedy what it might see as deficiencies in the market system. Its role is to establish the conditions within which the market can operate; government has a vital task in establishing a framework of law within which capitalism can operate. 'Hayek rejects the notion of social justice. There is nothing just or unjust . . . about market outcomes. What matters for Hayek is not the pattern of distribution established through the market, but that there should exist a market order, based on general rules, which guarantees everyone maximum opportunities. Actual distribution will be a lottery depending on skill and effort to a limited degree, but predominantly on chance – the chance of genetic and material inheritance and the manner in which opportunities arise.'[8] Thus, life is a lottery.

Hayek and others on the libertarian wing of the New Right, especially in the USA, have advocated constitutional restrictions on the ability of governments to manipulate the economy; Mrs Thatcher, conscious of the benefits to be gained from ensuring the 'correct' economic climate in the run-up to a general election, showed little interest in this aspect of his thinking.

Milton Friedman

Friedman is the most articulate and passionate spokesman for monetarism and in the 1970s led the attack on Keynesianism. He believes that if an increase in the money supply outstrips GDP it will produce inflation. He also believes in a 'natural' wage level at which people would find employment; interference with this by trade unions may, in the short term, produce higher wages, but only at the cost of higher unemployment and rising inflation. Thus there is also a 'natural' level of unemployment. Although in theory at least monetarism is politically neutral (monetarist ideas influenced Dennis Healey as Chancellor, especially after 1976) Friedman is an enthusiast for the free market, which he associates with freedom. He believes that planning is inefficient and a threat to liberty, that taxes should be cut, state industries and services privatised, and regulations relating to most economic and social matters scrapped. Virtually anything which stands in the way of the efficient working of the market should go. Government has a role in ensuring law and order and defence, as well as in protecting those groups, such as children, who clearly cannot protect themselves. In common with other New Right theorists, Friedman sees a connection between capitalism and personal freedom; he praised Hong Kong as an example of society to be emulated by Britain and other Western nations 'suffering' from socialism. His view of freedom is that of a classical liberal: it consists in making choices and being free from coercion by others. Like Hayek, Friedman advocates formal limitations on the power of government over the economy.

The Institute of Economic Affairs

This began in 1957 as a research and education body, devoted to studying the role of markets. It addresses a mainly academic audience and its work is devoted to influencing opinion-formers. Its principal aim has been to combat the ideas of Keynes; it is now the intellectual home of markets, liberalism and monetarism in Britain. The work of the IEA provides a clear guide to the ideas circulating in government. An IEA pamphlet published in 1984 called for a programme of privatisation including railways, coal, hospitals, and schools. This and other measures, such as the abolition of the Manpower Services Commission and ACAS, it is claimed, would enable the government to cut taxes; in turn, output would rise by 10 per cent and employment by 2.5 million.

There is no single, official IEA view, and the Institute provides a vehicle for writers from a number of mainly Right-wing perspectives. There is a belief in the market, in the generally malevolent influence of government, and in the primacy of the individual in the running of the economy. The IEA believes that financing government services by tax conceals the costs of these services, which do not respond to choice by consumers. The demand for such services is not limited, which leads to spiralling costs and increasing inefficiency. The Institute is also critical of the government monopoly or near monopoly in the provision of many services. Thus it has emphasised privatisation, the sale of council houses, opposition to universal social services and so on. The role of the state in the provision of education and health means, in reality, that the middle class benefit most; those in greatest need gain least. This is a recurring theme of the New Right; the policy of targetting benefits was taken up by the Thatcher government. The IEA favours reducing the role of government, limiting it to functions, such as national defence, which only it can perform, and freeing the market and the price system as ways of efficiently allocating resources. It supports neo-classical economics and the assault on Keynesianism. It speaks 'of the interaction of buyers and sellers as the democracy of the market place – "the daily referendum of the market".'[9]

The IEA has played a major role in changing the intellectual climate in recent years, and its views gained heavywight support in newspapers such as *The Times* and the *Financial Times*. Its influence on the Thatcher wing of the Conservative party has been deep and pervasive.

The Adam Smith Institute

This was established in 1977 to develop free-market policies. It is critical of the public sector, which one of its leading contributors, Madsen Pirie, describes as 'inherently evil'. It has been prominent in advocating privatisation of nationalised industries and a wide range of local authority services. Its main concern is to promote public debate and thus influence policy makers. Much effort went into the *Omega Project*, a review conducted by a number of groups of the whole range of government activities. The aim was to suggest what activities could be transferred from the public to the private sector, thus, in its view, widening opportunities for choice and enterprise. It favoured greater privatisation of central and local government services and industries, the replacement of the Welfare State by a system of private insurance, with more encouragement of private health insurance, as well as a policy of parental choice in and control over schools. Many of these ideas have since become government policy.

The Centre for Policy Studies

The CPS was established by Sir Keith Joseph in August 1974 with the aim of studying the operation of successful market economies, such as those of West Germany and Japan. Its establishment was in part because of Joseph's suspicion of official bodies, such as the Conservative Research Department, thought to be Heath-ite in orientation. The work of the CPS was one factor in Joseph's break with the post-war consensus and his attack on the Conservative leadership in 1975. When Mrs Thatcher became leader she used the CPS, a number of whose associates, such as Sir Alan Walters and Sir John Hoskyns, became her advisers.

The CPS publicises free-market ideas among party activists. A number of study groups have been set up; their reports have favoured market-oriented policies, generally opposing state economic involvement. It has advocated making strikes in essential services illegal, with fines or imprisonment for strikers whose actions cause death or serious injury to members of the public. Its interests go beyond economic policy; it has been critical of comprehensive education and its suggestion that the Inner London Education Authority be abolished was accepted by the government.

Other organisations

Many other organisations exist on the Right of British politics. The Social Affairs Unit is mainly concerned with social policy and so outside our immediate concern. However, its influence on government policy is considerable and can be seen as part of the general New Right assault on the consensus. *Aims of Industry*, founded in 1942 to protect private enterprise, is a propaganda body which has opposed nationalisation and more recently has favoured privatisation. It criticises what it sees as the high level of public spending, direct taxation and government regulation of industry on the grounds that these things stifle initiative. It has urged restrictions on trade unions and the abolition of the Greater London Council. The Institute of Directors campaigns for free enterprise, cutting public spending and tackling the unions, and is passionately committed to privatisation. It has been critical of the CBI, which it sees as favouring some kind of accommodation with the unions; during Mrs Thatcher's time the CBI was largely kept at arms-length. The Institute keeps in close touch with Whitehall and with No. 10 Downing Street and has influenced policy on tax and welfare benefits.

There are also several groups more directly linked to the Conservative Party. The *Monday Club* is mainly concerned with matters of immigration and similar issues, although it supports free-market economics. The *Selsdon Group* was formed in 1973 in reaction to the 'U-turn' and was particularly critical of the rescue of the 'lame duck' Rolls Royce and Upper Clyde Shipbuilders. It supports policies such as privatisation, major cuts in taxation and public spending and greater private provision in health and welfare. It is a 'free-market' pressure group and one of the leading proponents of economic liberalism. It believes that most public services should be provided by the market and paid for by the people as consumers rather than taxpayers. The task of government should be to maintain the framework within which markets operate rather than to provide services. The *Bow Group*, once a platform for 'One Nation' intellectuals in the Tory Party, has moved to the Right and favours economic liberalism. It has criticised the government for missing opportunities for radical tax cuts, reduced public expenditure and reform of the tax and social

security system. More recently formed organisations include the
No Turning Back group, largely composed of younger Tory MPs,
mainly elected in 1983, some of whom had become ministers by
the end of the decade. Another is the *Bruges Group*, formed after a
speech by Mrs Thatcher in Bruges, in which she criticised what
she saw as the excessive centralisation in the EC. The Bruges
Group campaigns for Thatcherite free-market policies in the EC
and for the maintenance of as much British sovereignty as
possible.

The impact of these groups can be seen in many areas of policy.
They had ready access to the Prime Minister, to members of the
Cabinet and to senior civil servants. Their work was, in various
ways, promoted by much of the media. They helped provide the
motive power for many of the radical policies of the last decade
and provided the theoretical justification for much of
Thatcherism. Though there were tensions between the groups
and Conservative politicians who had to be aware of electoral
pressures and the limits of what governments can do, there
remained great affinity between the basic set of policy preferences
of these groups and the agenda of Mrs Thatcher and her supporters in the Tory Party.

The New Right – main ideas

There is a 'gap' in New Right theories between liberalism on
economic matters and authoritarianism on social matters, which
has meant that 'rolling back the frontiers of the state' has been
selective. Thatcherism fuses free-market, neo-liberal and socially
authoritarian, neo-conservative ideas. Ruth Levitas points out
that neo-liberalism differs from the kind of social democratic,
welfare state liberalism so detested by the New Right.[10] Similarly,
neo-conservatism can be distinguished from the Conservatism of
the post-war consensus, which accepted a commitment to welfare
capitalism.

A full discussion of New Right ideology is outside the scope of
this book and I will concentrate on the economic aspect; however,
the interaction of theories of how the economy works and the kind
of society required for that economic system to succeed cannot be

ignored. A society where market forces predominate requires a disciplined work force, hence the emphasis on trade union reforms and restoring primacy to management. Critics have said that a factor in the educational reforms of the past few years has been to produce a more skilled and compliant labour force. Mrs Thatcher repeatedly emphasised the rights of property; the sale of council houses and the wider distribution of share-ownership were ways to bolster property, a theme common to both neo-liberals and neo-conservatives.

Gamble pointed to the comprehensive nature of New Right economics. 'The New Right has set out to change the agenda in economic and social policy. New Right economists argue for market solutions to economic problems and reject governmental ones. Their general catechism – markets good, governments bad – unites all strands of economic liberalism.'[11] Several themes need to be examined.

1. The so-called 'moral' dimension. The market is said to enable the public as consumers to exercise choice and self-reliance, both of which are restricted or eliminated in a planned economy. By fragmenting decision making in the economic sphere, political freedom is guaranteed. Government's sphere of responsibility is limited, the power of politicians to 'interfere' in people's lives is reduced, and government becomes once more responsible for those things which are properly its concern and ceases to be responsible for those things better left to the market and the individual. This link between free-market capitalism and political freedom is a theme joining all the various groups on the New Right, even though the emphasis may differ. Some libertarians go further and argue that, as property rights are absolute, any restriction is illegitimate; at its most extreme, this view argues for a free market in everything, including drugs, pornography and sex. It also means opposing limitations on immigration. Mrs Thatcher had some reservations in these areas.

2. Free-market thinkers are hostile to any government action which goes beyond the basic responsibilities for defence, law and order, and a system of justice which (among other things) guarantees the sanctity of contracts. Most New Right proponents also agree that basic public services must be provided by the state,

though there is much disagreement as to their nature and extent. Anything which restricts competition is attacked as inefficient. Controls are ineffective either because they are evaded or because they produce results less beneficial than their absence. Free markets are more successful than central planning because the central planner will never have as much knowledge as the market and will have no way of knowing whether its planning is efficient or not, because prices are not set by supply and demand. Government intervention is always flawed because the trial-and-error approach of the markets will mean that the best course of action will emerge spontaneously. This approach, known as the Austrian School, is particularly hostile to socialism, which is declared wholly illegitimate, in that it encourages envy among the ignorant and disadvantaged, and ignores the complexity of those institutions which have sustained economic progress.

3. Among free-market liberals, especially those of the so-called 'public choice school' there is distrust of politicians and of the political process generally. Politicians are seen as 'prisoners' of self-interested groups of producers, bureaucrats and pressure groups of every kind; in seeking to satisfy these pressures, often for electoral reasons or in search of financial or other support, they have taken 'popular' decisions which have had adverse economic consequences, such as encouraging inflation. This has had disastrous social consequences. Inflation, for example, is held to benefit some, such as borrowers or members of strong trade unions, at the expense of others, such as lenders, consumers and so on. The public has been encouraged to turn to government in the expectation that every problem will be solved. Government becomes 'overloaded' and cannot cope, and public services are increasingly faced with impossible demands. As expectations grow the capacity to deliver declines, and the system degenerates into chaos. Such was the picture painted of Britain at the time of the 'Winter of Discontent'.

4. With this distrust of the state comes a deep hostility to the Civil Service because its members do not fear redundancy and thus do not need to adapt their practices to the disciplines of the market. It is a powerful group, intent above all on maintaining its own interests; because of its role in policy formulation the bureau-

cracy can ensure that it is protected against the consequences of its own action. Mrs Thatcher had a fierce dislike of the Civil Service partly because she held it largely responsible for a generation of wrong policy advice; the Keynesian consensus suited the bureaucratic mind, with its preference for agreement, compromise and, as she saw it, drift. The 'vested interests' and protected position of civil servants (in terms of index-linked pay and pension arrangements) meant that they were unconcerned about inflation and so resisted efforts of successive governments to bring 'reality' to economic and other policy making. Finally, Mrs Thatcher shared the views of Right-wingers such as Sir John Hoskyns and Sir Alfred Sherman that civil servants generally lacked commitment to free-market ideas and would 'conspire' to prevent their implementation. 'Is he one of us' was said to be the touchstone for advancement in the Civil Service, even though this did not necessarily imply a party-political criterion.

5. Another theme is that of control of the money supply as a weapon in the fight against inflation, although it is important not just as a technical argument but as a way of attacking the whole social democratic consensus. It became more significant after 1972 when most major currencies were 'floated', that is, set free to respond to the pressures of supply and demand, thus greatly strengthening the practical and theoretical case for monetarism. Money supply figures gained greater significance as a sign of the authorities' determination to deal with and control inflation. If the markets felt that inflation was not being tackled with sufficient vigour, the currency concerned would be sold, creating an exchange crisis. 'The rise in influence of monetarism has to be understood against this background. Monetarism would have remained a technical debate among economists if conditions in the world economy had not altered so dramatically in the 1970s and made the control of inflation the top priority for government economic policy.'[12]

Though there are some technical disagreements among monetarists, they agree that politicians have seen increases in the money supply as a way of financing inflationary wage demands or expanding welfare provisions – as a method of 'buying' votes and thus ensuring their continued hold on power. Monetarists generally distrust the role of government in managing the economy and in providing social welfare.

6. Free-market liberals join with neo-conservatives in hostility to the public sector generally (although some areas, such as the police, generally escape). State action is widely seen to have failed when it has replaced the market in delivering services, particularly in health and education. It may also interfere with acts of charity and self-help which are essential aspects of freedom and self-will. This last point was increasingly taken up by the Thatcher administration, especially in social policy when there was an emphasis on 'care in the community' as a way of reducing the role of central and local government and placing the emphasis on the voluntary sector in caring for groups such as the mentally ill, the homeless and the elderly. Critics speculated that this was less a concern for charity than a way of reducing public expenditure.

7. There is a general antipathy towards trade unions. Libertarians dislike what they see as the coercive aspects of trade unionism, such as the closed shop and picketing, while free marketeers see unions as inhibitors and distorters of market forces and as a prime cause of lack of competitiveness, inefficiency, resistance to necessary technological change and of slow economic growth. In addition, both groups dislike the links between the unions and the Labour Party. Free-market proponents have supported legislative curbs on union activity, and also called for more government action to fragment labour markets, by devices such as local as opposed to national pay bargaining. This, they believe, would make for a more flexible labour force and would enable employers to respond more efficiently to economic change.

8. There is suspicion of any attempt to use concepts such as social justice as the basis for policy and especially as a criterion for the distribution of goods and services. While free marketeers support (at least in theory) the idea of equality of opportunity, egalitarian ideas are seen as both unrealistic because inequality is a fact of human existence and undesirable, poverty and insecurity being necessary spurs to effort. Social Darwinism, the survival of the fittest, is a theory which has great attraction for many New Right theorists, as promoting ideas of self-help, self-reliance,

competition and personal responsibility, although most accept the 'safety net' approach to social provision. At least by inference, many New Right thinkers believe that the poor are poor because of some deficiency of character. Gamble pointed out that these ideas are not new and quoted Herbert Spencer, a nineteenth century philosopher: 'Is it not manifest that there must exist in our midst an immense amount of misery which is the normal result of misconduct, and ought not to be dissociated with it.'[13] On the other hand, there is a need to reward the entrepreneur so that the benefits of his (or her) energies 'trickle down' to the less energetic. Taxes must be cut. 'The case for bringing down taxes hinges on the presumed effect of taxes on incentives. The economy, it is suggested, would be much more prosperous if taxes were lower, because individuals would work much harder and high earners would spend less of their energies in finding ways of avoiding paying taxes.'[14]

Summary

This chapter has examined the intellectual changes in the Conservative Party in the 1970s which were the background to the rise of Thatcherism. The tensions between the 'wets' and the 'dries' overshadowed the contradictions inherent in the differing aims of the neo-liberals and the neo-conservatives and help to account for the policy contradictions which became increasingly apparent towards the end of Mrs. Thatcher's time in office. The next chapter will consider Labour's twists and turns of ideology and the attempt of the centre parties to offer a convincing alternative to both major parties.

Notes

1   Leonard Tivey: Economic and Industrial Policy, in Leonard Tivey and Anthony Wright (eds.): *Party Ideology in Britain*, Routledge, 1989, p.134.

2   Robert Blake: *The Conservative Party from Peel to Thatcher*, Fontana, 1985, p.311. 'Dirigisme' means control by the state in the economic and social spheres.

3   Hugo Young and Anne Sloman: *No Minister. An inquiry into the*

Civil Service, BBC, 1982, pp.66–7.

4 Peter Riddell: *The Thatcher Decade*, Blackwell, 1989, p.204, quoting an interview in *The Financial Times*, 19 November 1986.

5 Robert Behrens: Social Democracy and Liberalism, in Tivey and Wright, *Party Ideology in Britain*, p.65.

6 Dennis Kavanagh, *Thatcherism and British Politics. The end of Consensus?*, OUP, 1990, 2nd edn, pp.76ff.

7 Ibid., p.77.

8 Andrew Gamble: The Political Economy of Freedom, in Ruth Levitas (ed.): *The Ideology of the New Right*, Polity, 1986, p.45.

9 Kavanagh, *Thatcherism and British Politics*, p.83.

10 Levitas, *Ideology of the New Right*, p.4.

11 Gamble, Political Economy of Freedom, pp.29–30.

12 Ibid., p.34.

13 Ibid., p.30, quoting Herbert Spencer: *Man versus the State*, Williams and Norgate, 1907.

14 Gamble, Political Economy of Freedom, p.39.

8

Economic policy and the political parties since 1945: Labour and the centre parties

Though the post-war Labour government laid the basis of the Butskellite consensus, the Labour Party became increasingly immersed in an ideological quagmire as it sought to define socialism in an increasingly hostile domestic and international environment. Divisions in the Labour Party provided the opportunity for the revival of centre politics, although the failure to establish an image clearly distinct from the two major parties ended the revival in bitterness and disappointment. This chapter examines the economic ideas of both left-of-centre parties.

The Labour Party

The Labour Party has lacked a clear and consistent creed; Herbert Morrison's statement that 'Socialism is what a Labour Government does' has proved an accurate definition. The founders of the Labour Party reflected many strands in Left-wing politics, from socialists hoping for a transformed society, to the mainly non-socialist trade union leaders, seeking to protect their members' interests. The Labour Party has continued to reflect the differing aspirations of those wishing to bring about a fundamentally different kind of society and those seeking to reform what exists, to make it fairer, juster or more equal. However, the founders of the Labour Party were agreed that capitalism was a socially unjust system which degraded and exploited working people. The 'free' market was in conflict with their ethical position, which saw co-operation as superior to self-interested capitalism. Capitalism produced waste and inefficiency; Fabian socialists in particular thought that rational planning by disinterested experts motivated by the common good would harness the productive capacities of modern science in the interests of society generally. Collectivism, the bringing together of individual talents and energies for the benefit of the community, marked Labour's loose coalition.

Labour and the 'parliamentary road'

Most of the founders agreed that socialism could be achieved through Parliament; thus the 'parliamentary road' has dominated Labour Party thinking and explains the efforts to get rid of Militant and other far-Left elements in recent years. Marxist theories of the class struggle with the state serving the interest of capitalist exploitation of the working class were rejected. The doctrine of the 'neutrality of the state' particularly attracted Fabians, many of whom were employed in the public service. The state could intervene to correct the inequalities and inadequacies of capitalism. Revolution was unnecessary. Since the majority of working men could vote, it was only a matter of time and education before socialism triumphed. However, more radical ideas were not wholly absent; some of the founders *were* Marxists, and particularly in the 1930s and the 1980s Marxism influenced some leading figures and local activists, though the bulk of the party remained unimpressed or hostile.

Until 1918 Labour was of minor significance in Parliament, seen as little more than a trade union pressure group. The socialists were a minority in the party compared to the trade unions, who still retained Liberal sympathies, even if growing progressively disillusioned with the Liberal Party. 'The dominant ideology of the new party was therefore Labourism, a fusion of trade union assumptions concerning the efficacy of free collective bargaining, and the Liberal conviction that parliamentary reforms were all that was required to create a more just society.'[1]

The 1918 constitution

The 1918 constitution gave the Labour Party a socialist basis. This was particularly evident in Clause Four:

To secure for the producers by hand or by brain the full fruits of their industry, and the most equitable distribution thereof that may be possible, upon the basis of the common ownership of the means of production and the best obtainable system of popular administration and control of each industry or service.

Coal, steel, railways and life assurance were to be nationalised, there was to be a mimimium wage and full employment, with heavy taxation of the rich to pay for social welfare and expanded education and culture for the people. But the Labour Party was not converted to socialism and the new constitution gave more power to the unions. This programme – a compromise between Marxism and piecemeal social reform – was the basis of the Labour Party's appeal to the electorate by 1945.

Although theory was increasingly important it did not provide much guidance about how to move towards socialism, and the two minority Labour governments achieved little. The second collapsed in 1931 as the world economy slumped following the 1929 Wall Street Crash. Ramsay MacDonald and his supporters joined the Conservatives and Liberals in a 'National' government; thereafter, MacDonald's 'betrayal' of the Labour Party was a stick with which the Left beat the Right, an issue which re-emerged as many social democrats left the Labour Party in 1981.

Labour was in opposition during the 1930s. Some members, despairing of democratic politics, turned to more extreme solutions of the Left and the Right. But these flirtations only affected a minority; most retained faith in parliamentary insitutions and democratic methods. The 'moderates' dominated policy making, supported by the trade union bloc vote at Annual Conferences and increasingly bolstered by Keynesian theories. Labour played a significant part in the war-time coalition under Churchill, and came to power with both a theoretical understanding of what needed to be done and practical experience of government.

By 1945 Labour's definition of socialism largely centred on the concepts of nationalisation and a virtually all-embracing Welfare

State. Economic planning of the kind envisaged by Keynes, still less that suggested by the Left in the 1930s, was absent from the 1945 manifesto and was only implemented (as far as it ever was) after the economic crisis of 1947. Nationalisation was advocated in terms of social justice and of national reconstruction. 'The industries on the list were generally described as 'basic', and this gave some plausibility to the claim that they would be the means of sustaining, and potentially steering, the rest of the economy.'[2]

Despite some minor differences there was general agreement in the party that economic change and state action had shifted the balance of power away from the employers towards the workers. The Welfare State had produced a system of social welfare which benefited working people and was part of a trend towards a more egalitarian society. This consensus about the nature of the post-war Attlee administration long survived; Aneurin Bevan never disavowed its achievements and even Tony Benn saw it as socialism in action. However, the problems faced by post-war Labour governments highlighted an inherent tension: 'in the very conception of the Labour Party: was it 'socialist' in the sense that it should promote the values and interests of society as a whole, or was it essentially a wing of the Labour movement? The dilemma proved insoluble.'[3]

Revisionism

After 1951 the parliamentary leadership favoured 'consolidation', while the Left viewed the reforms of 1945–51 as the first step in the assault on capitalism. The consolidators (also know as 'revisionists') dominated policy making; they were Keynesians who argued that management of the economy did not necessitate further public ownership. Full employment and greater equality could be achieved by other means, such as progressive taxation. Nationalisation, seen increasingly as an electoral liability, was defended in terms of taking into public ownership industries which were 'letting the nation down' rather than as part of the transition to socialism. They pointed to the dire example of the Soviet bloc, where virtually total economic control was accompanied by tyranny and inequality much more marked than in Western societies. The inefficiency of the 'command systems' was hidden and some on the Left argued that Soviet achievements such as the space programme meant that planned economies were inherently superior to the 'chaos' of Western capitalism.

The collapse of Communist bloc economies in the late 1980s forced a reappraisal of these views.

The leading revisionist thinker was Anthony Crosland[4] whose optimistic analysis was of a post-capitalist Britain, in which the ownership and control of private firms were in separate hands, with the managers, who had replaced shareholders as the predominant force, being concerned with more than profit maximisation and who would work with the state in pursuit of full employment, greater investment and so on. The pre-war capitalist system was gone. There would be a continuous improvement in the material conditions of all sections of society through a healthy 'mixed' economy, while socialism would be achieved through the progressive extension of equality and the eroding of the class system.

The main problem is that revisionism depends on economic growth. High public spending, necessary for the expansion of public services, requires economic growth. A stagnant or sluggish economy leads to resistance to public spending, making the attainment of socialism by consent impossible. The Wilson and Callaghan governments found that mounting economic crisis caused the shelving of reforms. By the time of Crosland's death in 1977 it was clear that his optimism was misplaced: the economy had ceased to grow, while taxpayers resisted efforts to redistribute wealth towards the less well-off and criticised the scale and nature of public spending.

The Left's critique

Aneurin Bevan became the spokesman for the Left. Though he accepted that the post-war government had achieved amazing results he did not agree that socialism had been achieved; he argued that much had to be done to eradicate capitalist exploitation of working people. Public ownership was essential to ensure that democracy became real and not just a slogan. It was only the first step towards socialism, though all-important, for without it the conditions for further progress would not be established. He said those who favoured a reduction of public ownership were frightened by the administrative problems involved, and he advocated greater industrial democracy as a way of dealing with poor labour relations in the nationalised industries.

However, the socialist aim of producing a society marked by wider choice and greater responsibility became the hallmark of the revisionists with their support for a mixed economy; the Left became increasingly defensive and in asserting the need for greater public ownership seemed out of touch with social and economic developments.

After 1959 the main emphasis was on modernising Labour's

appeal to take account of the 'affluent society' and working class aspirations. Hugh Gaitskell sought to reform the structure and policies of the party, following the example of the West German Social Democratic Party, which, in the Bad Gödesberg programme, had thrown off the last vestiges of Marxism. He sought to remove Clause Four from the constitution but underestimated the strength of symbols and the attachment of several unions to public ownership. The attempt to produce a new ideological basis failed; Wilson's stress on technological innovation and economic modernisation was sufficiently vague to appeal to almost all factions. However, it lacked both reality and intellectual rigour and left Labour struggling during the 1970s.

Wilson's modernisation strategy emphasised that the main task was to restore a sense of purpose by harnessing science to the service of the British people; the 'white heat of technology' was the road to economic and social progress. Planning was the centre piece of the policy, while the importance of public ownership was down graded. But as economic difficulties mounted pragmatism replaced socialism and both revisionist and fundamentalists became disillusioned and disoriented. Growing strains appeared in the party. Although by 1970 some of the economic problems had been dealt with, the sense of disappointment and betrayal felt by many ensured that the Left gained the initiative.

Revisionism in retreat

The confusion on the Right put public ownership back on the agenda. *Labour's Programme 1973* argued that the experience of Labour in government had made it evident that even the most comprehensive measures of reform could only succeed in masking the 'unacceptable and unpleasant' face of capitalism and could not achieve any fundamental changes in the power relationships dominating society. The Left's solution, the Alternative Economic Strategy, called for a major programme of nationalisation, including the 25 largest companies (a proposal vetoed by Wilson in February 1974), the imposition of statutory planning agreements with private industry, selective import controls, considerably increased public expenditure and higher taxation of the wealthy, including a wealth tax. The February 1974 manifesto called for 'a fundamental and irreversible shift in the balance of power and wealth in favour of working people and their families'.

The disillusion with the record of the 1964–70 government led many individual members to leave the party and contributed to its enfeeblement as an electoral force; many of those who stayed tried to ensure that Conference decisions, increasingly influenced by the Left, would be implemented by the parliamentary leadership. The same phenomenon can be seen following the downfall of the revisionist Callaghan government; this time constituency activists were joined by many trade unionists who felt betrayed by his call for continued wage restraint despite the sacrifices which they felt they had made to ensure the success of the Social Contract. It was widely felt that a Labour government had attempted to deal with a stagnant economy and high inflation by kow-towing to international bankers at the expense of its own supporters, the working class. The Left argued that by attempting to prove its fitness to govern by adopting orthodox economic policies, Labour had subordinated working class interests to capitalism. 'Labourism' or 'gradualism', the idea that socialism could come via the 'parliamentary road', was seen as a way of diverting the working class from the path of radical (and possibly revolutionary) political change. 'In a sense the 1974–9 government represented the triumph of the social democrats. There was precious little fundamentalist socialism involved in its legislative programme. Its *raison d'etre* was social democratic and it failed comprehensively on its own terms. No small wonder that the fundamentalists thought that enough was enough.'[5]

Tony Benn headed a disparate coalition of Left-wing groups to argue both for a return to socialist policies and for reforms in party organisation which would make Labour MPs responsible to (or, as critics put it, subordinate to) the extra-parliamentary party so that Conference decisions would be implemented, both in government and in opposition.

During the 1970s, and especially following the abolition of the proscribed list in 1973 (this was a list of far-Left groups, mostly Marxist or Trotskyite, membership of which was incompatible with membership of the Labour Party) there was a revival of Marxist thinking in the Labour Party. The Tribune Group, which had followed Bevan in the 1950s, grew in size but also became more fragmented. The Labour Co-ordinating Committee and similar groups became briefly of greater significance, developing a whole range of alternative strategies. After 1979 Benn rejected both the monetarism of the Thatcher government and the corporatism of the Wilson–Callaghan era, putting forward a package of what he called 'democratic socialism' and leading the battle for changes to policy and organisation.

For a while Benn led a coalition of groups against the parliamentary leadership. However, there was tension between those who stressed that the way to socialism was through greater participation and the kind of grass-roots democracy which had been pioneered by the Liberal Party in the 1970s and those, like Militant, who demanded widespread nationalisation and increased state power over the economy generally as the road forward; though both perspectives were agreed in rejecting the 'parliamentary road' to socialism, they were agreed on little else. The tendency of the Left to fragment could not be overcome simply by opposition to revisionism.

The 1983 election manifesto, *The New Hope For Britain*, restated Labour's commitment to the Alternative Economic Strategy and the policies adopted at Conference. This manifesto, which Labour MP Peter Shore called 'the longest suicide note in history', summed up for many Labour members and voters all that had gone wrong over the past few years; the Left was blamed for one of the most humiliating results for Labour in its history. The Left fragmented, and many on what came to be called the 'Soft' Left joined with the Centre-Right to mount a counterattack against the Bennites and the various groups which had entered the party in the previous decade. Neil Kinnock of the Soft Left was elected leader in the place of the discredited Michael Foot, while Roy Hattersly, a leading revisionist, became deputy leader. Then began the search for an alternative to Thatcherism which would be electorally popular and which would carry conviction as a restatement of the aims of the Labour Party. A purge began of far-Left elements, symbolised by the struggle against the Militant

infiltration of the Liverpool Labour Party, seen by the parliamentary leadership as a necessary cleansing operation and by elements
of the Left as a form of McCarthyism, aimed more at bolstering
Labour's image of respectability than at building socialism.

The emphatic defeat suffered in the 1987 election, all the more
bitter because of the progress made in refurbishing Labour's
tattered image, did not lead to a prolonged process of
recrimination. Instead, in the search for electoral success, two
documents were issued: *Statement of Democratic Socialist Aims and
Values and Social Justice and Economic Efficiency*.

Labour's policy review

The 1987 Conference agreed to a thorough review of policies
which would put forward a clear alternative to Thatcherism and
demonstrate Labour's commitment to a positive conception of
freedom, giving people the economic and political strength to
assert their rights.

A number of policy groups were established. The group which
considered the economy stated that the market had a central place
in satisfying consumer demands; the state, however, had a major
role in ensuring competitive success by providing training,
research and long-term investment. Public ownership was still
part of Labour's policy, but each case should be judged on its
merits. 'Central to the reports is that Labour should be a party of
economic efficiency as much as of social justice and that state
intervention should be justified on both these grounds.
Thatcherism is condemned not only for being morally wrong but
also for being economically inefficient.'[6] The review was conducted under conditions which ensured a firm grip for the leadership; Kinnock had a major imput into the process, guiding it to an
acceptance both of the market economy and the altered class
structure. The general aim was to demonstrate Labour's changed
ideological image. 'The success of the moderate democratic
socialism espoused by Kinnock is threatened by the image of
extremism portrayed by some Labour activists. Similarly, a party
which claims to represent the interests of the consumer cannot be

seen to be dominated by the organisations representing the producers.'[7]

The diminished significance of the Left was demonstrated at
the 1988 conference when Benn challenged Kinnock for the
leadership, while Eric Heffer and John Prescott stood against
Hattersley. The Left argued that 'the priority for the Labour party
was to be as unbending in support of the interests of the class it
represented as the Conservatives were in support of the class they
represented. Only in this way would it continue to advance and
win support around a programme of radical economic and social
change.'[8] However, Conference gave the challengers an emphatic
thumbs-down. Their poor showing demonstrated the extent of
the decline of the Left; Kinnock's leadership was consolidated.

The policy review culminated in a document entitled *Meet the
challenge Make the change. A new agenda for Britain*, published in
July 1989. It criticised the Tory government and Thatcher for
neglecting social values. It maintained that the state in the hands
of the Tories is intrusive and centralising where it should hold
back, and passive and neglectful where it should protect and
enable. Labour promised what it called the 'enabling state', which
would be an instrument for creating opportunities and advancing
the freedom of the individual and, cumulatively, of the whole
community.

Turning to the economy, the Thatcher government was
attacked for failing to tackle the 'fundamental weaknesses' of the
British economy. Labour realised that improving the quality of
people's lives depends largely on generating the wealth necessary
to pay for it. That, in turn, depends upon success in achieving greater competitiveness. This was to be emphasised by
spokesmen in an effort to counteract Conservative attacks on what
they said would be the economic consequences of a Labour
government. There was a lively debate on Labour's taxation
policies. The Conservative attack concentrated on the cost of the
programme and its effects on taxpayers, while Labour emphasised
that 'it would not spend what it did not earn'. Though Labour
promised greater social justice than the Tories, it was at pains to
emphasise that it would put economic efficiency ahead of greater
equality.

The report went on to attack the Conservatives for imagining that the market could solve every problem and advocated what it called 'supply-side socialism'. The economic role of modern government is to help make the market system work properly, and to replace or strengthen it where it is deficient. Labour would create the conditions whereby enterprises could be more successful and competitive, but where they would fulfil their obligations to their workers, the consumers and the environment. It attacked the 'short-termism' of the Conservatives, accused of having produced an unsustainable consumer boom, which had to be corrected by severely deflationary policies. Labour advocated macro-economic policy which would serve Britain's general economic and industrial objectives. Reliance on interest and exchange rates would end, and there would be an emphasis on sustaining and encouraging the competitiveness of British industry in international markets.

The question of public ownership was addressed. The policy review had rejected the Morrisonian model on the grounds that its bureaucratic structure excluded worker participation and diminished the interests of the consumer. While asserting that 'natural monopolies' such as water and electricity should remain in 'social ownership and control', the report recognised that the rigid boundaries between the public and private sectors had dissolved, leading to a new mix of public and private enterprise.

The report was accepted by the 1989 Party Conference. Public reaction, as measured by polls (but also by Labour's much improved showing in by-elections, local elections and the 1989 Euro-election) was generally favourable, though concern was expressed about Labour's ability to deliver economic growth and a future Labour government's domination by the unions. It was no coincidence that Kinnock embarked on a campaign to reduce the role of the affiliated unions in Labour's policy making process. The Left attacked the whole exercise, and in a meeting in Chesterfield (Benn's constituency) reasserted its belief in fundamentalism, including taking major companies into public ownership and withdrawal from the EC.

In May 1990 the Labour Party published *Looking to the Future*, claimed as an agenda for government. It 'was aimed at reassuring voters that Labour would handle the economy prudently, limit income tax increases only to the better-off and not spend wildly'.[9] Labour promised not to spend more than the country could afford, and committed itself to achieving the highest possible levels of employment rather than promising to restore full employment. There was a greater emphasis on the role of private investors, who would be encouraged to join the public sector in financing infrastructure projects. Labour's plans for common ownership were re-emphasised and there were promises that although some of what were regarded as 'unfair' restrictions on trade unions would be removed, there would be no return to the pattern of industrial relations which had cost Labour so dear in the past. The rights that would be given to the unions would be exercised peacefully and fairly. *Looking to the Future* also reasserted Labour's increased commitment to Europe, already spelled out in the 1989 document.

The review exercise has produced much debate about the nature and extent of Labour's changed ideological stance and about its chance of winning the support of the electorate. John Callaghan, commenting on Labour's rejection of 'the intrusive state' in favour of 'the enabling state' pointed out 'it is a state . . . which will have all the old problems to contend with – many of them reminiscent of Wilson's project of modernization from the early 1960s – in a context where socialist programmes which are purely national are severely constrained by the more integrated global economy of the present, and where old forms of state intervention command less popular support and intellectual credibility'.[10]

A criticism of the ideological shift of the review came from Tudor Jones. He attacked 'the virtual abandonment of Labour's traditional commitment to public ownership and of its antipathy towards a market economy'.[11] Jones believed that since 1918 public ownership had been central to Labour's thinking, pro-grammes and strategy, the main strand of its socialist ideology, a vision of the Socialist Commonwealth. He criticised previous revisionist attempts to downgrade or eradicate the concept of public ownership and argued against Kinnock's 'second-stage' revisionism on two grounds. The first, while paying tribute to

Kinnock's courage in challenging entrenched Labour assumptions, doubted Kinnock's own commitment to such revisionist ideas. Jones saw Kinnock as more a traditionalist than a moderniser, with his roots in the distinctive culture, ethos and language of the Labour movement. The second reason involved the mass membership; Jones doubted whether they had undergone a mass conversion to the market economy. The goal of a transformation of society, with public ownership as an essential element, still commands widespread support among the active party membership. Jones' conclusion was that 'Labour's overriding aim has . . . been both moral and economic – the gradual replacement of capitalism by an economically, socially and morally superior alternative.'[12]

This view was countered by Raymond Plant who pointed out, firstly, that the revisionist assumptions of Crosland and others had foundered in the 1970s with the crisis brought on by the quadrupling of oil prices. This led to 'the loss of intellectual confidence in the assumptions of what might be called postwar Keynesian social democracy on which the Labour Party had in practice built its policies'.[13] Secondly, the Left's solutions have been eroded, partly by changes to the class structure and partly because of the impact of events in Eastern Europe. It no longer made sense to see the Labour Party as part of the class struggle, defending the working class and seeking more planning and public ownership of the economy. Plant pointed out that Labour, especially at the time of the 1983 election, had seemed a prisoner to a coalition of interest groups and that the wider public interests had been ignored. His conclusion was that 'the policy review is in many ways an attempt to bring the official outlook of the party into line with what has been the dominant form of its political practice in the postwar world, while at the same time recognising that the growth of individualism and affluence requires a different approach to the public sector than that which prevailed in the 1960s'.[14]

Despite Labour's lead in the polls during 1990 and 1991 voters still had reservations about Labour's competence in office. Voters judge competence largely in economic terms; governments which go to the polls during a boom tend to win another term of office, while those which face election in a time of economic difficulty gain a reputation for incompetence which may be hard to live down. 'British governments from 1955 to 1987 have been re-elected on the strength of falling commodity prices and the resulting boom in real incomes more often than on the strength of anything for which they could decently take credit.'[15] The aims of the Labour Party are still equality and the eradication of poverty and want, though the new emphasis is on a much more decentralised political system, designed to disperse power throughout the community. 'The key issue is how this project can be achieved in an economy increasingly susceptible to decisions taken beyond its shores, and in a party where ideological coherence is notoriously difficult to achieve.'[16]

The centre parties and the economy

The Liberal Party

Liberalism as a set of political ideas developed during the eighteenth and nineteenth centuries. It stressed government by the consent of the governed, the end to the privileges of the aristocracy and the church, freedom of thought and expression and, above all, the freedom of the individual, especially in economic affairs. The state should not obstruct individuals in search of their own economic advantage, except in so far as it was necessary in the common good. 'In classical liberalism, the more the individual received free scope for the play of his faculties, the more rapidly would society advance. In this view, unrestricted competition was the mainspring of progress. At home an existing harmony of interests required only limited government to maintain order, enforce contracts, and protect individual property rights.'[17] The harmony of interests would be ensured by Adam Smith's 'Invisible Hand'.

By the end of the nineteenth century tension grew between those Liberals who clung to orthodox ideas of individualism, free trade and minimal government, and those attracted to what came to be called the 'New Liberalism'. This accepted that the state had both social and economic obligations to the people at large and that government should be more active in tackling poverty, unemployment and so on. The 1906 Liberal government introduced a programme of interventionist legislation, including old age pensions, insurance against unemployment, sickness and industrial injury, the establishment of labour exchanges, and some limited redistribution of wealth from the rich to the poor.

During the First World War the party split; the damage done put it on a downward spiral of decline until the 1960s. During the 1920s and 1930s much of its support went either to Labour or to the Conservatives. David Lloyd George, the party leader, was influenced by Keynes, and in 1928 the Liberal Party issued the *Yellow Book*, which advocated government planning and a public works programme to deal with unemployment. Another leading Liberal, Lord Beveridge, produced the report on which the Welfare State was constructed after the Second World War. Thus two of the major planks of the post-war settlement were the work of Liberals, while the party itself almost disappeared from the political scene in the 1950s; a case of lots of chiefs but few Indians.

After 1945, the Liberals sought an economic policy which would reflect the acceptance of state action in economic management, while preserving the role of the individual as much as possible. This reflected liberalism's emphasis on the individual, while taking account of the realities of the modern world and the divided nature of the Liberal Party itself, containing as it did both those who hankered for minimal government and the inheritors of the 'New Liberalism' of the early twentieth century. It was also an expression of the need to try to distinguish the Liberal Party from its two larger rivals. The electorate, though favourably inclined to its moderate, centrist image, found it difficult to identify anything that was distinctively Liberal. Most of its support in this period, at least outside pockets of traditional Liberalism in Scotland, Wales and the West Country, was essentially negative. The Liberal Party tended to pick up protest or tactical votes at by-elections, which it was unable to translate into votes or seats at general elections.

Thus the Liberal Party gave general support to the mixed economy with a role for both public and private enterprise and government planning, supported by a prices and incomes policy, but tended to be suspicious both of nationalised industries and of large corporations. Liberals found it difficult to adjust to the increasingly important role played by the unions and called for co-ownership of industry, with workers sharing responsibility with management. Profit sharing would increase the involvement felt by workers in the running of their enterprises. Liberals believed that although the market offered advantages to too few people, it was the most efficient and democratic way of running the economy. Excessive inequalities should be reduced through co-ownership and partnership in industry (though not by nationalisation), and there should be a wider spread of private wealth and property. From early on, the Liberals advocated British membership of the EEC which they believed would re-vitalise the British economy. It was also seen as a move towards free trade, which had been a Liberal rallying cry in the nineteenth century and something to which most Liberals had clung during the first half of the twentieth century.

The Liberal Party also evolved a critique of the constitutional structure of the United Kingdom; it came to believe, especially in the 1970s, that Britain was over-governed from London. In calling for devolution to Scotland and Wales (with England following suit later), and for the decentralisation of power generally, the Liberal Party suggested that this would help to regenerate economic growth, especially outside the relatively prosperous south east. People would become more responsible for the success of their region and of their firm. 'Small is beautiful' was a slogan of the 1970s with which most Liberals easily identified.

The Social Democratic Party

The emergence of the Social Democratic Party (SDP) and the subsequent alliance with the Liberal Party was welcomed by David Steel as the chance to 'break the mould' of British politics. In a party political broadcast on 28 August 1981 he hailed it as a great new political alliance which would make the mixed economy work and turn the country back from the long record of division and decline.

The appearance of the SDP early in 1981 was the product of a combination of factors. One was the growing division in the Labour Party. The second was the existence of the Liberal Party; social democrats in the Labour Party felt that some kind of alliance could prove electorally popular. Thus to split from Labour would mean not political extinction but the opportunity to offer to the electorate the kind of Butskellite policies which they had supported but which were under threat as Labour moved to the Left. Finally, the Conservative government was deeply unpopular; the monetarist experiment was producing results which the electorate found unacceptable. The Alliance quickly overtook both its main rivals in the polls and won some spectacular by-election victories; by the end of 1981 almost half of those questioned said they would vote for Alliance candidates at the next election.

Yet it was the divisions in the Labour Party which most explain the emergence of the SDP, and the growing split over economic policy had a major part to play. Following the 1979 election the Left, led by Benn, began an assault on the mixed economy; this, and the growing pressure for organisational changes aimed at reducing or eliminating the primacy of the parliamentary party in policy making, alarmed many social democrats, who saw this as more than a matter of intra-party democracy. The mixed economy, with its commitment to political pluralism and individual liberty, was in danger.

Another major source of division was Europe. Social democrats in the Labour Party, with few exceptions, were passionately committed to British membership, while the Left was opposed. A symbol of the growing gulf was the decision of Roy Jenkins to leave British politics to become President of the EEC Commission. His conviction grew that the two-party system had become frozen and lifeless and was in large part to blame for many of Britain's economic problems. When he returned to Britain in 1979 he developed his ideas. His view of the role of the state, especially in the running of the economy, was close to Liberal thinking. He argued that the free market was important in providing economic growth. The state, which 'must know its place', would intervene to avoid gross inequalities and indifference to unemployment. Similarly, market forces were insufficient left to themselves.

At the time of the founding of the SDP the 'Gang of Four' (Roy Jenkins, David Owen, Shirley Williams and Bill Rogers) expressed their continued adherence to democratic socialism saying that it was the Labour Party which had left them, rather than the other way round. The Limehouse Declaration which announced the founding of the SDP called for a mix of private and public sector in the running of the economy. But in the months which followed, their praise of democratic socialism quickly ceased; in a number of ways, particularly in terms of economic policy, there was a distinct move to the Right.

The early emphasis on greater equality soon faded. The Alliance manifestos for the 1983 and 1987 general elections aimed to revive the economy without changing the balance between the public and the private sectors. The 1983 manifesto, 'Working together for Britain', called for a programme of selective increases in public investment to reduce unemployment by one million in two years. There would be 'a fair and effective pay and prices policy', accompanied by action to limit the power of the unions. There would be no further nationalisation and no further denationalisation. In 1987 the manifesto, 'Britain United. The time has come' said that in three years an Alliance government would reduce unemployment by one million. The emphasis would be on targeting resources on output and exports and by what was called an 'incomes strategy'. There was a commitment to join the EMS with the aim of achieving currency stability. Privatisation was viewed more favourably and there were calls for greater union democracy, much along the lines being followed by the Conservatives. The Alliance stressed themes such as profit-sharing, employee share-ownership and works councils as ways of promoting partnership in industry.

The social market

David Owen became leader of the SDP after the 1983 general election. It was the adoption of what was called the 'social market' strategy which marked a decisive shift to the Right in SDP policy; this was to be a significant factor in the break-up of the Alliance after the 1987 election. The 'social market' is a rather complex concept, meaning several different things when seen from different political perspectives. The term originated among German liberals in the nineteenth century to denote support for a *strong* state which would favour a market economy of small property owners. After 1945 it became the expression of the economic policies of the Christian Democratic Party; in turn it was adopted by the

West German Social Democrats to signify their acceptance of competition and rejection of Marxism. After 1975 the Thatcher/Joseph wing of the Conservative Party took up the theme; finally Owen adopted it as part of his 'tough and tender' approach (when critics dubbed him 'Thatcher with Brylcream').

The market is accepted as the most efficient method of allocating resources and running the economy; the basic institutions of a market economy, in particular private ownership of the means of production, would be protected. Central planning of the economy is rejected. But beyond this there is much disagreement about the scope of market forces and the limits on government intervention. The mainstream New Right in Britain largely limit market forces to the operation of the economy; libertarian New Right ideas about extending the concept to the fullest possible extent, including legalising drugs and the sale of human organs, have been rejected. 'The family, national defence and traditional morality remain protected domains from which the corrosive power of markets is to be excluded.'[18]

Social democrats broadly accepted that market principles should apply in the private sector of the economy, but believed that the state had a significant role in services such as education and health (though increasingly they accepted private health and private education, a far cry from the demands for greater equality of the early days).

However, Owen and his followers seemed increasingly to lean in a Thatcherite direction regarding the efficacy of the market. Owen believed that the disciplines of the market were necessary in order to achieve industrial competitiveness. Echoing Jenkins, Owen called for more restraint from the state whose task was to assist the market by encouraging technological adaptation and skills-training, and by exposing as much as possible of the public sector to the market. Those less able to help themselves in a competitive market would be helped, though it was important to do this without stifling initiative or imposing a centralized bureaucracy. Owen proposed a targeted social policy that would improve the prospects of the worst-off without aiming to level down society or to provide services on a universal basis. This is the nearest the Alliance got to developing a distinctive theme, in that its combination of market liberalism and egalitarian social policy expressed the 'tough and tender' approach. However, this combination, especially with increasingly minimised 'egalitarianism', was a source of division rather then unity. The SDP came increasingly to resemble a 'one-man band' and a vehicle for Owen's policies and ambitions, and the social market approach symbolised the divided state of the party and of the Alliance. Owen's support for a nuclear defence strategy and for the market meant that he increasingly seemed to favour an accommodation with Thatcher should an election produce a 'hung' Parliament, whereas Steel seemed more to favour other strategies.

As the 1987 election approached, criticism of Owen grew (though largely in private). In the SDP supporters of Roy Jenkins, who had been leader from the founding of the party until after the 1983 election, criticised the excessive market-orientation of Owen. They favoured a genuinely mixed economy in which there would be state intervention to direct market forces to the public good. Jenkins and his supporters stressed the need to offer a distinctive alternative to Thatcherism and criticised Owen for drawing attention to what they regarded as 'minute' policy differences with the Liberals. Owen, aiming to avoid a fusion with the Liberals, took every opportunity to emphasise the distinctiveness of the SDP. Liberals increasingly distrusted both Owen's style – increasingly charismatic and intolerant of diverging views – and some of his policies, especially on defence and the market. Owen's readiness to do a deal with Thatcher was particularly repugnant.

The Liberal Democrats

These factors combined to produce a deeply disappointing result in 1987. Within a few days Steel called for a 'democratic fusion' between the two parties. Owen continued to argue for a partnership of separate parties. Amidst intense recrimination the merger battle began which resulted in a split in the SDP. Many members opted for a new grouping; a minority remained in a rump SDP under Owen's leadership. Many others, disillusioned with the whole process, left politics altogether.

The Social and Liberal Democratic Party (SLDP) emerged in March 1988. In agreeing to merge 'Liberals said goodbye to the historic Liberal Party, and Social Democrats rejected a narrower commitment to redefine social market ideas ambiguous in their relationship to Thatcherism because of their emphasis on market-led recovery.'[19] Shirley Williams had already drawn attention to the need to moderate Owen's emphasis on the social market when she called for measures to protect weaker groups in society and to hold private sector companies to account for their actions. She stressed the continuing need for public provision in areas such as health and education and pointed out that private sector mono-polies are not necessarily subject to market disciplines. The welfare of workers and the need for long-term investment in industry were also important factors in economic prosperity which might be sacrificed by market forces.

The first leader of the SLDP, Paddy Ashdown, was faced with the task of asserting its primacy in the centre of British politics. At the 1988 conference he called for 'enhanced citizenship', which would give 'real choice' by setting a minimum income and defining access to education, housing and health care. He attacked what he saw as the 'myth' of the economic miracle claimed by the Prime Minister; Britain was faced with the decline into a third rate, uncompetitive economy, whose main function was to assemble goods made elsewhere.

At the 1990 Conference Ashdown stressed his faith in the free market and promised to break up the privatised monopolies created by the Thatcher government. He claimed that the Liberal Democrats wanted to open up the economic system, and called for choice, competition, quality and enterprise to be the cornerstones of economic policy. He urged that market mechanisms be increasingly used in the provision of services such as health and education, with the aim of government becoming 'enablers' not providers and regulators.

The Liberal Democrats' policy stance was left of centre; the aim was still to replace Labour as the alternative to Thatcherism. With Labour's move back to the centre, and despite the announcement by Owen of the winding-up of the SDP in 1990, this aspiration seemed doomed to follow the other attempts to 'break the mould'.

Summary

The last two chapters have traced the changing relationship between party ideology and attitudes to the economy since 1945. In the Labour Party the dominance of revisionism was challenged in the 1980s but then made a recovery in the guise of what might be called Kinnockism. Similarly, 'One Nation' Tory paternalism suffered a rude assault from the economic liberals, led by Mrs Thatcher and her supporers, 'red in tooth and claw'. Yet in many respects, Major's political attitudes seem to hark back to a more consensual age. This change in the political atmosphere will be examined in the Conclusion.

Notes

1   John Callaghan: The Left: The Ideology of the Labour Party, in Leonard Tivey and Anthony Wright (eds.): *Party Ideology in Britain*, Routledge, 1989, p.25.

2   Leonard Tivey: Economic and Industrial Policy, in Tivey and Wright, *Party Ideology in Britain*, p.132.

3   Ibid., p.134.

4   C.A.R. Crosland: *The Future of Socialism*, Cape, 1956.

5   Stephen Ingle: *The British Party System*, Blackwell, 1989, 2nd ed., p.119.

6   Robert Garner: Modernisation and the Policy Review: The Labour Party Since the 1987 Election, *Talking Politics*, Vol. 1, No. 3, Summer 1989, p.102.

7   Ibid., p.103.

8   Andrew Gamble: The Future of the Labour Party, *Talking Politics*, Vol. 2, No. 2, Winter 1989/90, p.68.

9   *The Independent*, 25 May 1990.

10   Callaghan, in Tivey and Wright, *Party Ideology in Britain*, p.46.

11   *Contemporary Record*, Vol. 3, No. 2, November 1989, p.6.

12   Ibid., p.7.

13   Ibid., p.8.

14   Ibid.

15   Alan Ryan: Party Ideologies Since 1945, in Anthony Seldon (ed): *UK Political Parties Since 1945*, Philip Allan, 1990, p.84.

16   Callaghan, in Tivey and Wright, *Party Ideology in Britain*, p.46.

17   Behrens, in Tivey and Wright, *Party Ideology in Britain*, p.80.

18   Gamble, in Ruth Levitas (ed.), *The Ideology of the New Right*, Polity, 1986, p.51.

19   Behrens, in Tivey and Wright, *Party Ideology in Britain*, p.95.

Part Four

Corporatism

9

The role of unions in British politics

This chapter and the next examine the place of trade unions and business groups in the post-war British economy. 'Corporatism' or 'tripartism' arouses much controversy.[1] Debate exists about whether and to what extent corporatism as a description of post-war policy making actually existed. Some deny that anything even remotely like a corporatist state existed in Britain in this period; this debate concerns definitions and will be examined later. At another level, the merits of corporatism as a model of economic policy making and as a method of conducting the business of government generally are disputed. Before 1979 organised interests such as unions and employers' organisations had a significant role in policy making. The decline of this relationship will also be examined.

Introduction

During the 1960s and the early 1970s a close relationship between government and powerful interests such as unions was thought essential. However, since the general turning-away from the economic role of government, corporatist-style planning has declined. The Thatcher government claimed to keep pressure groups at arm's length. In 1986 Home Secretary Douglas Hurd called them 'strangling serpents' that distorted the relationship between government, Parliament and the electorate, making it more difficult for ministers to take decisions in the 'public interest'. Mrs Thatcher was less committed to consultation and consensus-building than any post-war Prime Minister and largely ignored both the TUC *and* the CBI. But this picture is over-simplified, and the relationship between government and organised interests is complex.

Corporatism

Although the concept has a number of meanings[2] in this context it refers to the state working with significant interest groups in making economic and possibly other forms of policy. This has been labelled neo-corporatism or tripartism, 'A system, usually Liberal-Democratic, in which the Government has formal links with both the owners of industry and commmerce and with the trade unions. The "Tripartite" bodies which are established then assist the Government in policy-making.'[3]

Co-operation between government, the employers and the unions in many aspects of economic organisation grew during the Second World War, but declined after 1945, although both sides of industry continued to be consulted about various aspects of policy making and their co-operation sought when necessary. By the late 1950s, however, the view gained ground that some institutional structure was required to deal with growing economic problems.

The NEDC began an experiment in planning which was briefly part of the political consensus. There were several aspects.

1. It aimed to achieve a more efficient economic system.
2. It was part of a deeper concern that political institutions such as Parliament were failing to achieve social harmony or to represent adequately important interests in society.
3. Trade union power was growing as full employment and an expanding economy allowed employers to grant wage increases and other concessions which previously they would have resisted. Union members were less willing to accept calls for restraint by their leaders; the 'never had it so good' syndrome was beginning to have an effect on the behaviour of

workers.

4. The employers were comparatively unorganised, leading to problems in responding to government policies on investment, regional planning and so on, as well as in co-ordinating action to deal with the unions. The establishment in February 1965 of the CBI, which merged the main employers' federations, was in part the result of this perceived need for greater unity.

Thus corporatism was not just about the economic system; it also reflected a view of the nature of society itself, in which there was both a premium on co-operation and a realisation that unity meant strength and isolation weakness.

Corporatism: the arguments

Corporatism involves a particular kind of relationship between organised groups, particularly economic interests, and the state. Decisions are made through consultation and negotiation between the various interests, with government being only one element in the process. To a degree government gives up its claim to primacy, to being the authoritative allocator of values and resources; instead, it becomes one of several sources of power and influence, bargaining with other powerful groups in an effort to achieve its ends. This is but one aspect of corporatism which has attracted the anger of the New Right, dedicated simultaneously to reducing the role of the government in economic management and increasing its authority over subordinate groups.

Corporatism requires the existence of a range of governmental and other institutions through which negotiation can proceed. This has led to a number of criticisms.

1. During the 1960s and 1970s critics said that Parliament was being bypassed, that vitally important economic and social decisions were being made by government and representatives of powerful pressure groups in virtual secrecy, perhaps over 'beer and sandwiches in No. 10'. Parliament had become virtually a formality, with MPs deprived of influence and left to 'rubber-stamp' decisions. An example was the bargain struck by Healey and the TUC in 1976, when in return for TUC

acceptance of a pay policy, tax allowances were raised to increase take-home pay in the hope of avoiding inflation.
2. That various powerful and well-organised groups become too powerful and gain privileged access to the decision making process. A cosy relationship exists between government and groups to the detriment of the public interest. Both sides expect to benefit: the groups expect access to the policy makers to ensure their own interests, whilst the government expects to gain the co-operation and consent of groups and help in implementing decisions, some of which may be repugnant to the ordinary members of the group concerned. Some critics have explained the failure of prices and incomes policy in these terms.

Some Right-wing commentators attacked corporatism for delivering government into the hands of powerful economic interests, rendering it powerless to assert a common interest in the face of greedy and unrepresentative cliques. The unions have been seen as the prime culprit, although employers' organisations (especially the CBI) have been attacked for their role in de-legitimising government. Left-wing critics saw corporatism as subordinating unions to governments, both Labour and Conservative, intent on imposing incomes policies which bolstered capitalism by depressing wages. Thus, corporatism was a kind of conspiracy against the interests of the working class.

The Social Contract illustrates these various criticisms of corporatism. It seemed that major economic interests were becoming part of the economic policy making process, while also providing evidence that government was becoming too reliant upon them for the success of its strategy. Alternatively, the Left saw it as another act of betrayal by the Labour leadership, intent on asserting its 'respectability' and reassuring foreign financial interests by disciplining the workers. Corporatism was associated with incomes policy, which needed the active co-operation of both unions and employers. The weakness of the TUC and the CBI, however, meant that both 'lacked the authority to ensure that their members complied with agreements arrived at with government. All too often, it looked as if legislative concessions were being given, particularly to the unions under Labour, in return for promises of cooperation which turned out to be of little value.'[4]

Although corporatism has fallen out of favour, it can be defended.

1. The representation of important groups is inevitable. Most individuals are represented through membership of various groups, and their interests are more effectively secured by such membership.
2. Because governments need the co-operation of important groups, they have to remain constantly responsive to the wishes of significant sections of society; they cannot simply win power in an election and then ignore the public until the next election.
3. Parties need programmes which will gain the support of a wide coalition of interests and so are less likely to become prisoners of their most extreme activists. Thus moderation goes hand in hand with practicality.
4. Whatever the ideology of particular governments, the complexity of modern economic systems means that the co-operation of significant interests is required though the interests consulted will differ according to the political complexion of the government and the circumstances of the time. The hostility of the Thatcher government to the unions was aided by mass unemployment; the weakness of the unions both permitted and ensured their exclusion from power. Similarly, government policy towards manufacturing meant that the CBI lacked sufficient political 'clout' to ensure attention.

Some deny that 'corporatism' had any real meaning in post-war British politics. Wyn Grant, while agreeing that such tendencies existed in the 1960s and 1970s, believed their impact was exaggerated, being related to the special political and social attitudes of the time.

Corporatism since 1979

Mrs Thatcher was hostile to corporatism for a number of reasons.

1. Government should provide leadership towards clearly stated

goals, not to attempt to bring about some kind of consensus (seen as the negation of honesty and consistency of purpose) between producer groups more concerned with self-interest than with the general good.

2. She saw corporatism, involving incomes policy, economic planning, conciliation of groups (particularly the unions) and so on, as interference in the free play of market forces and the enemy of economic 'realism'. Far from being the *solution* to Britain's economic ills, corporatism was a central part of the *problem*.

The reaction against corporatism has also affected the opposition. Labour rejects incomes policies and detailed economic planning, and the relationship between a future Labour government and the unions will probably lack the closeness of the past. Labour's policy review acknowleged that in the past the party was identified with the producers; it promised to take greater account of the interests of consumers.

The role of trade unions in British politics has been a major source of controversy, especially since the 1960s. The significance of business interests, though of central importance, is less well documented. Both require examination.

Trade unions in British politics

One of the major issues in post-war British politics has been the position of the unions. They have been accused of being too powerful, of exerting an undue influence on successive governments and, in the process, misusing their power by obtaining unrealistic pay rises unrelated to productivity, while resisting innovation and efficiency. Union power, some say, contributed to the downfall of a number of post-war governments. Others feel that union power has been exaggerated; it has been essentially negative, the power to prevent things happening rather than to ensure that government policies would advantage the unions and their members.

The development of trade unions[5]

Initially trade unions were seen by governments as dangerous, even revolutionary, bodies, and by employers as a threat to their economic interests and to their right freely to run their enterprises. Trade unions and trade unionists were under threat from the law. Judges were hostile to the *collective* nature of trade union activity. They assumed that an employer and an individual employee were of equal strength in the bargaining process and saw collective action by workers as illegitimate pressure.

Attitudes had gradually changed and unions become more 'respectable' and acceptable to those in authority. By the last quarter of the century it was widely assumed that unions had a special status in law and thus could not be sued by an employer who had suffered from the effects of a strike.

This assumption was challenged by the employers in a series of cases in the 1890s when the legal immunities of the unions were whittled away by the courts, culminating in the Taff Vale case of 1901. The Amalgamated Society of Railway Servants called a strike on the Taff Vale Railway and was sued by the employers who claimed breach of contract. The case reached the House of Lords, which found against the union and awarded damages of £23,000. The union movement realised that without a change in the law successful strike action would be impossible. The Taff Vale judgement was a significant factor in influencing the unions to support the Labour Representation Committee; increasingly they saw the need for a separate party in Parliament to represent their interests.

The position of the unions was restored by the Trade Disputes Act, 1906, passed by the Liberals under pressure from the Labour Party. The disablities imposed by Taff Vale were removed. Unions could not be sued for civil wrongs committed on their behalf and strikes could be called without crippling and unsustainable penalties. The Act also clearly legalised peaceful picketing.

Another blow to the unions (and to the Labour Party) was the Osborne judgement of 1909. Labour was largely financed by contributions from affiliated trade unions. Some unions paid from their general funds, while others had instituted a separate fund to help maintain Labour MPs, most of whom, in the absence of a parliamentary salary, had no other source of income. A member of the Amalgamated Society of Railway Servants named Osborne, who was financed by various employers' organisations, took legal action to prevent his union from financing the Labour Party. The case went to the Lords, which found in his favour.

A series of cases followed which resulted in some 25 unions being barred from involvement with the Labour Party. The party and the unions then began a vigorous campaign to get the law changed and to end legal restrictions on the political activities of unions. However, the campaign was only partly successful.

The unions regarded the 1913 Trade Union Act as an unfair and discriminatory piece of legislation because it placed no restrictions on employers. It was only accepted as a provisional and temporary measure. The Act:

1. Legalised political expenditure by trade unions, though with conditions.
2. Such expenditure was to be made only from a separate Political Fund, to be set up after a ballot of members.
3. Any union member was to be allowed to 'contract out' of the political levy, that is, to declare he did not wish to contribute to the Political Fund.

'Contracting out' was replaced in 1927 by 'contracting in' (whereby a union member has to declare his or her desire to pay the political levy), a consequence of the defeat of the trade union movement in the 1926 General Strike. This was reversed in 1946 and remains the position. However, the issue of the political levy was raised again in the 1984 Trade Union Act. 'The Conservative Party, and Conservative governments, have in fact returned again and again to the business of amending legislation in order to reduce the contribution of the trade unions to the Labour Party. The 1984 Act is thus simply the latest, and perhaps the most potent, manifestation of a long tradition.'[6]

The position of the unions was enhanced by the First World War, but declined during the inter-war period, dominated by Depression and mass unemployment. The unions were again accepted as vital to national survival during the Second World War, and after 1945 the unions and the Labour government generally agreed about political aims and industrial methods. This harmony between government and the unions (shared, though sometimes grudgingly, by the employers) continued under Conservative administrations; the 1950s were fairly peaceful on the industrial front and Tory Ministers of Labour had good relations with the largely Right-wing trade union leadership. Many disputes were settled over beer and sandwiches at No. 10.

The system of industrial relations was termed 'voluntary', one in which the law played little part in the system of collective bargaining. Unions and employers preferred to solve industrial problems themselves. 'Until the 1970s the enduring legal landmarks in British industrial relations were few. There was no law giving trade unions rights to recognition and no law requiring employers to bargain with them. Collective agreements were not directly, legally enforceable.'[7] Though the state intervened in areas such as health and safety and attempted to protect the most vulnerable groups of workers, the system of voluntarism made the British system of industrial relations one of the least affected by legal regulation.

In the 1960s the position changed, and industrial relations worsened. Between 1945 and 1967 there were only three years when days lost exceeded 4 million and only one above 8 million. Between 1968 and 1978 there was only one year with less than 4 million days lost, while in six of the ten years over 8 million days were lost. The year 1979, with over 20 million days lost, was the worst since 1926, which included the General Strike.

By the mid-1960s many in the Conservative Party were arguing for a reduction in union power, a view commanding growing public support. A clear majority disapproved of the activities of trade unions and more people laid the main blame for Britain's economic woes on them rather than on either government or the employers. There was an increasing tendency to see strikes as *the* prime cause of the troubles of the British economy.

The Labour government and the unions 1964–1970

From 1964 strikes, many unofficial, increased markedly, affecting foreign confidence in the British economy. Faced with a deepening sterling crisis, the government first deflated the economy and then instituted a statutory incomes policy. In 1965 Harold Wilson appointed a Royal Commission on the Reform of the Trade Unions and Employers' Associations, headed by Lord Donovan.

The Donovan Report 1968

Its recommendations, which endorsed 'voluntarism, were widely seen as inadequate. Donovan rejected legal curbs on unofficial strikes and recommended voluntary agreements and the establishment of an Industrial Relations Commission, without powers of enforcement, to examine disputes and suggest changes. The law *as a major means* of stimulating change was rejected. Donovan did suggest that if voluntary change failed, then legal remedies should be considered.

A minority report called for the unions to be brought within the law, stressing that it was no longer possible to regard a dispute between an employer and workers as a private fight; society was increasingly interdependent and affected by industrial action. Unions should be required to accept certain minimum standards of behaviour and collective bargaining should no longer be 'outside the law'. Unions should not be able to avoid contractual obligations and to escape public regulation of their activities. Increasingly, opinion in the Conservative Party moved in this direction.

'In Place of Strife', 1969

Although the government supported the bulk of Donovan's conclusions, which rejected the view that collective agreements should be made legally enforceable and that the government should itself take action against those striking in breach of an agreement, it did announce in a White Paper entitled 'In Place of Strife' that some legislation was necessary.

1. An independent body would be established to settle inter-union disputes which the TUC had failed to solve.
2. The government would take powers to require a return to work for a

conciliation period of twenty-eight days to allow for negotiations or an enquiry.

3. Trade unions were to be required to hold a ballot before a strike, and the failure to comply with these conditions might lead to the imposition of fines on unions or on individual strikers.

Although the Minister of Labour, Barbara Castle, strenuously denied that there was a prospect of strikers being sent to prison under legislation passed by a Labour government, it was pointed out that if, as a matter of principle they refused to pay fines, they could be imprisoned for contempt of court.

In April 1969 a short bill was announced, covering the penal clauses. Though the TUC tightened up its procedure for inter-union disputes, it expressed its 'unalterable' opposition to the proposals. Resistance also grew within the Labour Party; in the Cabinet and on the National Executive Committee it was led by Jim Callaghan, and in the PLP it spread across the spectrum and included many normally loyal MPs sponsored by trade unions. It became increasingly clear that there was a real danger that the bill would be defeated in the Commons. After a bitter and public battle the government dropped its proposals in return for a 'solemn and binding' undertaking by the TUC to use its influence to stop unofficial strikes, something which had little effect in curbing such action. This humiliating failure to reform industrial relations was electorally damaging to Labour, and a factor in its defeat in 1970.

Heath and the unions 1970–1974

The Tories were committed to a comprehensive framework of law to deal with what they saw as the abuse of trade union power. The Industrial Relations Act of 1971 was a departure from both the spirit and practice of voluntarism. It had a number of provisions.

1. The National Industrial Relations Court (NIRC) was established with power to impose financial penalties of up to £100,000 on unions which breached legally enforceable collective agreements, organised sympathetic strikes, imposed penalties on non-union members and so on.

2. A register of unions was established and registered unions had to agree to conform to the principles of the Act; in return they would gain rights regarding recognition by employers, bargaining and so on. Unregistered unions would no longer be

immune from liability for inducing breaches of contract; in effect this made strikes by unregistered unions illegal.
3. Unless specifically declared to the contrary, collective agreements were to be legally enforceable.
4. The Secretary of State for Employment could apply for an order prohibiting industrial action which he thought harmful to the economy. There could be a 'conciliation pause' of up to sixty days to allow negotiations to take place.
5. Ballots on strike action were to be compulsory.
6. 'Unfair' industrial practices, such as sympathetic strikes, actions against non-unionists and the imposition of pre-entry closed shops, were to be made illegal.

From the start the Act was opposed by the TUC and virtually all the unions. The TUC recommended its constituent unions not to register under the Act, to exclude legal enforcement, not to co-operate with the NIRC and so on. Those few unions which *did* register were expelled from the TUC.

Industrial relations worsened and the number of days lost grew rapidly, largely because the duration of strikes increased sharply. By 1972 few unions had registered, and when the government forced a pre-strike ballot on the railwaymen in 1972, there was an overwhelming vote in favour of a strike. Some strikers were imprisoned and then released in the face of a fresh wave of strikes in ways increasingly humiliating to the government. Other disputes were settled, with or without industrial action, without reference to the Act. Increasingly the 'crucial' Industrial Relations Act was seen as a failure.

The most spectacular examples of the failure of the Industrial Relations Act came in the miners' strikes of 1972 and 1973–74. The 1972 strike was settled by the Wilberforce tribunal, whose award breached the government's pay policy. In effect the Act was put on ice; its failure was shown in the first full year of the Act when 23 million working days were lost in strikes and other disputes, the highest since 1926. The 1973–74 strike, again about pay, resulted in massive dislocation to industry and to ordinary life and was intensified by the massive cut in oil supplies caused by the Yom Kippur War which led to the price being quadrupled.

Heath's government was seen to have mishandled the strike, making tactical errors during the negotiations and misjudging public opinion, which increasingly sympathised with the miners. The 'Who Governs?' election failed, and instead of the Tories getting a mandate for 'resolute' action, a minority Labour administration came to power with the miners back at work on *their* terms. Although it is an oversimplification to say that the miners brought down the Heath government, they certainly helped in its suicide.

The Social Contract: Labour and the unions 1972–1979

In this agreement Labour promised to restore the legal position of the unions and to follow policies advantageous to working class interests. In return the TUC agreed to help moderate wage demands. A Labour Party–TUC liaison committee was formed in 1972, and there was some TUC influence on government policy, at least in the early years. The aim was to involve union leaders more closely in policy making and to ensure the co-operation of their members in possibly unpalatable decisions. This effort, though successful for a while, ended in the chaos of the 'Winter of Discontent'.

Legislation initially reflected this philosophy. The Trade Union and Labour Relations Act, 1974, amended in 1976, abolished the 1971 Act, restoring and extending the privileged position of the unions and strengthening the closed shop, whereby membership of a union became a condition of employment. The Employment Protection Act 1975 established the Advisory, Conciliation and Arbitration Service (ACAS) with powers to arbitrate in industrial disputes and introduced a series of collective rights for trade unions and unionists such as advance notice and conciliation when redundancies were declared, protection against unfair dismissal and so on. Generally, the policies were designed to improve the economic and social position of working people, although a gulf with the unions appeared after the IMF loan of 1976.

These concessions did not bring moderation in wage demands. Inflation and pay rises chased each other in an ascending spiral.

The TUC adopted a voluntary pay policy, which had limited success. In 1975 wages rose 31.7 per cent, far above the rise in the cost of living and an all-time record. In 1976 Jack Jones, the General Secretary of the Transport and General Workers Union helped to persuade the TUC to agree to a £6 per week limit to wage increases. Under pressure from the IMF public expenditure was cut and other deflationary measures taken. The TUC, faced with increasing unemployment, accepted tighter wage restraint. For a while, Britain's economic prospects looked brighter; the rate of inflation fell considerably and the balance of payments improved as sterling rose in value. But the attempt of Callaghan in 1978 to get the unions to accept a 5 per cent limit on pay rises failed and collapsed amidst massive disruption.

This did much to ensure Labour's defeat in 1979 and to end 'voluntarism'. Public disgust at the excesses of 1978–79 was shared by many trade unionists, and it is significant that Labour's vote in this section of the electorate fell markedly. A survey in April 1979 during the election campaign found widespread support among Labour voters for Conservative policies such as cuts in social benefits for strikers' families and the outlawing of secondary picketing. A MORI poll published in November 1979 discovered that as many as 73 per cent of trade unionists polled thought that the unions had too much power, 91 per cent believed that strikes should be called only after the holding of a secret postal ballot among the members involved and 86 per cent said secondary picketing should be outlawed. The Conservatives came to power with a clear commitment to pursue union reform as a matter of priority.

The trade unions and the government since 1979

Prior to 1979 the Conservative Party had emphasised their opposition to voluntarism and their support for a far-reaching legal framework, but before the 'Winter of Discontent' the Tories had had a major political problem in convincing the electorate that they could cope with the unions. They were widely seen as a party likely to provoke industrial confrontation, while Labour was able to boast of its ties with the unions. However, the highly unpopular strike action of 1978–79 came to the aid of the Conservative Party and ended Labour's claims to a special relationship. Mrs Thatcher and successive Secretaries of State, especially after the departure of Jim Prior, kept the unions very much at arm's length.

The Tories came to power determined on basic reform while avoiding the mistakes of Heath. The aim was to weaken the unions significantly. Mrs Thatcher and her supporters wished to see a pattern similar to that in the USA and Japan, where unions are often closely tied to individual firms and largely free from involvement with political parties. Ties with the Labour Party were to be weakened, with major changes in the way workers viewed unions, 'a diminution of concepts of trade unionism as a movement, a loosening of solidaristic bonds across industry and a greater identification of the union and its membership with the needs of the enterprise'.[8] To distract union members from wider concerns of class solidarity the sale of council houses and of shares (especially in the newly privatised public sector) was encouraged.

Industrial confrontation failed to materialise; disputes fell, both in number and length, and union membership declined substantially. Whereas in 1979 more than half of the workforce were union members, with TUC-affiliated unions having 11.5 million members, by 1986 the percentage had fallen to 40 per cent, with TUC-affliated unions having only 9.2 million members. Some unions suffered badly. However, despite Thatcher's dislike of public sector unions, they have in general suffered less than those in the private sector. The relative docility of the shop floor was matched by the almost total inability of the TUC leadership to change government policy, as shown by the failure of several long and bitter strikes, most spectacularly the year-long miners' strike of 1984–85.

The decline of corporatism

After 1979 union leaders were virtually excluded from the policy making process. Unions were seen as an obstacle to the changes necessary to 'turn round' Britain. Contacts were largely at the initiative of the government, being largely seen as an opportunity for Mrs Thatcher and other ministers to lecture union leaders on their failings. TUC representatives were removed from a range of consultative and advisory bodies, and although remnants of corporatism such as the NEDC and ACAS remained, trade union influence was low. Following the 1987 election the government announced, with no consultation, that the NEDC would meet quarterly instead of monthly and the Chancellor would only chair one meeting a year. TUC involvement with bodies concerned with education and training also declined.

A number of explanations have been put forward for the lack of union militancy since 1979.

1. The Thatcher government's legislation was successful in severely restricting the unions. Heath's legislation was comprehensive and unworkable, while that of Thatcher achieved its objectives, largely because no attempt was made to enact anything like the all-embracing Industrial Relations Act. 'Within the broad contours of a strategy developed prior to coming to office, Mrs Thatcher's industrial relations policy has been cumulative and adaptive. Its details were not graven on tablets of stone. The policy developed and evolved. Far from rushing her fences like Edward Heath, she has worked for success in one area before building on it in another. She has been prepared to retreat, or trim her sails when expedient, while successful policies have yielded further alternatives.'[9] Nothing like the NIRC was established as it both prolonged and politicised strikes. Legislation after 1979 concentrated on aspects of industrial relations, gradually tightening the screws on the unions and transferring responsibility to the employers or dissident union members. The attitude of the judges to the unions was a major factor; the law, both civil and criminal, was consistently interpreted to the detriment of the unions. Critics pointed to the resurgence of nineteenth century common law attitudes and to the striking coincidence of attitudes between the Thatcher government and the judiciary.

2. Mass unemployment blunted the militancy of the workers. The record levels of the early 1980s deterred industrial action; workers were encouraged to feel that high wage settlements would jeopardise their jobs. Mrs Thatcher led a chorus of ministerial warnings about people 'pricing themselves out of a job'. While the Right saw this as a long-overdue dose of economic 'realism', the

Left interpreted it as another weapon with which to destroy union power and create fear among working people. The general elections of 1983 and 1987 showed that unemployment was not a disaster for the Tories; the electorate failed either to 'blame' the Tories or to accept that Labour or the Alliance had a viable alternative.

3. There was no formal incomes policy. The attempts by governments before 1979 to deal with inflation by means of an incomes policy led to conflict with the unions. The Thatcher government avoided this; free collective bargaining left the responsibility for settling disputes in the hands of employers and unions, while the deflation of the early 1980s made it difficult for employers to pass on increased wage costs in higher prices. The government, at least publicly, said that its only responsibility was in the public sector, where, as part of the battle to reduce expenditure, it took a tough line on wage claims. Cash limits and norms were to keep public sector pay under tight control. Cash limits meant that a certain figure was laid down for public sector pay which could not be exceeded whatever the circumstances. An alternative strategy was that of 'norms', whereby a percentage rise for a part of the public sector would be fixed; efforts would then be made to keep other pay rises as close as possible to the norm. This 'hands-off' approach to private sector bargaining was largely for public consumption; in reality ministers were using public sector pay norms as an attempt to indicate to private sector employers what was an acceptable level of pay rises at any particular time. To some extent a covert pay policy was in operation, though one which enabled the government to avoid the politically damaging consequences of open involvement in pay negotiations.

However, mass unemployment as a factor depressing wage levels rapidly weakened. As the economy slowly recovered from the recession of the early 1980s, and especially when Lawson unleashed a consumer boom in the run-up to the 1987 election, inflation reappeared as a major economic and political problem for a government which had staked virtually everything on its claim to have squeezed it out of the British economy. It again sought to explain inflation in terms of excessive wage claims and emphasised the desirability of ending national pay bargaining. It was hoped that regional pay bargaining would reflect the pattern of unemployment and act as a downward pressure on wage levels generally. This would also weaken the power of unions nationally, and set groups of workers in different parts of the country against each other. However, most employers showed little interest in such moves; they found national bargaining with one union more effficient, less time-consuming and less likely to result in a chaotic situation of leap-frogging pay claims throughout the country. They also feared that an end to national negotiations would result in a rapid movement of workers, searching for higher pay in more economically advanced parts of the country.

4. There were major changes in the union movement itself. Powerful leaders such as Jack Jones and Hugh Scanlon, although resolute in protecting the interests of their members, were committed to the maintenance of Labour in power and were prepared to accept pay restraint as part of the price. Jones was instrumental in persuading the TUC to accept a £6 per week limit on wage increases as part of the Social Contract. Their successors were much more subject to pressure from members for wage increases virtually regardless of the political consequences. Moss Evans, Jones' successor as leader of the TGWU, led the fight against the 5 per cent limit on pay rises in 1978–9, while Len Murray and Norman Willis, successive TUC General Secretaries, failed to rally effective opposition to legislation after 1979. The divisions in the trade union movement were reflected in splits over issues such as single union deals.

5. The government was generally successful in handling industrial disputes. Initially Mrs Thatcher had to accept defeat on two major issues. During the 'Winter of Discontent' Labour, to postpone the settlement of some major public sector claims, asked Professor Hugh Clegg to consider the issue of comparability with the private sector. In the course of the election campaign Mrs Thatcher promised to implement Clegg's findings. His report, which the new administration accepted, recommended large rises for parts of the public sector. This was the last exercise of its type. The Conservatives attacked the concept of comparability, instead referring to the government's responsibility to judge pay claims in the light of existing economic circumstances and the 'willingness'

of the taxpayer to finance them. The second setback came in 1981. The NUM made a substantial pay claim; the Energy Secretary, David Howell, favoured resistance but was overruled by the Prime Minister, fearful of a costly and politically damaging strike during another oil crisis, this time sparked off by the fall of the Shah of Iran. However, preparations were intensified to deal with the NUM and its leader, Arthur Scargill, rapidly occupying a central place in Mrs Thatcher's demonology. After 1981 the government won most of the battles in the public sector, while allowing the private sector to fight its own battles in a legal climate which favoured the employers.

6. The government did much to depoliticise industrial relations by the way it used the legal system. Rather than being a matter for the criminal law, breaches of trade union legislation were civil matters to be pursued by those directly affected. The courts could then inflict such civil penalties as injunctions, compensation and sequestration of union funds; the latter was used to devastating effect in the miners' strike. At all costs the Thatcher government was determined to avoid the error of the Heath government which itself took legal action against unions and their members, as in the 'Pentonville Five' incident, in which the imprisonment of five London dockers led to widespread sympathy strikes and a hasty climb-down by the government.

The post-1979 legislation gave employers and individual unionists (often assisted by Right-wing organisations such as the Freedom Association) the responsibility to seek redress. If a union failed to hold a pre-strike ballot the employer or any union member directly affected could ask the High Court for an injunction to prevent the strike taking place. If a union failed to comply damages could be awarded against it or its assets could be seized. Thus *individual* trade unionists would not be imprisoned, avoiding the creation of 'martyrs' which was such a feature of Heath's period in office.

The approach was step-by-step, in contrast with that of Heath. New legislation was introduced gradually, often in an attempt to deal with the unintended consequences of previous attempts, and was largely successful in winning public support. Opinion polls suggested that the main changes commanded the approval of the electorate, including that of the majority of trade union members. There were five major Acts.

1.   The Employment Act 1980

Following the 1979 election victory, Mrs Thatcher appointed Jim Prior as Employment Secretary. Prior sought to end what were seen as the worst excesses of union power and to produce some kind of agreement with the TUC and the CBI.

Prior had been a member of Heath's Cabinet and feared that Mrs Thatcher's hostility to the unions would lead to a repetition of previous confrontations. Thus the legislation was limited and rather cautious. It attempted to deal with secondary industrial action by limiting lawful picketing to an employee picketing at or near his own place of work. It would no longer be lawful for someone to picket a firm in which he or she was not employed, in the hope of spreading a strike or of putting pressure on workers or employers not directly concerned in an existing strike. This tactic of secondary picketing had been used with considerable success in the 1970s, and with much effect in the 1973–74 miners' strike, when power stations were brought to a stop by 'flying' pickets. Secondary industrial action which was not directed at the business of the employer in the dispute was made illegal, and employers adversely affected could ask the courts for an injunction.

The Act also limited the scope of the closed shop, which most Conservatives attacked as a denial of individual liberty and a threat to the rights of management, as the union effectively decided who could and who could not be employed. A worker who lost his membership, perhaps for protesting at union actions, would then have to be dismissed. However, the government realised that to repeat Heath's attempt to ban the closed shop entirely would fail, possibly bringing the whole programme of reform to a premature halt. The strategy was step-by-step.

Compensation was made available for unfair dismissal for a number of categories of workers in a closed shop, including employees when the agreement came in and those having a con-scientious objection to union membership. Employees working in a closed shop were to be protected against being unreasonably expelled from their union (and thus losing their job). Secret ballots were required for *new* closed shop agreements and an 80 per cent majority of the workers concerned was required.

Secret ballots were encouraged though not yet made compulsory. Public money was to be made available to unions to pay for postal ballots on issues such as the calling or ending of strikes, the election of union officials and so on.

The Secretary of State was given power to publish codes of practice for the conduct of industrial relations following consultation with ACAS. The law on unfair dismissal and maternity leave was also amended to remove some of the advantages gained by employees during the 1970s.

The Act made it more difficult for the unions to be effective by narrowing the definition of lawful picketing and secondary action. Picketing was restricted to a person's own workplace and a Code of Conduct issued with the Act defined a 'reasonable' number on a picket line as six. This was seized on by the courts; judges were ready to grant injunctions to stop picketing by more than this number, thus rendering strikes much less effective than in the past. Most sympathetic industrial action was made unlawful.

This comparatively modest Act aroused the anger of Mrs Thatcher and was a major factor in the eventual demotion and departure of Prior. It was followed by the much more penal 1982 Act.

2. The Employment Act 1982

Prior's replacement was Norman Tebbitt, who said that the aim of the new legislation was, firstly, to safeguard the individual worker from an abuse of power by the unions, and secondly, to improve the operation of the labour market by redressing the balance between unions and management. In particular, the closed shop was to be further weakened.

The Act had a number of provisions. Trade unions could be sued if they organised 'unlawful' industrial action. Lawful trade disputes were limited to ones between workers and their own employers about matters such as pay, conditions and so on. If there was no dispute between an employer and his employees,

then a trade union could not take action over any matter –
including lack of union recognition. Thus unions could not
organise 'blacking' or other secondary action against non-union
firms. A very significant clause stated that if an employer had given
the requisite notice of dismissal to strikers, those dismissed could
not claim unfair dismissal. This allowed employers to pick and
choose which workers to re-employ after a strike.

The circumstances in which dismissal for non-membership of
a union was unfair, especially for those 'unreasonably' expelled
from their trade union were widened. The compensation for
individuals dismissed for not being trade union members in a
closed shop was increased, and compensation could be claimed
from the union as well as from the employer. At the same time,
Tebbitt announced that this was also to apply to those dismissed
for their union activity thus claiming to adopt an even-handed
approach. The requirement for secret ballots was made more
stringent. *Existing* closed shops had to win the support of 80 per
cent of the workers concerned.

In limiting the legal definition of lawful trade disputes to those
between an employer and his own workers, 'political strikes', such
as those in the public sector against privatisation, were made
illegal. 'However, the crucial element of the 1982 Act was that
which returned the unions into the area of liability in tort [i.e. a
private or civil wrong]. This represents a major step into the
central ground of industrial relations. The resurrection of the
spirit of Taff Vale renders the unions no longer the beneficiaries
of immunities they have enjoyed since 1906. The Act makes them
liable to claims for damages of up to £250,000 from any person
whose business is damaged by "unlawful means", within the new
narrower concept of a trade dispute.'[10]

The 1980 and, especially, the 1982 Acts were designed to
weaken the economic and political role of the unions, to enhance
what were seen as individual liberties and to redress the balance of
power in the workplace decisively in favour of the employers. The
next episode in union reform had a different motive. As expressed
by Mrs Thatcher, it was 'to give the unions back to their members'. It reflected the view among many Conservatives (a view
evidently shared by many rank and file trade unionists) that trade

union leaders and activists no longer reflected the wishes and aspirations of members.

3. The Trade Union Act 1984

Following the Conservatives' sweeping victory in the 1983 general election further legislation was introduced. The Trade Union Act 1984, introduced by Tom King, was directed at the internal organisation of unions.

a. *Part One: union elections*
The voting members of a union's governing body must be elected by secret ballot and may not remain in office for more than six years without re-election. With few exceptions, all members of the union are entitled to vote which must be by ballot paper, in secret, free from interference. This was an attempt to deal with the highly criticised phenomenon of mass meetings taking decisions about strike action by show of hands, often in rather chaotic conditions amid allegations of vote rigging and intimidation. A postal ballot is the preferred method and public funds can be made available. No union member can be unreasonably excluded from standing as a candidate.

b. *Part Two: the political activities of trade unions*
Unions which have adopted resolutions under the Trade Union Act 1913 to enable them to spend money on political objectives must renew them at least every ten years by a ballot of all members. The rules governing the ballot must be approved by the Certification Officer each time such a ballot is held.

The deduction by employers of the political levy from wages where an individual has declared in writing that he wishes to 'contract out' was made illegal. The system of 'contracting out' as opposed to 'contracting in' remains. However, the TUC issued a statement on the action which affiliated unions should take to ensure that members are informed of their rights on the subject.

c. *Part Three: ballots before industrial action*
A union which authorises or endorses a strike or other industrial

action involving breach of contract loses its immunity at law unless, within the previous four weeks, it has tested members' opinion on the matter in a secret ballot and approval has been given by a majority of those voting. The ballot can be either postal or workplace; the question on the paper must be so framed as to require an answer Yes or No, and the people entitled to vote must be informed of the result. Otherwise the requirements on the conduct of the ballot are similar to those for union elections, including the need for secrecy and convenience of voting and for freedom from interference. If a union fails to hold such a ballot, anyone who suffers loss through the industrial action may sue the union (or the union official responsible) for an injuction to stop the action and for damages.

The Act concentrated on the internal organisation of unions. The aim was to redistribute power within the unions by requiring secret ballots for union elections. The provision for compulsory secret ballots before strikes aimed at weakening the power of unions both nationally and locally and thus at strengthening the power of management. Another aim was to reduce the political effectiveness of unions by weakening the links with the Labour Party. The original proposal to substitute 'contracting in' with 'contracting out' was changed 'to subject the very existence of political funds to the repeated ordeal of recurrent ballots. This ingenious measure would mean that trade union political expenditure could be completely terminated if ballots fell during a period when Labour support was going through a bad patch.'[11] Thus the Act was of considerable political significance; critics pointed out that its aim was to weaken the main opposition party without subjecting corporate donations to the Tory Party to the same test by requiring ballots to be held among shareholders.

A number of strands in the New Right's attacks on the unions were highlighted by this Act. 'In accordance with the Thatcherite principle of individualism, the Conservative Party placed great emphasis on the "rights" of individual trade union members, rather than the "rights" of trade unions as corporate bodies. The liberty of trade unionists was accorded higher priority than the freedom of trade unions *per se*.'[12] Left-wing critics saw this as a clear example of the way Mrs Thatcher and her supporters turned political ideas upside down. The populist strand in Thatcherism emphasised the Conservative aim to save the 'downtrodden' worker, not from wicked capitalist exploiters, but from 'Marxist bully-boy' union leaders such as Arthur Scargill. An important aspect was the political gains expected to be reaped from trade unionists grateful for their 'liberation'. 'That this gratitude might benefit the Conservatives in subsequent general elections obviously added piquancy to their proposals on trade union reform.'[13]

The hope that the Act would result in the reduction in the number of unions having Political Funds was dashed when secret ballots brought majorities for their continuation, and therefore for continued links with the Labour Party. An effect of the new legislation was to make it necessary for some unions previously without a Political Fund to ballot to create one, as much union activity unconnected with party politics was now at risk without the legal protection conferred by the existence of such a fund. 'The politicisation of unions without an electoral tradition or who were not affiliated to the Labour Party was inevitable when it became clear that, despite the assurances of the government, the courts would take a restrictive attitude as to what constituted union political expenditure.'[14] Thus the Act legitimised union activity and helped to encourage attempts by unions to extend participation by members.

4. *The Employment Act 1988*
This was given the Royal Assent on 26 May 1988.

Section One allows a union member to apply to a court for an order preventing industrial action in the absence of a secret ballot in which a majority votes in favour of such action. Any member of the union can apply to the courts for an injunction to prevent the strike; failure to obey will lead to action for contempt of court, with fines or sequestration of union property as the sanction. Members may also have grounds for action against the union trustees for failing to use union property properly.

This principle was extended to allow the worker to continue working even if the ballot had produced a majority for strike action and was attacked by critics as a 'scabs' charter'. It was prompted by the News International dispute, when the National Union of Journalists fined members for ignoring an instruction not to continue working on newspapers owned by Rupert Murdoch. The government's view was that an important principle was at stake in that the decision whether or not to work was a matter for the individual. Critics replied that the principle was being restricted to the unions; no other voluntary organisation worked on the assumption that members could in effect ignore decisions taken after a ballot.

The closed shop was further limited when mechanisms for creating 'approved' ones were ended and legal immunity removed from industrial action to maintain a closed shop. Section Ten makes it unlawful to organise or threaten industrial action to establish or maintain any sort of union closed shop. Section Eleven provides that dismissal of an employee for not being a member of a trade union is unfair in all circumstances.

Section Twelve reinforced the principle of the 1984 Act relating to the election of union executives. It extended the requirement to union general secretaries and presidents and to all non-voting members of the principal executive committees. It is clear that the ability of the executive of the NUM (and especially Arthur Scargill) to evade the requirements of the 1984 Act led to this attempt to further limit the actions of union leaders; it was hoped that fear of election defeat would induce Scargill and others to 'moderate' their activities. In the event, Scargill resigned as President in order to force an election, which he won easily.

A Commissioner for the Rights of Trade Union Members who would help members take legal action for breaches of employment legislation by underwriting legal costs, assisting with preparation of cases and on some occasions taking action in his own right, was created. The Commissioner became involved in the allegations that money from Russian miners donated during the 1984–85 miners' strike had been wrongfully diverted to an international organisation in which Scargill and others were involved. In June 1991 the charges against Scargill and others collapsed.

5. *The Employment Act 1990*

The Act received the Royal Assent on 1 November 1990,

although it had been foreshadowed at the 1988 Conservative Party Conference, when Employment Secretary Norman Fowler said that it would deal with 'wildcat' unofficial strikes. Such strikes, which accounted for three-quarters of all industrial disputes, were 'the weapon of the militant – the tool of the wrecker'. Fowler also announced that the same bill would ban the remaining forms of secondary action and outlaw closed shop agreements entirely. It was a reaction against disputes on the railways and London Transport during 1988. The government had accused a 'small group' of shop stewards of organising the unofficial disruption of London Transport.

The bill was introduced into the Commons on 20 December 1989. Fowler said that it aimed to tackle three 'long-standing problems': the closed shop, secondary action and unofficial strikes. He foreshadowed the final end of the closed shop, recalling the decision by the European Court of Human Rights that the dismissal by British Rail of three workers who refused to join a union following the 1976 Act was a breach of the European Convention of Human Rights. The bill aimed to forbid pre-entry closed shops, whereby people applying for jobs were required to be in possession of a union card. It also aimed to make it unlawful to deny people a job because they were union members. The bill would also tighten the law regarding secondary action. Citing the unsuccesful attempt by the Ford Motor Company to build a new factory in Dundee in the face of threats of secondary action by the Transport and General Workers Union (TGWU), Fowler said that the bill would remove immunity from all forms of secondary industrial action.

However, the main target of the proposed legislation was unofficial industrial action, which Fowler referred to as 'a deep-rooted and long-standing problem'. He claimed that nearly one and a half million working days had been lost in 1988 through unofficial strikes which were called without the authority of the union concerned and without a secret ballot.

The Labour Party and the TUC attacked the proposed legislation, although both organisations had already announced their acceptance of the end of the closed shop as required by the European Social Charter. The government remained bitterly opposed to the Charter, which envisaged a package of protection for workers, including a legal right to trade union membership, while the Labour Party and the TUC saw this as a way of redressing the balance tipped so decisively towards the employers.

The Act contains a number of far-reaching requirements.

i.   It is unlawful to refuse to employ a person because he or she is or is not a trade union member, or because he or she will not agree to become or cease to be a member. Any person refused employment for such a reason may complain to an industrial tribunal. The government claimed that this effectively outlaws the closed shop.

ii. Immunities for secondary action are removed, including action in support of an employee dismissed while taking unofficial industrial action.

iii. The Act extends existing legislation enabling employers and others to take legal action against a union which calls industrial action without holding a proper secret ballot. Unions must state on the ballot paper who is authorised to call for industrial action. The aim is to prevent unauthorised union officials from calling 'premature' action.

iv. The Act widens the circumstances in which unions are legally responsible for organising industrial action. Unions will be potentially responsible for the organisation of industrial action by any of its officials, including shop stewards. To avoid liability, unions have to issue a written notice of repudiation to every member who has taken (or may take) industrial action in response to that call, warning them of the possibility of dismissal, and to every employer of any such member. No employee dismissed while taking unofficial action can claim unfair dismissal.

v.   The scope of proceedings for which the Commissioner for the Rights of Trade Union Members may grant assistance is extended. The Commissioner can assist in action brought by union members alleging breaches of the union's own rules on matters such as election to union office, disciplinary proceedings by the union or the authorising or endorsing of industrial action.

The reaction of the unions

The legal, economic and political background of the 1980s was hostile to the unions whose position deteriorated. Certain patterns appeared. The legislation was increasingly used by employers, although mainly in printing, publishing and shipping. The courts were hostile to unions and gave their full backing to government policy. Injunctions to prevent strikes were readily granted to employers, sometimes without union representatives being present. Ministers were not overtly involved in the operation of the law as they had been in the Heath era. Individual employers and in some cases, most notably during and after the miners' strike, members of unions themselves took action in the courts. There was a comparatively modest increase in the use of ballots, most of which produced majorities in favour of strike action, which seldom followed, as unions used the ballot as a weapon with which to bargain with employers. Although it is difficult to assess the legal impact of the legislation, combined with the general economic and political climate it clearly *was* significant.

There were different reactions in the union movement. The predominant view among union leaders was that, while they should press for a role in policy making, they should not appear to challenge the legally elected government, however much they may have opposed the changes. Initially they hoped for a 'U-turn' once unemployment had reached a certain figure, but when that hope was ended by Thatcher's massive victory in 1983, union leaders began to reassess the situation. Some, while not liking the changes, accepted that they had to come to terms with Thatcherism. These were the views of those union leaders often referred to as 'moderates' or 'new realists'. They rallied behind the 'Dream Ticket' of Neil Kinnock and Roy Hattersley, were prepared, if possible, to work with the government and were sympathetic to moves to reduce union domination of the Labour Party.

Others, dubbed the 'militants' or 'old fundamentalists' opposed the legislation to such an extent that they urged that the law be ignored or broken. The defeat in 1983 of the National Graphical Association over the attempt to enforce a closed shop at the

Stockport Messenger, with the awarding of injunctions, fines and sequestrations against the union, led to the owner, Eddie Shah, becoming a hero of the New Right. When the TUC tried to organise a national newpaper strike in December 1983 it was declared illegal by the High Court, and was called off; this was to be followed by many other legal decisions banning strikes in a variety of industries. Shah's example was followed by Rupert Murdoch, whose *News International* operations were moved from Fleet Street to Wapping against massive union opposition. However, the printing unions were defeated after a year-long strike which saw much violence. The role of the Electrical, Electronic, Telecommunications and Plumbing Union (EEPTU) in ordering its members to continue working, thus ensuring the failure of the strike, enraged the printing unions and their supporters at the TUC and divided the trade union movement. Militants also pointed to the banning of trade union membership at GCHQ, Cheltenham, as evidence of the depth of Conservative hostility to the unions. The division between the two groups was reflected in the conflict over the miners' strike: the 'fundamentalists' wanted all-out support against pit closures, while the 'realists' urged caution and were highly critical of Scargill's leadership.

Public opinion, though somewhat divided about the merits of the strike, blamed the miners for the violence and ignored evidence that the government needed scenes of disorder in order to justify its own position. The bulk of the press was wholeheartedly, even hysterically, on the side of the government. Thatcher and her supporters hailed the defeat of the NUM as a triumph for firmness and a vindication of her policies on the running of the economy and the management of the nationalised industries. To some extent, the general approval given by the public was a factor in the 1987 general election. It was also an element in the changing relationship between the trade unions and the Labour Party. The strike typified much of the politics of the 1980s: the arrogance and intransigence of Scargill, increasingly intent on a political challenge to the government, was met by the determination of Thatcher to inflict what she hoped would be a fatal blow to one of the bastions of collectivism.

Divisions widened in 1988 with the decision to expel the

EETPU from the TUC because of its involvement in single-union, no-strike deals with employers. However, differences in the union movement over the extent to which a future Labour government should be committed to the repeal of legislation passed since 1979 declined as the Labour Party made it clear that no wholesale changes were envisaged.

The Labour Party and the unions

Following Labour's third successive defeat the question of the relationship between the political and industrial wings of the labour movement became acute. The problem was that the unions saw Labour's election as *the* answer to the problems posed by Thatcherism. However, a major reason for Labour being unelectable was the perception in voters' minds that it was union-dominated. This view was based on organisational factors, such as the role played by the union bloc vote at Conference, the crucial importance of union funds in the running of the party and so on, as well as on episodes such as 'In Place of Strife' and the 'Winter of Discontent'. Following the 1987 election moves began both in the party and the unions to loosen the connection, but Labour's search for a more electorally credible policy stance made this highly complicated and controversial. The leadership needed union support at Conference and in the National Executive Committee (NEC) for its efforts to drop commitments to nationalisation, withdrawal from Europe and, above all, unilateral nuclear disarmament. At successive Conferences, Labour's revisionist leadership gained the necessary support for its policy review and attention shifted to reform of the organisation in an effort to diminish the size of the bloc vote and other aspects of the past without alienating the unions on which Labour will continue to rely unless and until it can build up its individual membership to fill the vacuum.[15]

The unions – too much or too little power?

The unions' role became a matter of political controversy in the 1960s. The increasing difficulties of the economy led politicians,

economists, businessmen and others into a search for an explanation. Many critics accused the trade union movement of a major
responsibility for economic decline; this was often coupled with
attacks on the political role of the unions, the links with the
Labour Party, and allegations of anti-democratic and even
'revolutionary' aims. Those more favourable to the unions, while
not blind to defects in structure and organisation, saw most of the
criticisms as hysterical overreaction, as the search for a scapegoat
and as politically motivated. 'For many observers after 1945 the
trade unions proved to be useful scapegoats in helping to explain
Britain's postwar decline. But they mistook the cause for the
effect. Much of the voluntarist analysis, symbolised by the
Donovan report, was complacent, insular and inadequate. The
troubles of the economy did require urgent and radical action in
the labour market, but tackling the perceived inadequacies of the
unions tended to divert political attention from more fundamental
reasons for the poor performance of the economy after the 1950s.
Trade unions and workers were like almost everybody else in the
postwar period – trapped by attitudes of mind that they inherited
from long ago when Britain was the first industrial nation and the
workshop of the world.'[16]

The unions have been increasingly attacked by Conservative
politicians, alleging that some trade union leaders have pursued
revolutionary aims by seeking to replace parliamentary democracy
with some kind of Marxist 'dictatorship of the proletariat.' The
links with the Labour Party have been attacked; the unions have
been accused of having too much influence on policy, making
Labour the servants of a section rather than of the nation. Union
leaders have been attacked for fostering outmoded class antago-
nisms. The structure and organisation of most unions have been
condemned as undemocratic, giving power to a minority of politically motivated militants, referred to as 'union bully boys', while
leaders such as Scargill have been portrayed as 'robber barons',
out of touch with their members. A somewhat different line of
criticism emerges when union members come to a decision not to
the liking of ministers. In such cases the unions are attacked as
'anarchic', with leaders unwilling or unable to exert a 'moderating'
influence on members careless of the 'national interest'.

These attacks are inseparable from criticisms of the economic role of unions. Trade unions are portrayed as having adverse effects on the efficient working of the capitalist system and on Britain's ability to compete internationally. The assumption is that if the power of the unions is reduced (or possibly destroyed), Britain will be much stronger both internally and internationally. Thus the alleged monopoly power of the unions has been seen as *the* prime cause both of inflation and loss of competitiveness, a point repeated by ministers with the return of double-digit inflation in the late 1980s. Critics, including those not hostile to the unions, have pointed to the fragmented and decentralised nature of wage-bargaining in Britain, and to the tendency for leap-frogging pay demands as one group uses a settlement for another group as a base from which to advance. Trade unions have also been criticised for restrictive practices, for hostility to new technology and for maintaining outdated craft distinctions. Some have suggested that the unions as a whole are over-powerful, while others have concentrated more on the divisions between different types of union and between central bodies and local organs such as shop stewards.

Supporters of the unions have been on the defensive in recent years. They point out that union members, in selling their labour in a market system dominated by self-interest, are motivated by much the same interests as owners and shareholders whose aim is to maximise their wealth. Union power is narrow and limited. The success of the government since 1979 in limiting unions has given the lie to allegations of excessive union power. It is clear that the commitment of successive governments to full employment was *the* key factor in determining the role played by trade unions. The mass unemployment of the 1980s enabled an ideologically motivated government and what has been termed a 'macho' style of management to erode union power substantially.

To some extent, both opponents and supporters of unions have exaggerated the effects of the period since 1979. The high-point of union power ended in 1976 when the Labour government accepted the terms imposed by the IMF. After 1979 Mrs Thatcher and her supporters gained political capital out of the claim to have 'tamed' the unions; it was in the interests of the Tory

Party to picture the unions as weak and toothless (while urging the need to keep up the pressure). The Left warned of the social and economic damage caused by what they saw as the vindictive class-warfare tactics of the Tories, intent on destroying what was left of working class solidarity. 'A dispassionate scrutiny of the contemporary evidence suggests that neither the Prime Minister's dramatic self-congratulatory assertions nor the hysterical exaggerations of her enemies in the Labour movement reflect what has really been happening. The complex impact of Thatcherism on the unions does not warrant sweeping conclusions.'[17]

Membership has fallen by around 3 million since 1979, nothing like as severe a fall as in the inter-war Depression, something from which the unions managed to recover. Membership figures have recently shown a slight increase, at least in some sections of the workforce. There are fewer strikes, fewer workers involved and fewer days lost. National industrial action has not disappeared, however, and may sometimes command considerable public support, as was shown by the successful dispute with British Rail in 1989. Since 1982 wage increases have exceeded the rate of inflation, leading to periodic lectures from ministers on 'economic responsibility', hence their embarrassment in 1991 at pay rises given to directors of the privatised monopolies. For a while, the demand for different types of labour meant that competition for workers in many parts of the country reappeared at the same time as the reduced significance of unemployment lessened the impact of fear on wage bargaining. Use by employers of the new legislation has been limited. 'In Britain – despite Thatcherite hostility – we witnessed no rolling back of the unions by aggressive employers as occurred in the United States under President Reagan.'[18] These factors need to be taken into account in assessing the contemporary position of the unions.

Summary

The unions have clearly suffered a major diminution in political significance. Many government policies proved popular with workers already inclined to reject the collectivism of their leaders. The unions have almost totally failed to alter policy since 1979, and the electoral decline of the Labour Party has added to their woes. There is no certainty that an improvement of economic conditions will produce full employment, nor that the eventual return of Labour will mean dramatic changes in the statutory and legal position. However, the public distrust of unions, a factor of crucial importance in 1979, has largely declined. Opinion surveys find strong support for trade unions as a way of protecting the interests of working people, but such support clearly depends on the unions accepting their diminished power. Public opinion would react adversely to any future attempts by the unions to re-establish the conditions of the 1960s and 1970s and neither Labour nor the union wish to recreate the Social Contract. The future remains uncertain for the union movement in this country.

Notes

1 For a discussion on the concepts of corporatism and tripartism, see Wyn Grant: Corporatism in Britain, *Social Studies Review*, Vol. 2, No. 1, September 1986.

2 See David Robertson: *Dictionary of Politics*, Penguin, 1986, p.71.

3 Keith Pye and Richard Yates: *British Politics. Ideas and Concepts*, Stanley Thornes, 1990, p.171.

4 Wyn Grant: Pressure Groups, in William Wale (ed.): *Developments in Politics*, Vol. 1, Causeway Press, 1990, p.78.

5 For a fuller treatment, see Henry Pelling: *A History of British Trade Unionism*, Penguin, 1987, 4th edn.

6 Ken Coates and Tony Topham: *Trade Unions and Politics*, Blackwell, 1986, p.121.

7 John McIlroy: *Trade Unions in Britain Today*, MUP, 1988, pp.73–4.

8 Ibid., p.47.

9 Ibid., p.46.

10 Jeff King and Dave Marsh: The Unions under Thatcher, in Lynton Robins (ed.): *Political Institutions in Britain*, Longman, 1987, p.219.

11 Coates and Topham, *Trade Unions and Politics*, p.64.

12 Peter Dorey: Thatcherism's Impact on Trade Unions, *Contemporary Record*, Vol. 4, No. 4, April 1991, p.9.

13 Ibid.

14 Andrew J.Taylor: Into the 1990s. Trade Union Political Activity in Britain and the Thatcherite Legacy, *Talking Politics*, Vol. 2, No. 2,

Winter 1989/90, p.73.

15   See Richard Kelly: Party Organisation. Developments Since 1983, *Contemporary Record*, Vol. 4, No. 4, April 1991, pp.6–8.

16   Robert Taylor: Trade Unions Since 1945: Scapegoats of Economic Decline?, *Contemporary Record*, Vol. 1, No. 2, Summer 1987, p.10.

17   Robert Taylor: Trade Unions Since 1979, *Contemporary Record*, Vol. 1, No. 3, Autumn 1987, p.20.

18   Ibid., p.22.

10

The role of business in British politics

This chapter examines the place of business groups in British politics. Employers' organisations and financial interests such as the City of London play a major role in policy making and have a particular affinity with Conservative governments. However, friction occurs even with administrations as favourable to business as that headed by Mrs Thatcher.

The role of business in British politics

There is controversy about the extent and nature of involvement by business interests in politics. The Left, particularly the Marxist variety, sees the influence of business and capital as malignant. Capital uses its economic and social power to preserve the interests of capitalism to the detriment of the working class. The persistence of inequality and the survival of capitalism are seen as proof of the privileged position of business within the economy and society. Capital is not seen as one of a number of competing interests, all seeking to influence government from a position of comparative equality; its power is qualitatively as well as quantitatively different. 'Of course, there is recognition that there are certain issues of no moment to business (such as abortion, or capital punishment), but within their particular sphere of concern the Left regards the business interest as overwhelmingly influential, and trade unions (in particular) are seen as in an inferior position. Government cannot be indifferent to the long-term success of business. If it does not facilitate economic growth and expansion then it limits its capacity to raise taxes and so cuts into the public revenue on which its own power depends. More-over, because depression, inflation, or other economic distress can bring down a government, and because jobs, prices, produc-tion, the standard of living, and the economic security of everyone, all tend to rest on the performance of business, politicians and administrators alike have to regard business as *more* than just another interest group.'[1]

The Right agrees with those parts of the analysis which point to the crucial importance of capitalism as a generator of wealth and as a vital factor in the success or failure of governments. But far from this being a malign influence, the source of exploitation and oppression, capitalism is seen not merely as the only workable economic system but as the one which guarantees freedom and choice. Thus the political influence of business is both necessary and desirable and something which should be facilitated.

However, despite the ideological enthusiasm of the Thatcher government for capitalism and market forces, mistrust and mis-understanding between government and business did not dis-appear. In contrast to the Left's view of the privileged position of business under Thatcher, some commentators see business as politically weak, finding it difficult either to define its interests or to select the best political strategy. The business community has differing interests, and though capable on occasions of acting cohesively if it perceives its interests to be under threat, this is rare. While business has not been without political influence, leadership increasingly has been provided by politicians with their own vision of what business needed. This has been especially true of Thatcherism, which had 'a clear view of what is needed to secure a revival of business enterprise.'[2] But is is not clear that this vision of what is called 'the enterprise culture' is really what is in the interests of British business; it may be that the need is for a relationship of mutual support with government, a point made by Heseltine during the Tory Party leadership contest in November 1990.

The political influence of business

The political influence of business has had a long history, pre-dating that of other pressure groups such as the unions. Eighteenth century governments had close ties with the merchants and financial interests of the City of London, while in the nineteenth century business groups influenced the development of policy towards the Empire. Many Members of Parliament had close links with particular concerns, such as railways, and used their positions to advance those interests. The significant role played by business interests in the political process was enhanced by the evolution of the Conservative Party in the latter part of the nineteenth century as the voice of commerce and industry, as well as that of land. This form of business representation was essentially personal and informal; leading businessmen would often combine their careers as entrepreneurs with that of membership of the Commons. Andrew Bonar Law, leader of the Tory Party from 1911 to 1921 and again from 1922 to 1923 was a Glasgow iron-master, while his successor, Stanley Baldwin, was a member of a steel-making family. Alfred Mond, one of the founders of ICI, was an MP for a number of years. 'In such circumstances lobbying was as likely to be for the narrow interests of the particular individual concerned as for the collective interests of the business community.'[3] More recently, it has become increasingly rare for businessmen of this kind to enter the Commons. They may be found in the Lords but are rarely regular attenders. Instead, the political influence of business has become institutionalised; business is represented by formal organisations directing their efforts primarily at the decision makers, ministers and civil servants.

Methods of exerting influence

Moran identified four types of organisations through which the political interests of business may operate.

1. *Giant firms*
Companies such as ICI have considerable advantages in dealing

with government. They are run by managerial bureaucracies closely linked with the public sector bureaucracies. Large firms are rich and can hire experts to deal with details of public policy of concern to the enterprise; some may have special departments devoted to relations with government. Their decisions on employment, investment and so on will often have a crucial impact on the economy; governments will be aware of the need to consult with and listen to them in the hope of influencing those decisions.

2. *Employers' organisations*

Organisations such as the Engineering Employers' Federation play a major role. Many originated in the late nineteenth and early twentieth centuries as a response to the growing significance of trade unions and were active in the courts at the turn of the century with the aim of eroding the immunities won by the unions. Employers' organisations continue to influence many areas of public policy concerning the economy, especially in recent years in matters relating to education and training.

3. *Trade associations*

In the late nineteenth century, as part of the attempt to limit competition between firms in the face of intensified foreign competition, trade associations began to lobby governments for protective measures. With the growth of state intervention in the economy, governments sought close ties with trade associations, seeing them as valuable sources of advice and expertise, and as a means of implementing policies such as the attempt to decrease capacity in, for example, the textile industry when markets shrank in the 1950s.

4. *'Peak associations'*

These concentrate on representing interests rather than on the regulation of an industry or negotiation with workers. They are generally loose federations of trade and employers' associations and individual firms. Most aim to speak for particular sections of business; for example, the Retail Consortium claims to represent the retail trade, although in practice it is dominated by the large chains.

The Confederation of British Industry

Some peak associations claim to speak for the business community generally. The best known of these is the *Confederation of British Industry* which was founded in 1965 from three other associations largely at the urging of government, which wanted to deal with a single body representing business. Though it has been only partly successful in this respect, the CBI has established itself as the most prominent group promoting the business interests, at least in the eyes of the public. Its large and well-financed staff maintains continuous contact with governments of both parties, and it nominates members to a wide range of public bodies. Thus it is in the centre of a potentially highly influential network of influence and pressure.

However, the CBI has failed to become the acknowledged voice of business in Britain. Business has remained divided in its policy objectives; trade associations maintain their autonomy, while many large firms remain aloof from the CBI, preferring to deal with government on an individual basis. The greatest source of weakness of the CBI is that it is dominated by large firms in the manufacturing sector; small businesses are underrepresented, while the service sector, the most successful in the last decade, tends to stand aloof. Multinational firms, for various reasons, also tend not to become associated with the CBI. Nevertheless, a criticism often voiced concerns the wide range of firms it represents. However, the significance of the CBI that it does speak for most of the large manufacturing firms should not be underestimated. This is its main source of influence.

Relations between the CBI and successive governments have fluctuated. George Brown managed to persuade the leaders of the CBI to sign the Joint 'Declaration of Intent on Productivity, Prices and Incomes' in December 1964 as part of the ill-fated National Plan, although relations between Labour and the business community soon worsened. Initially there was considerable closeness between the views of the CBI and the Heath government. But friction developed when statutory price controls were imposed and when Heath tried unsuccessfully to woo the unions after 1972. A further complication was the Prime Minister's dislike of the CBI; he often openly abused the organisation and its members. In particular he was bitterly critical of what he saw as British industry's failure to invest on the scale he thought both necessary and possible. Heath's reference to the operations of Lonrho (a giant company with interests in Africa) as 'the unacceptable face of capitalism' demonstrated his prickly relations with an interest supposedly at one with his attempts to revitalise the economy. The comments of the then Director General of the CBI, Campbell Adamson, just before the February 1974 election, widely taken as a repudiation of the Industrial Relations Act, were thought to have cost the Tory Party votes and so to have contributed to Heath's narrow defeat. A number of leading firms resigned from the CBI in protest.

Under the presidency of Lord Watkinson, a former Cabinet minister, and with John Methven as Director General, the CBI began a period of greater political activism. Organisational changes enabled it to act in a more coherent and effective manner and 'the policy programmes produced by the CBI in the late 1970s and 1980s were as comprehensive, and probably better researched and documented, than anything of an equivalent character produced by a political party'.[4]

During the 1974–79 Labour administration the CBI had several significant political successes. It played a major part in modifying the industrial strategy from one of state intervention (including a 'commitment' to planning agreements, a concept deeply disliked and distrusted by industrialists) to one of co-operation. Wilson's main aim was to preserve the confidence of the City and industry. The shifting of Benn from Industry to Energy and his replacement by Eric Varley, who shared Wilson's views on industry (including hostility to planning agreements), symbolised the desire to accommodate rather than to alienate the CBI in this period. However, Left-wing commentators saw the successful campaign waged by the CBI against the implementation of the proposals on industrial democracy made by a committee headed by Lord Bullock as the epitome of the power of business to protect its own interests. In this and other episodes, the CBI had considerable influence and exerted direct pressure. Watkinson threatened to withdraw CBI co-operation if the recommendations on industrial democracy of the Bullock Committee were adopted. The need to retain the co-operation of the financial sector for its economic policies was a major constraint on Labour's freedom of action.

The CBI and the Thatcher government

In many ways Conservative governments pose greater problems for the CBI than do Labour ones. If the CBI does not get its way through 'back door' lobbying with Labour it can go on the offensive in ways which will please its members. This is a much more hazardous operation when most members of the CBI support the government and would be alienated by too open and public a rift, whatever the issues concerned.

These difficulties were illustrated in the first two years of the Thatcher government. The combination of a world recession and government policies, especially over the appreciation of sterling combined with high interest rates, led to significant falls in industrial production. CBI members, especially in hard-hit regions such as the north west, alarmed at the increase in bankruptcies, protested. Sir Terence Beckett, Director General of the CBI, promised a 'bare-knuckle' fight with the government. This led to several leading firms leaving the CBI, whose prestige suffered further when it totally failed to persuade Mrs Thatcher to alter course.

Over the next few years relations, at least in public, improved, though in private discussions with civil servants, especially from the DTI, criticisms continued to be voiced. In particular the policy of high interests rates was a continuing source of friction, leading to increasingly open criticism from leading figures of the CBI, who complained bitterly that British industry was unable to compete internationally because of high costs, of which the cost of borrowing was a major factor. The reappearance of high inflation, coupled with evidence of a recession at the end of the 1980s, revived these criticisms.

The Institute of Directors

Under Walter Goldsmith and his successor as Director General, Sir John Hoskyns (the former head of the Prime Minister's Policy Unit), the Institute has effectively lobbied for the adoption of free-market policies. It has supported Thatcherism enthusiastically in all its manifestations, but especially in its curbing of the unions. Hoskyns in particular saw the Thatcher government as tackling the fundamental problems of the British economy. The Institute has been hostile to the somewhat more hesitant approach of the CBI, which has tended to favour more of a 'partnership' approach to industrial and economic problems. In particular the Institute has wholeheartedly favoured the privatisation policies of the Thatcher government, while the CBI has been somewhat inhibited by its association with corporatist bodies such as the NEDC and ACAS, and by the fact that nationalised industries are among its members. The Institute has a Policy Unit and maintains regular contacts with senior civil servants, Whitehall political advisers and the No. 10 Policy Unit. The Institute has pressed for major cuts in public expenditure, especially in the field of welfare. 'The IOD's interests in free enterprise and its hostility to public ownership leave little doubt about which party it prefers at the end of the day.'[5]

The political role of the City

The role of the financial sector in the British economy is so important that its political impact requires examination. However, there is little agreement about the nature or significance of the role of the City in the running of the British state.

Marxists see the fiscal policies pursued by successive British governments as clear evidence of the power of big business and in particular of the finance sector. The commitment of British governments since 1945 to maintaining the value of sterling and the emphasis on the balance of payments, often to the detriment of domestic needs such as full employment, has been interpreted as evidence that British governments not only share the views of the City but that the City has been uniquely able to ensure that *its* views prevail. Dearlove and Saunders accepted the basic premises of this argument. The 1964 Labour government struggled against devaluation of the pound, which led to the abandonment or dilution of much of its social and economic programme. Throughout the post-war period domestic demand has been sacrificed to the needs of sterling and the balance of payments. 'This predisposition on the part of British Governments to support major financial institutions has never been clearer than under the Conservative Governments from 1979 onwards.'[6] The abolition of exchange controls, the policy of high interest and exchange rates, the squeeze on domestic demand, with its consequences for employment, and the attempt to control public expenditure, are evidence that big business and finance capital are uniquely able to ensure that governments, regardless of colour, will see the world through 'City-coloured spectacles'.

Moran, however, warned against simplistic assumptions about the power of capital, pointing out that though until recently government intervention in the City was limited, this in turn meant that the City kept out of Whitehall. The intermediary role of the Bank of England as the link between the City and government meant that 'City interests were poorly represented in many important parts of the machinery of economic policy making'.[7] When the then Governor of the Bank of England, Lord Cromer, echoed City criticisms about public spending during the 1960s, this was seen by the Left as an example of the City's power. However, Moran believed that 'the reverse is true. The way to cut public spending is to kill commitments at the policy-making stage, not to grumble about them afterwards. The Governor's complaints reflected the way the City was marginalised in key areas of policy.'[8] Relations between the Bank of England and the government since 1979 have at times been frigid. The Governor, Lord Richardson, was uneasy at the reliance on interest rates to deal with economic management and was not on good terms with the Prime Minister. His replacement, Robin Leigh-Pemberton, was more acceptable to Mrs Thatcher, but during the repercussions over the collapse of Johnson Matthey Bankers, Bank officials felt 'in the doghouse' when they were blamed for the collapse. For a while the Bank was excluded from influence over economic policy. The uproar in May 1991 over Leigh-Pemberton's 17 per cent pay rise may again strain relations with the government, increasingly desperate to ensure wage restraint as part of the battle against inflation.

Another example of the limited political influence of capital was given by Margaret Reid.[9] She reported Mrs Thatcher's anger at pay awards made by the clearing banks in 1980–81 at a time when the manufacturing sector was in recession. Shortly afterwards, banks were subjected to an exceptional 'one-off' £400 million tax. Protests from the banking sector were brushed aside. Thus, although relations between financial institutions and Conservative governments are generally closer than they are with Labour, the City cannot take any government for granted, a point examined later.

Grant agreed that 'The economic strength and political influence of the financial services sector is an important feature of British business.'[10] 'The City' consists of a variety of institutions, such as banks, the Stock Exchange, commodity markets and exchanges, insurance companies and so on, which has traditionally relied little on formal lobbying or organised pressure. Its power has depended on the freedom to run its own affairs with a minimum of government regulation; this freedom has been greater than that accorded to other major interests. The geographical significance of the concentration of these various forms of financial activity imposed by their location in the square mile of the City of London has been reinforced by social factors. The City has 'been dominated by a social elite far more exclusive than is the case in manufacturing industry. A small number of families, often connected to each other by kinship and by economic interests, and drawn from upper-class society, have exercised disproportionate influence in City life.'[11] Because so much of the relationship was informal and by word of mouth, little was written down; thus little became public knowledge. This distinctiveness is largely related to the role of the Bank of England, which has traditionally organised City interests and represented their views to governments. The intermediary role played by the Bank is the reason that the City for long had little incentive to work with other parts of business or to go directly to government on its own behalf.

However, much of this picture has now changed. Vast changes have overtaken the City. The 'big bang' of 27 October 1986 introduced fundamental changes to the way it does its work. For example, large institutions, both British and foreign, are now allowed to acquire full control of Stock Exchange firms. These changes have come about as the result of international as well as internal developments in the financial sector and are intended to facilitate the operation of market forces and encourage greater competition. Traditional barriers between institutions have broken down, for example the blurring of the distinction between banks and building societies through a combination of deregulation and market forces.

Yet it is unlikely that these changes, which have produced a considerable concentration of capital, have led to a similar concentration of political power or influence. 'What must be emphasised is that the emergence of enterprises straddling traditional boundaries in the financial sector has not produced a new political unity of purpose.'[12] The role of the Bank of England has changed recently, distancing it from City interests, and transforming it from 'a City institution with a voice in government; now it is a government institution with a voice in the City'.[13] Government intervention has in some respects increased, eroding the self-regulatory nature of financial organisations. Direct contacts between government departments and the City have increased, while the social cohesion has declined. The City is thus beginning to resemble the formally organised interests usual elsewhere in the business community.

The financial sector exerts its political influence in several ways. Direct pressure can be put on governments by, for example, a co-ordinated refusal to buy government stock. There is an informal network of links with the Conservative Party through individual Tory MPs with City interests and through bodies such as the backbench finance committee. However, the key to the influence of the financial sector lies in what Grant called its 'exceptionalism', 'the long-standing freedom of the financial sector from extensive government intervention and the way in which issues which might be awkward to it have not appeared on the political agenda'.[14] It has a marked ability to ensure that matters vital to it are seen to be of no concern to politicians. In general, the wish of the City that such matters remain outside politics has been shared by the Treasury and the Bank of England. One such issue has been the external value of sterling; acceptance of the need to maintain its value even at the cost of a depressed domestic economy was and is part of orthodox thinking about Britain's world role. One result of this 'exceptionalism' has been that the City has been able to settle key issues through private negotiation inside the financial community.

However, this relatively privileged position enjoyed by the City (a term quickly losing its utility as financial institutions spread beyond the square mile) is being threatened. The old social cohesion has largely gone, and with it a system of operations based on trust and shared values. The enormous changes which have taken place in the financial sector and especially the internationalisation of markets have meant changes to relationships both within the financial sector and with government. A series of highly publicised scandals, including the Guinness affair, when a number of leading business figures received prison sentences (the leniency of which also drew criticism), attracted much unfavourable comment. A number of Conservative MPs, uneasy at the damage being done to confidence in the financial system of this country as well as at the possible electoral damage to their party, called for tighter control over the activities of the City. The Banking Act of 1979, passed by the Labour government, and the Financial Services Act of 1986 have been part of a steady growth in regulatory activities, despite the lip-service still being paid to self-regulation. The City has been obliged to enter the political process in ways formerly seen as unnecessary. Though City interests have been highly successful in defending their positions, the necessity of actually mounting a defence is a novel experience. By conferring a range of powers exercised by private institutions such as the Securities and Investments Board the 1986 Act created a range of corporatist institutions which in effect became agents of the state. The government's hostility to corporatism, it seems, has limits.

Business and the political parties

Though business generally supports the Conservative Party, the policies of Tory governments, particularly since 1979, have not always been to its liking. Where the two have conflicted, party ideology has prevailed. An important factor is the electoral damage of being too closely associated with an interest which can arouse public anger should it be felt to be abusing its position; this is an ever-present danger for the Labour Party, often seen to be too closely identified with the unions. The Tories need to appeal to a broad electoral coalition, some elements of which may be suspicious of if not actually hostile to big business. The institutional links between Labour and the unions are absent in the relations between the Conservative Party and business; instead, the connection depends on a community of interest and informal links which may be strained when particular policy issues are examined.

Grant examined four aspects of the relationship between business and the political parties.

1. *The connections between the outlook of the parties and the interests of business.* Though the business community often has reservations about aspects of party policy, the majority of business people are inclined to support the Conservative Party. Criticism may well be muted; opposition from within business organisations may be handicapped by the feeling that 'our party' must be supported, virtually come what may. Yet relations with some Conservative leaders *have* been strained; Heath's anger with British business was often open and vehement, while Mrs Thatcher expressed impatience at the failure of business to realise what was good for it. In turn, leaders of business organisations, particularly of the CBI, have sometimes openly criticised Tory governments. Sir Terence Beckett's 1980 threat of a 'bare knuckle' fight over policy towards industry was repeated in 1985. In 1990 John Banham, the Director General of the CBI, urged the government to 'get its act together' over a range of policies, including interest rates and the Unified Business Rate, both seen as sources of much business woe.

Such difficulties are not the result of poor communication but are related to the central problem, which is that of deciding what is the best political strategy for business. 'Converting the general goal of profit maximisation into a political strategy is a difficult task, given the range of options available.'[15] Yet for many business people, whatever reservations they may have about Tory policies, these are nothing compared to the fears aroused by Labour, especially in the 1970s and the early to mid-1980s. Labour's move to the Left aroused fears of a state takeover of business on a large scale. These anxieties helped dampen criticism of Thatcherite policies, such as that of ending aid to 'lame duck' industries. The Conservative Party is the nearest thing to a party for business which is available.

Since Neil Kinnock became leader, Labour has been trying to improve its relations with the business community, aware of the crucial importance of capital. Several policy commitments, including withdrawal from the EC, have been dropped and others, such as reversing some aspects of privatisation or trade union reform, have been soft-pedalled. In the past, business has been prepared to work with a Labour government following periods of Conservative rule which it perceived as having been economically unsuccessful. This is clearly behind the attempts by Labour's Shadow Treasury team, led by John Smith, to convince leaders of the business community of Labour's 'realism' and 'moderation' in the run-up to the next election. The Labour Finance and Industry Group, consisting of individual business people including senior managers in nationalised industries, accountants and others, acts as a bridge with the business community and as a think-tank for ideas. It provides a broader input into party policy making than could be provided by the trade unions alone. Members of the Group help with various aspects of the party's work, including campaigning, and were active in the 'Jobs and Industry' Campaign.

2. *The formation of party policy.* The Thatcherite wing of the Tory Party defined the interests of business, with the leaders of the business community largely acquiescing in their analysis. This was because Britain was seen to be in a crisis so severe that business feared for its survival. In the circumstances the lead offered by Mrs Thatcher and her supporters seemed to be the

only way out; as Mrs Thatcher kept repeating 'There is no alternative.' Business, failing to offer alternative policies, could only follow, allowing politicians to define the political strategy for business. Despite the efforts of the CBI to develop policy initiatives, both for business and for more general issues of political reform, most businessmen continued to feel that such matters were for politicians to solve. 'If business as a social category is not prepared to develop its own sense of political direction, or respond to those who are trying to provide such a sense of direction, it is not surprising that the task of defining what is in the interests of business is left to conviction politicians with a sense of mission.'[16]

3. *The role of businessmen in political parties.* Although most business people are too busy to pursue an active political career, many, especially small businessmen and the self-employed, do become active in local Conservative Party politics. Around one-third of Conservative MPs have a business background as have about 10 per cent of Labour MPs. However, the business experience of most Tory MPs is gained in the City and relatively few MPs have direct experience of industry. A number of people in the Lords have business experience, and a report of the House of Lords Select Committee on Overseas Trade in 1985 was highly critical of much government policy.

4. *Business financing of political parties.* This is something which arouses considerable passion. Despite the requirement of the 1967 Companies Act that firms publish details of donations of more than £200 for a political purpose, the definition of a 'political purpose' is not comprehensive enough to prevent 'conduit' organisations such as the British United Industrialists (BUI) collecting money for transmission to the Conservative Party, which then claims that it receives only part of its income from industry. Figures show that the BUI channelled over £9.5 million to the Conservative Party between 1949 and 1980 and that in the same period the party's income from donations of all kinds totalled over £31 million.[17] In 1989 there were allegations in the press about so-called 'river' companies, formed specifically to channel money to the Conservative Party in ways designed to avoid public scrutiny. It was suggested that these companies (named after British rivers) allowed it to receive company donations without

having to pay tax on certain kinds of donations. The secrecy of
Tory fund-raising has led to accusations of secret understandings
between the party and business, to the detriment of the public
interest. Attempts to change the law to allow shareholders to block
political donations from their companies were resisted by the
government, who overturned a Lords' amendment to the 1989
Companies Bill. Criticism of the links between the Tory Party and
business have also been raised in connection with the Honours
List; the link between honours and company donations has often
been pointed out. A number of businessmen who were prominent
contributors to Tory Party funds were rewarded in Mrs
Thatcher's resignation list. Nevertheless, the proportion of companies donating to the Conservative Party is quite small, although
some are clearly large givers. In recent years the party has become
reliant on fewer companies, who pay an increasing share of the
sums donated. Increasingly, companies are consulting their
shareholders before making donations.

Finance and property companies, food, drink and tobacco firms
and construction companies are especially prominent in providing. It was estimated that in 1983 29 per cent of donations came
from banking, insurance, property and investment trust companies. Links between the Conservative Party and the food, drink
and tobacco industries were forged in the nineteenth century, and
critics of the relationship pointed to the successful campaign
waged during 1989 by the big breweries against government
proposals to force them to sell 22,000 pubs, a significant proportion of their tied public houses. The aim of the scheme was to
increase competition and choice for the consumer, aspirations
said to be dear to Mrs Thatcher. The defeat of the plan was a
major blow to Lord Young, then Secretary of State for Trade and
Industry.

The brewers are among the largest contributors to party funds.
In 1987 Allied Lyons contributed £97, 100 directly and a further
£5,000 through the BUI. Whitbread gave £76, 500 and other
breweries smaller sums. A member of the Cabinet, George
Younger was a member of a brewing family, while another, John
Moore, was the son of a publican. Neil Hamilton, deputy chairman of the Tory backbench Trade and Industry Committee, was

also the Brewers' Society's paid parliamentary consultant, and helped to co-ordinate resistance to Lord Young's plans. Though one or two breweries may have threatened to withdraw their support for the Conservative Party their real power is much more subtle. 'Their great advantage is their strong regional presence and the position of the beerage in the local squirearchy and constituency parties. Furthermore, many brewing families enjoy a paternalistic position within the local community that goes back generations and is part of the local Conservative tradition.'[18] A press and poster campaign by the brewers was backed up by intensive lobbying of MPs, peers (many of whom had brewing connections) and others. Ten influential members of the 1922 Committee wrote to Mrs Thatcher, condemning the proposal; they were joined by Mr Thatcher 'who apparently made his views (on the side of the brewers) known to Lord Young in no uncertain terms'.[19] The proposals of the DTI were swiftly watered down.

The precise significance of business donations to political parties is hard to assess because of the difficulty in obtaining full and reliable information, either about the extent or the sources of funds. Between one-fifth and one-quarter of total Conservative Party income comes from business in a non-election year, with the total rising to over one-third in an election year. Concern at the role played by business and the unions in the financing of political parties led the Hansard Society to establish a committee of investigation. Its report, *Paying for Politics*, was published in 1981. It said that 'Many people are concerned that, because of their small membership, the two major parties have become over-reliant upon institutional sources of finance – companies and trade unions. This is seen as an unhealthy development in a democracy where there are a large number of other interests which seek representation.'[20] The report recommended state aid for 'duly qualified' political parties on the basis of a matching contribution to that raised by the party itself; for every £2 raised by the party in individual donations, £2 would be given from public funds. There would be a limit to the total sum available and a formula would determine the meaning of 'duly qualified' and how much each party would receive. The committee hoped that the proposals would lead the parties to broaden their appeal, to seek new members and to encourage them to seek a large number of individual donors rather than to rely on a small number of large donations. No action has been taken on this report, and as it envisaged reducing the flow of institutional money to the two major parties, none is likely in the future.

How powerful is business?

Those who believe that business is exceptionally powerful in Britain base their opinion on two main propositions.

1. Business has the ability to influence government by lobbying. Successful businessmen are part of an elite of wealth and can use their position to lobby other elites, such as ministers and civil servants. They have the expertise with which to influence policy, or they can hire experts such as tax lawyers to do it for them. Business can influence opinion generally through access to the media or by other forms of public campaign; in this respect business is aided by the fact that much of the media, especially the national dailies, are sympathetic to capitalism.

2. Business can obstruct and evade government decisions by its activities in the market place. Marxists in particular argue that in a capitalist economy private interests and individuals make key decisions about investment, employment and so on. Governments have to defer to business because their own success is intimately related to that of capitalism.

Marsh and Locksley pointed out that it is not easy to distinguish between the direct and indirect influence of capital. On occasions there is direct influence on government policy. 'However, often the influence is less direct stemming either from the structural position in the economy which capital enjoys, or from the fact that the interests of capital underpin the ideological background against which policies are made.'[21] They examined several episodes between 1974 and 1979 when policies were changed in ways which pleased business but infuriated the Labour Left. Business interest made repeated representations to the government. Even more important were the statements by the Prime Minister and Chancellor on the need to retain the confidence of industry and the City at a time when sterling and the economy generally were in deep trouble. 'This appears to be another example of the other faces of power at work – the interests of capital shaped government policy not merely, or perhaps even mainly, because of the direct representation of its agents but because their interests were identified with the national interest.'[22] This point about the tendency of opinion-formers to equate business interests with the national interest was taken up by Miliband. 'When politicians and others tell the electorate that we must "tighten our belts", accept cuts in public services, see our wages reduced and curb the tendency to strike in order that business may increase its profits, they are simply expressing the logic of a system of production in which profits must be sustained if economic activity is to continue.'[23]

Yet this picture of British business as a particularly effective lobby can be questioned. There are deep differences of interest separating the various sectors, such as industry and finance, which make a unified approach to government unlikely except in the most extreme cases. Despite the resources at its disposal, the business community often fails to get its way with governments. Many policies have been pursued in the face of intense business opposition; an obvious example is the determination with which the Thatcher government carried out its deflationary, monetarist experiment in the 1980–81 period, despite the howls of anguish from many sections of the business community. The record levels of bankruptcies in this period hardly endeared the government to business. Despite the resources available to many business pressure groups, there are doubts about their effectiveness; the CBI is a case in point. Nor has business some magic wand to wave when it wants to keep an issue off the political agenda. Finally, there is the point that in a complex society like Britain there are countervailing forces. Trade unions, despite their reduced role, still offer opposition to business interests, as recent government anxiety about the level of wage settlements testifies. Employers still need to take account of the wishes of their employees, despite the record levels of unemployment in recent years. Consumer and environmental groups can limit business freedom in a number of ways, as in the successful campaign to force petrol companies to produce a lead-free variety, a campaign which also persuaded the government to introduce a differential tax rate. Governments, even one as friendly to business as that of Mrs Thatcher and her successor, limit, regulate, tax and control business in a myriad of ways, few of which business welcomes. This complex picture of mutual interaction may be one in which business has a great deal of power, but not one in which it exerts the kind of dominance suggested by some critics.

Summary

The last two chapters have examined the rise and fall of corporatism. After reaching its peak in the 1960s and 1970s, trade union influence on goverment declined sharply in the 1980s in the face of public reaction against what was widely seen as a gross abuse of power. The New Right found it easy to promote its dislike of collectivism in all its manifestations. Paradoxically, the success in curbing the unions has removed a mill-stone from around Labour's neck; public fear of union militancy has declined dramatically and the Labour Party seems to be emerging from the shadow of the 'Winter of Discontent'. The political influence of business has been examined and a complex picture has emerged. The power of financial interests is marked and has grown since 1979, while manufacturing has frequently been at odds with Conservative governments. The present recession has deepened the gulf.

Notes

1   John Dearlove and Peter Saunders: *Introduction to British Politics*, Polity, 1984, pp.67–8.

2   Wyn Grant with Jane Sargent: *Business and Politics in Britain*, Macmillan, 1987, p.9.

3   Michael Moran: *Politics and Society in Britain. An Introduction*, Macmillan, 1989, 2nd edn, p.125.

4   Grant and Sargent, *Business and Politics*, p.121.

5   Dennis Kavanagh: *Thatcherism and British Politics. The End of Consensus?*, OUP, 1990, 2nd edn, p.92.

6   Dearlove and Saunders, *Introduction to British Politics*, p.233.

7 Michael Moran: City Pressure, *Contemporary Record*, Vol. 2, No. 2, Summer 1988, p.29. See also Margaret Reid: Mrs Thatcher's Impact On The City, *Contemporary Record*, Vol. 2, No. 6, Summer 1989, pp.20ff.

8 Moran, City Pressure, p.29.

9 Reid, Thatcher's Impact, p.22.

10 Grant and Sargent, *Business and Politics*, p.70.

11 Moran, *Politics and Society in Britain*, p.128.

12 Grant and Sargent, *Business and Politics*, p.74.

13 Moran, City Pressure, p.30.

14 Grant and Sargent, *Business and Politics*, p.80.

15 Ibid., p.169.

16 Ibid., p.180.

17 *The Independent*, 16 January 1989.

18 *The Independent*, 18 July 1989.

19 Ibid.

20 Hansard Society for Parliamentary Government: *Paying For Politics*, 1981, p.10.

21 David Marsh and Gareth Locksley: The Influence of Business, in Martin Burch and Michael Moran (eds.): *British Politics. A Reader*, MUP, 1987, p.216.

22 Ibid., p.222.

23 Quoted in Dearlove and Saunders, *Introduction to British Politics*, p.234.

Conclusion

This book has traced the rise and fall of Keynesian demand management, which was an integral part of the Butskellite consensus. Other parts of that consensus, such as the need to conciliate the trade unions, have also disappeared; perhaps only the commitment to the Welfare State remains more or less intact. Mrs Thatcher and her supporters claim to have created a new framework within which governments will have to work. What this is (and whether it actually does exist) will be examined later.

With the departure of Mrs Thatcher a process of evaluation is taking place. Within the Conservative Party there is much debate about the scale of her achievements; ministers (including John Major) have been lavish in their praises while trying desperately to distance themselves from many of her policies and attitudes. History is being rewritten daily. Senior figures in the Labour Party pour scorn on the 'economic miracle' while asserting their 'respectability' by promising to accept the kind of economic 'realism' stressed by Mrs Thatcher.

Yet whatever the achievements of the Thatcher years, in two crucial respects Thatcherism failed. The first was a failure of ideology. A major aspect of the agenda was to disengage government from economic management, to 'roll back the frontiers of the state' and to transfer responsibility to the individual. The state would merely establish the framework within which market forces would operate, which would then determine both rewards and penalties, with government retaining a minimal role in providing a welfare 'safety net'. However, it is clear that the electorate refused to accept this stern message. The main factor determining the popularity of the government is still its ability to manage the economy and to deliver prosperity and rising living standards; other issues, such as the debate about sovereignty within the EC, are only significant in so far as they relate to this central concern. The salience of economic issues most clearly distinguishes British politics post-1945 from its pre-war counterpart.

A number of factors brought about the downfall of Mrs Thatcher, but clearly it was growing unease about her government's competence in economic management which was *the* crucial factor, if only because it coincided with concern about her style of leadership. Despite eleven years of claiming responsibility for good economic news and blaming others for setbacks, and despite constant moralising about 'individual responsibility' and 'market forces', the electorate still persists in clinging to pre-Thatcherite values about the economic role of the state, while accepting a more limited set of objectives for governments to pursue.

The second, more specific, failure concerns the much-vaunted 'economic miracle'. Ministers have now ceased to use the term; after much hesitation they now accept that Britain is in deep recession. The claims made by the Conservatives at the time of the 1987 election have largely turned to dust.

Yet the Labour Party has so far failed to become the emphatic beneficiary of the changed public mood. In the last few months of Mrs Thatcher's premiership Labour built up a massive lead in the opinion polls and snatched two Tory strongholds in by-elections. Major's accession saw this lead transformed into a deficit, and although Labour's position improved, the gap between the two big parties remained small. To a considerable extent the argument is about competence; neither party has yet announced a 'great idea', perhaps sensing the electorate's suspicion of the grandiose claims which marked the Thatcher years. The Tories are trying to convince the electors that the recession will be short-lived and that they can be trusted to bring about recovery, while a Labour government would mark a return to the 'bad old days' of corporatism, government extravagance and subservience to trade unions. Labour politicians have stressed their 'realism'; the excesses and failures of previous Labour governments, especially in public expenditure, are freely admitted. Yet, despite the wooing of City opinion by Shadow Chancellor John Smith and his deputy Margaret Beckett, public doubts remain about Labour's economic competence. In addition, despite the much-reduced significance of trade unions, concern about Labour's links with the unions is another significant handicap for the main opposition party.

The nature of post-war economic management

Thatcherism is the latest in a number of attempts to rejuvenate the flagging British economy. 'Rolling back the frontiers of the state' and unleashing 'market forces' have gone the way of 'setting the people free', harnessing the 'white heat of technology', and killing off 'lame ducks'. As the 1990s began both major parties seemed to have tired of slogans and there was a more cautious approach to what governments can do to ensure prosperity and growth.

In a number of crucial respects Mrs Thatcher forced a funda-mental re-evaluation of economic management. But on present evidence, she has failed in her basic aim to turn the British economy around.' It is not difficult to see why the extreme neo-liberalism of the early and mid-1980s should have started to pall by the 1990s. Whatever else it may or may not have achieved, the neo-liberal experiment has not ended the century-long decline of the British economy.'[1] The debate about economic decline is beyond the scope of this book but it is clear that there are severe limits to economic management in Britain.[2]

Foster and Kelly sum up post-war economic management. 'Two broad conclusions seem to emerge from a study of govern-ment economic policy since the War; first, that any notion of government meticulously applying economic doctrines is facile – the need to respond flexibly to unforeseen circumstances (e.g. prior to Heath's 'U-turn') precludes any such 'texbook' approach; secondly, and of vital interest to students of British politics, economic policy seems to have been shaped primarily by external economic circumstances (for example, the Oil Crisis of the early 1970s) over which governments have little control.'[3]

Economic policy making, like all other aspects of government activity, is essentially political. 'Economic policy-making is best understood as the outcome of political bargaining, in which rational decision-making procedures may provide a subsidiary input.'[4] Whatever the prevailing rhetoric, post-war governments have realised that the chances of re-election depend primarily on how well they are considered to have managed the economy. The knowledge that voters want results in a hurry and are impatient of references to the 'long haul' and the necessity for sacrifices for the long-term good of the economy brings an element of urgency to economic decision making. The electoral cycle produces 'short-termism' in economic management, summed up by the phrase 'stop–go' and demonstrated by Lawson's 'dash for growth' around 1987. While governments are concerned for the 'national interest' their interpretation of that concept is limited by their ideological presuppositions and by the nature of their support. Labour governments have been attacked for an overemphasis on the interests of the trade unions, which supply much of the funding of the party, while one of the main criticisms of the Thatcher government was its concern for the City of London at the expense of Britain's manufacturing base.

The electoral system, which in recent elections has delivered power on the basis of around 40 per cent of those voting and which has emphasised the regional nature of party support, is also said to have contributed to a situation in which parties concentrate on *their* particular section of the electorate rather than having a concern for the nation at large. The adversarial nature of British politics, in which two class based parties face each other in a gladiatorial combat and in which there is a dramatic reversal of policies on a change of government, is also held to blame for the inconsistent nature of economic management since 1945. It is likely that both criticisms are somewhat misguided, especially given the nature of consensus politics. Critics cannot have it both ways; either the system emphasised consensus (at least up to 1979) *or* it stressed conflict. The electoral system puts a premium on making an appeal across class and other divisions, as Labour found to its cost in the 1980s, while 'U-turns' (as in 1972 and 1987) are as likely to occur *during* the lifetime of a government as on a *change* of government.

Yet these criticisms of the British political system should not be ignored. 'Voters and politicians have ignored evidence on the economic constraints and pursued infeasible objectives, such as too rapid a rate of growth or too low a rate of unemployment. They have been unwilling to make the unpleasant choices involved in trading off one objective against another, such as welfare state expenditure versus private consumption, and so have pursued inconsistent objectives. Policy objectives and policy measures have been chopped and changed as different political parties took office. Short-term political expedients have dominated policy-making at the expense of more considered and effective long-term strategies. Governments have allowed policies to be moulded by the need to accommodate powerful political interest and have failed to take a more detached view of the overall implications of their measures on the economy, on a broad spectrum of interests and over the longer term.'[5]

Another factor limiting the ability of governments to manage the economy is 'that government has limited control of the behaviour of all the economic agents in an economy whose inter-actions largely determine the amount and composition of national output.'[6] One of the features of the end of Keynesian demand management is a recognition that the ability of government to control the behaviour of agents (individuals, companies and so on) in the private sector and even in the public sector, that part of the economy supposedly under the direct control of government, by tax changes, alterations to interest rates and so on, is limited and difficult to predict. People's expectations of the effects of govern-ment policies change, thus affecting their behaviour, which in turn alters the intended effect of the policies. 'It is notable that over the years both the simple policy rules of Keynesians and then of monetarists have not worked out as expected by their advocates.'[7] As Mrs Thatcher found, social attitudes are hard to change; the British people did not behave like the Japanese and wealth did not become *the* aim. Poor training and a lack of skills could not be rectified overnight, especially by a government so dedicated to cutting public expenditure.

Another vital factor is the health of the world economy. In an economy as open and as dependent on exports as Britain's, the international situation plays a vital role in domestic economic management. 'Stop–go' was related to international confidence in the value of sterling and the policies of the Thatcher government were dominated by a concern for the external value of sterling, with its effects on domestic inflation. Optimism that the 'peace dividend' would substantially contribute to an easing of Britain's economic problems has been shaken by recent events in the Middle East and in the Soviet Union and Britain remains heavily dependent on the success of the German and American economies.

Economics is an imperfect science. There is 'the absence of a tried and accepted body of knowledge concerning how mixed market economies, linked to others through international trade and finance, actually work'.[8] Ideological presuppositions affect economists as much as they do politicians and condition the advice given by 'experts' as much as those receiving and acting on that advice. Dennis Healey's comments on the limitations of economics have already been noted, and a number of commentators have drawn attention to the weaknesses and inadequacies of Treasury economic models.[9] The collapse of consensus has added to the confusing variety of policy prescriptions offered to government. This has produced a new situation. 'What appears to be a new development – arising out of the situations in which the expertise of leading economists can be brushed aside as questionable or of dubious relevance – is the propensity of modern governments to invent their own bastard economics to justify their policies.'[10] Deane refers to the 'supply-side' economics of Right-wing regimes in the 1980s as an example.

Despite the difficulties facing governments, it is clear that there can be no return to the 'hands-off' posture of pre-war administrations. Both major parties are trying to come to terms with a situation of considerable complexity, one in which both Keynesianism *and* monetarism are 'the gods that failed'.

Political economy in the 1990s: the parties and the economy

In some respects John Major's priorities clearly differ from those
of Mrs Thatcher. In a speech in June 1991 he stressed the need
for a helping hand to be offered to those unable to take advantage
of the 'opportunity society'. Some took this to be a signal that the
government would accept a more positive role than was the case
under Mrs Thatcher.

Another change was in Major's attitude to the public services.
After a decade of almost constant denigration of the public sector,
the government has responded to the electorate's unease at the
state of education, the NHS and other highly visible services. In a
clear departure from the spirit of Thatcherism, Chris Patten said
'Private provision will and should continue. But I think that a
proper target for 2010 or before is to raise standards in the public
sector so high that no one will seriously believe that the private
sector should be an automatic choice for those who have the
resources to opt for it.'[11]

As the Conservative Party struggled to find a theme for the
1990s, the concept of the social market came back to the agenda,
although in a form very different from that promoted by Sir Keith
Joseph in the early 1980s. Commentators defined Conservative
policy as free-market economics combined with social reform –
Thatcherism turned to a social purpose, with 'Citizen John'
relating to all his fellow citizens. The 'Citizens' Charter' was seen
as potentially the 'big idea' which would catch the attention of
voters in the way that privatisation did in the 1980s. Rather than
stressing how quickly and thoroughly the state should divest itself
of functions, Major's stated aim was to improve the quality of
public services such as the NHS, local government and British
Rail. It is too soon to assess the effect of this new departure, and
only time will show whether John Major really has become 'Citizen John' rather than Mr Micawber, waiting for something to turn
up.

Clearly, Major's style differs considerably from Mrs
Thatcher's. 'In place of confrontation, there is a new consensus,
or an attempt to behave as if a new consensus were in existence.'[12]
This is the social market consensus, based on that of the German

Christian Democratic Party, admired for providing both economic success and social solidarity. 'There is a feeling that while we need to continue to apply some of the economic lessons that we've been attempting to learn in the 1980s, there's also a feeling that we need to be more explicit about the social responsibilities that should go with successful individualism. We have to emphasise both the importance of the collective and the community and the need to find ways of using market mechanisms more effectively without appearing in the process to devalue those services.'[13] This rediscovery of a positive role for the state poses problems for the Labour Party.

As Labour recovered from the shock of the 1987 defeat and moved into a clear lead in the polls, attention began increasingly to be paid to its economic policies. Labour has taken seriously criticism that a Labour government means economic crisis, inflation and an inability to control the unions. Though committed to 'restoring public services and helping those left behind in the 1980s', Neil Kinnock and his Treasury team of John Smith and Margaret Beckett have been restricting spending commitments by other Shadow ministers. The two firms pledges – an increase in old age pensions and a restoration of child benefit to the pre-1987 value when it was frozen by the Conservatives – would be paid for by removing the ceiling on National Insurance contributions and raising the top rate of income tax from 40 per cent to 50 per cent. Everything else would have to wait for an upturn in the economy and be financed out of economic growth. However, Labour also contrasted what it saw as the Conservatives' 'primary objective' to cut the standard rate of income tax, with its own determination not to do so; this would enable a future Labour government to spend more on vital areas such as education and training. Critics are divided about whether this package of commitments adds up to a realistic programme for government.

Labour's relations with one of the 'social partners' – the trade unions – have come under scrutiny. Though Kinnock stressed a more arm's length relationship, Conservatives claimed that Labour would be dependent on union funds and tried to resurrect memories of the 'Winter of Discontent'. Labour's plan for a national minimum wage ran into difficulties; although few believed Conservative accusations that it would destroy 2 million jobs, most academic studies pointed to some job losses and a possible 'ripple' effect on inflation. Leaders of skilled unions expressed reservations about the eroding of differentials. John Smith's suggestion of a National Economic Assessment (NEA), in which discussions between the government, unions and employers would 'develop a broad understanding of what is feasible in the light of Britain's economic circumstances'[14] has come under attack, not just from ministers and employers' representatives, but from sceptical union leaders such as Eric Hammond of the EEPTU and Bill Jordan of the Amalgamated Engineering Union, who expressed opposition to anything reminiscent of an incomes policy. Clearly, Labour leaders have a lot of work to do to convince their own supporters, let alone the voters, that the NEA will work and will not just be another to add to the long list of failed attempts to do a deal with the unions.

A new consensus?

Both parties have shifted much ground and discarded much ideological baggage recently. The Labour Party has abandoned virtually everything which made it unelectable throughout the 1980s; the alternative economic strategy, nationalisation, support for trade union militancy, unilateral disarmament and withdrawal from the EC have all gone. Instead, there is an acceptance of the central role of the market in generating wealth and that detailed economic planning or even Keynesian-style attempts to manipulate the economy are no longer realistic options. Under a Labour government the bulk of the economy will remain in private hands; like Continental Social Democratic parties Labour has come to the conclusion that debates about ownership are sterile and do nothing to ensure either enhanced efficiency or democratic accountability. Similarly, while pledged to remove some of the more blatantly unfair restrictions on the unions, Labour is determined not repeat the mistakes of the past by granting them a privileged status; 'social partners' must remain at arm's length. Labour's enthusiasm for EC membership stems from several imperatives, partly electoral, partly to ensure through the Social Charter the gains denied by a decade of Thatcherism, and partly the recognition that Britain's economic prosperity is increasingly dependent on the health of the European economy. Labour has been effective in demolishing the myth of the 'economic miracle'. Whether it can convince enough of the voters that it can do better than the rather more pragmatic Major government will be decided when the election eventually comes.

While Labour has accepted the virtues (or at least the inevitability) of the market, the Tories have rediscovered the attractions of good public services. To some extent this is the result of electoral pressures. But it also demonstrates that the government's agenda for the 1990s is being made by 'One Nation' Tories such as Chris Patten; there are very few Thatcherites left in the Cabinet, and most of Mrs. Thatcher's leading supporters will be leaving the Commons at the next election. John Major, in so far as it is possible to give him a label, appears more in sympathy with the paternalist tradition than with economic liberalism.

It appears that the ideological battles of the 1980s are over, to be replaced by a more restrained argument about competence. The social market, in which Keynes has been abandoned but Beveridge retained, seems to be the new consensus. 'Because the British people are . . . serious social marketeers, we are beginning to see the political struggles of the 1990s turning into a struggle over management rather than purpose and direction. The argument is not now about the direction we should take. The two major parties agree about that: we move towards a social market. For although the Labour party doesn't call it that, that is what it means. The argument is about who can lead us more successfully in the agreed direction; about whether the Conservative Party are better managers than the Labour Party, or *vice versa*.'[15]

The volatility of the electorate, plus the unpredictability of events, means that the next election is wide open. As the proverb says: 'Fortune is a wheel that turns with great speed.'

Notes

1   David Marquand: A Language of Community, in Ben Pimlott, Anthony Wright and Tony Flowers (eds.): *The Alternative. Politics for a*

Change, W.H. Allen, 1990, p.3.

2   See Andrew Gamble: *Britain in Decline. Economic Policy, Political Strategy and the British State*, Macmillan, 1990, 3rd edn.

3   S. Foster and R. Kelly: Keynesians or Monetarists? Post-War British Government and the Economy, *Talking Politics*, Vol. 1, No. 3, Summer 1989, p.114.

4   Rosalind Levacic: *Economic Policy-Making, Its Theory and Practice*, Wheatsheaf, 1987, p.3.

5   Ibid., p.360.

6   Ibid., p.358.

7   Ibid., p.359

8   Ibid.

9   See Bill Martin: Seeking Stabilisers for the Economy, *The Independent*, 19 August 1991.

10   Phyllis Deane: *The State and the Economic System*, OUP, 1989, p.193.

11   *The Independent*, 6 July 1991.

12   David Marquand: The Meaning of Major, in Gareth Smyth (ed.): *Can the Tories Lose? The Battle for the Marginals*, Lawrence and Wishart, 1991, p.16.

13   'The power to change'. David Marquand interviews Chris Patten, *Marxism Today*, February 1991.

14   *Newsnight*, BBC 1, 20 June 1991.

15   Marquand, The Meaning of Major, pp.16–17.

Index